DATE			

BAKER & TAYLOR

HOW TO SUCCEED IN ADVERTISING

WHEN ALL YOU HAVE IS TALENT

Laurence Minsky
Emily Thornton Calvo

NTC Business Books
a division of *NTC Publishing Group* • Lincolnwood, Illinois USA

ACKNOWLEDGMENTS

We wish to thank these individuals for their contributions and support: Bob Boyer, Phil Gayter, Wayne Johnson, Wally Peterson, and Kim Fouch of Leo Burnett/Chicago; Leslie Cole and Rebecca Willis of Burrell Advertising; Carol Madonna of Chiat/Day Inc; Mike Tardif and Jeanette Settino of Backer Spielvogel Bates/NY; Diane Mercier of Ally & Gargano and Nancy Cuttito of Amil Gargano & Partners; Keri Lannigan of Grace & Rothschild; Mary Brackin and Jackie Lenigan of DDB Needham Worldwide/Chicago; Cindy Rowe of BBDO/Los Angeles; Leigh Donaldson of FCB Communications, Inc./San Francisco; Nina Bertoncini of McCabe Communications; Heidi Lilli, formerly of McElligott Wright Morrison White; Jodie Skerritt and Tom Monahan of Leonard Monahan Lubars & Kelly; Richard Needham; Debbie MacKaman, formerly of Rice & Rice; Jean Howe of The Richards Group; and Patrick Hanlon of Hal Riney & Partners.

We also wish to thank:

Our editors, Anne Knudsen and Karen Shaw; Gerald Linda of Gerald Linda and Associates; Karen Wenzel and Joan Andrew of Bell & Howell; transcribers Jean Mamola, Rhonda Present, Lynne Van der Sitt; Hildy Hoppenstand, and Christy Calvo; Bob Straussman of Crest Communications; David Alabach of Ketchum Communications; Sandy Wade of Sandy Wade & Company; Bill Sharp of Sharp Advertising; Nick Savastio of Scott Foresman; Mary Warlick of the One Club; Ellen Young of the American Association of Advertising Agencies; Brian Sternthal, Kellogg School of Management, Northwestern University; and our attorney, Richard Alexander.

Finally, we wish to thank our dads, Joseph Minsky and Gregory Thornton, for introducing us to the industry; our families, friends, colleagues, and people on the street who are tired of hearing us talk about this project.

Library of Congress Cataloging-in-Publication Data information is available from the Library of Congress

Published by NTC Business Books, a division of NTC Publishing Group
4255 West Touhy Avenue
Lincolnwood (Chicago), Illinois 60646-1975, U.S.A.

4 5 6 7 8 9 0 VP 9 8 7 6 5 4 3 2 1

Contents

Foreword

Richard H. Needham
Former Senior Vice President
DDB NEEDHAM WORLDWIDE, INC.

Many of the men and women who have contributed chapters to this book have had their share of false starts and rejection. But their burning desires to create have ultimately rewarded them with success.

As you start reading, I issue you a warning. You're about to walk down a road with some of the most inventive and persuasive people in this country. They're going to give you some great advice, but there's a catch. Every one of them was born with creative talent. They won't teach you how to be creative, but if you *are* creative, they'll tell you how to use your talent to maximum advantage.

Here are some advertising headlines you may remember:

"You deserve a break today."

"Lemon."

"Fly the friendly skies."

All these lines are based on relevant marketing strategies. They sold billions of hamburgers, automobiles, and plane tickets and made Keith Reinhard, Bill Bernbach, Leo Burnett, and their associates famous.

Such ideas aren't originated, or accepted, easily. Nobody has said that creating great advertising is easy. But when an idea survives all the approval layers and successfully works itself into the marketplace, the originator's exhilaration is beyond measure. That's what makes the advertising business, with all its travail, so rewarding.

Just what *is* the advertising business? Well, it's many things. It's organizations who advertise (advertisers); it's the broadcast and print vehicles that carry advertising messages; it's a variety of broadcast and print suppliers. And at the heart of the advertising business are the thousands of agencies who create, produce, and place the millions of advertising messages we see and hear.

If and when you go to work for an advertising agency, you'll find that clients are served by teams made up of account management, media, research, and, of course, creative people. You may wonder why an agency requires anyone beyond the "creatives." After all, *they* do the ads and commercials. Well, the fact is there's a lot more to serving a client than producing advertising messages. There is information about consumer attitudes to be gathered. There is a need to make a sophisticated determination as to where advertising messages are to be placed. There are marketing plans to be developed and presented.

The research and media people provide creative people with a road map that tells them who the target audiences are and describes the environments in which those audiences will be receiving advertising messages. Without that information advertising dollars are almost certain to be misdirected.

Account managers are the people responsible for the total delivery of an agency's services. They are the leaders, coordinators, and administrators of the teams assigned to clients. A skilled account manager has an enormous impact on the successful development, execution, and *sale* of creative work. Mature creative people understand how indispensable good account people are.

I'm proud to have been in the advertising business. For well over a century advertising has been an essential lubricant in greasing the wheels of commerce. It has fueled our system of mass distribution at affordable prices.

One frequently hears the lament these days that the advertising business isn't the fun it used to be. There's some truth to that. Global competition and bottom-line pressures have taken their toll, and advertising has become a big, tough business. When I joined Needham, Louis & Brorby in 1949 our total billings were eleven million dollars. As I write this piece, Needham has become an operating unit of the Omnicom Group, which bills twelve *billion* dollars. Good glory!

But there are some things which have not changed:

- Advertising continues to be produced by small groups of individuals who have the maturity and good sense to be team players.
- Advertising still attracts people who are intellectually curious and fun to be with.
- Advertising will remain a viable industry for the foreseeable future. Its shape may change, but marketers will continue to rely on mass communication.
- Talented advertising people will *always* be handsomely compensated.

If you have the talent and the motivation, read on. You'll be glad you did.

How to Create Great Advertising

Patrick Hanlon
Vice President, Creative Director
HAL RINEY & PARTNERS/CHICAGO

Someone once said that advertising is the toy department of the business world.

Someone else said that advertising is the most fun you can have with your clothes on.

It's also one of the few professions where you can make as much as a doctor or lawyer and come to work in blue jeans.

But only if you are great.

To be great, you must start by writing 100 headlines.

Do 100 layouts.

Then do 100 more.

Many people have the talent to become great, but only a few have the energy.

Great advertising requires energy. You'll find that most people want to be home by five o'clock. They want to go to the bars. They want to do their laundry.

Forget it. Advertising is much better than having a social life.

Advertising is a competitive business. You must always *always* work harder than your competition.

One writer (in this book and in the Copywriter's Hall of Fame) was a high school dropout. Another great writer (not in this book, but her mentor is) started out as a secretary. Other writers and art directors have been lumberjacks, ministers' sons, surfers, and the sons and daughters of people already in the business. Advertising is one of the few professions that will accept anyone who can work hard, think smart, and do great work.

What more could you ask?

How to Succeed in Advertising When All You Have Is Talent

Bill Bernbach once purportedly said that "the memorable never emerged from a formula." There may be rules for a particular client, a set of things one should or shouldn't do. But there are no hard and fast laws—except, perhaps, making sure that people remember your client's name.

So how do you approach a book like this one? A book filled with advice in each chapter. Advice that may seem like rules or even advertising laws.

You think. You pick and choose. You find the ideas that are right for you—in your current situation. Advertising is problem solving. And every problem is slightly different.

Some of what you read will even contradict other parts of this book. Everybody has a different viewpoint, and what has worked for one person may not work for another. What's more, advertising is a quickly changing field, always looking for the new and the fresh. Ideas that succeeded in the past may never work again. Yet others may inspire the future. Again, your job is to figure out what ideas are best for you.

But we want you to do one more thing when you read this book. Please, sit back, relax, and enjoy. Advertising is an exciting profession. We hope that this book captures that excitement.

LAURENCE MINSKY
EMILY THORNTON CALVO

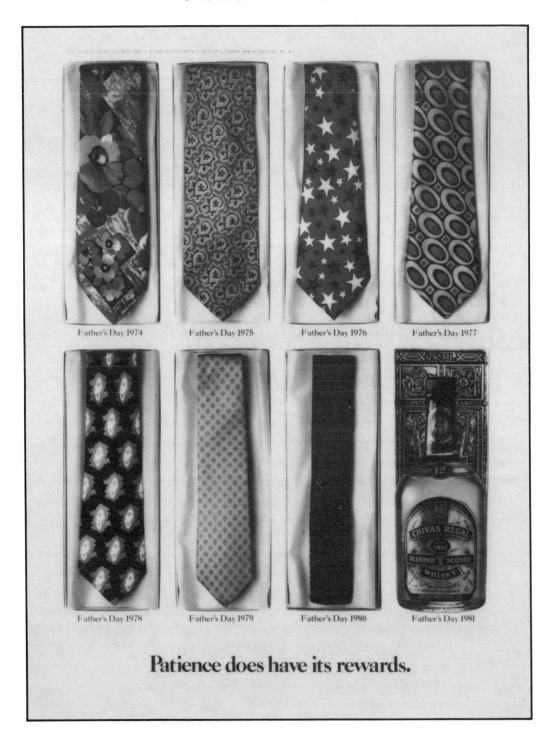

Father's Day 1974   Father's Day 1975   Father's Day 1976   Father's Day 1977

Father's Day 1978   Father's Day 1979   Father's Day 1980   Father's Day 1981

Patience does have its rewards.

Ted Bell

"There are two kinds of people in this business," says Theodore Bell, president and chief creative officer* for Leo Burnett USA. "There are those who 'get it.' And there are those who don't."

In this chapter, we'll examine basic ideas for putting together a portfolio, as well as explore what it means to "get it." Having held senior creative positions at both Doyle Dane Bernbach and Leo Burnett, Ted Bell clearly gets it. His career demonstrates how creative talent alone can foster a successful career in advertising—no matter what types of clients, products, or organizational politics may exist. He has created spots for Chivas Regal and Dewars, Memorex, McDonald's, and Volkswagen, and has earned numerous awards including golds at both The One Show and Cannes.

A graduate of Randolph-Macon College, Bell began his writing career at a small agency in Hartford, then moved to Tinker Dodge & Delano, a New York agency. Later he moved to Doyle Dane Bernbach and rose to senior vice president. He joined Burnett in 1982.

Bell lives in Chicago with his wife and daughter. When he's not guiding Burnett's quest for award-winning work, he enjoys sailing, hunting, and riding a Harley Davidson, an interest he developed while shooting a commercial for Dean Witter featuring this product. But his primary interest outside of work is reading historical biographies and fiction, evidence of his lifelong romance with words and literature.

*Bell has since moved on to a creative position with Young & Rubicam.

THRIVING IN THE BEST OF BOTH WORLDS

DO YOU HAVE WHAT IT TAKES TO SUCCEED? AS THE TITLE OF THIS BOOK IMPLIES, YOU CAN make it in creative advertising—and make it big—if you have one thing. Talent. But what is talent? And what else needs to be learned if you have talent? Perhaps a look at how Ted Bell's career developed can shed some light for you.

Bell didn't always display his talent for advertising. While in college, he expected to earn a degree in English in order to teach English literature. But during his senior year he realized that he would have to learn more than Shakespeare's sonnets to survive the academic environment; he discovered that faculty rivalries and tenure squabbles were as much a part of the job as were literary pursuits. Recalls Bell, "I thought I'd be better off in the real world than involved with the isolation and politics of academic life. At least that was my 21-year-old perception."

With this new perspective—and financial support from his grandmother—Bell decided to move to Europe and try his hand at completing a novel begun in college. He settled in a tiny town in Switzerland where the sheep population seemed to outnumber the two-legged residents.

The location had the solitude a budding novelist needed, but lacked the stimulation a young man exploring Europe craved. Consequently, he drove every weekend to Milan to visit with a Swedish friend of his—a friend who led a glamorous life as one of Europe's hottest fashion photographers. As a result, he was introduced to Milan's leading advertising people. His interest in the industry was born. It was a creative and, luckily, remunerative field.

But considering the language difference, he knew that it was probably a bad idea to start his career in Milan. Although he could have learned Italian, he knew that he would have trouble writing with enough idiomatic familiarity to create effective advertising. So he decided that perhaps England would be a better place to pursue his career.

Unfortunately, Britain in the early '70s was in recession, and to ensure that jobs didn't go to foreigners, visits of non-nationals were limited to only six weeks. Bell decided to make good use of his time, and during those weeks he sent three-page letters to London's agency directors to try to land a position.

"It wasn't a straightforward business letter," says Bell. "I talked about myself, my background in creative writing and English literature, and communicated how strongly I believed my creative energy could be channeled into something I could *do*, namely advertising. Also, I tried to make the letter funny."

In sum, Bell's letter detailed his background, his experiences, his passion for advertising in an interesting way—which managed to cut through the clutter. To his delight, a few of the creative directors took an interest in him, agreed to meet, and offered him encouragement. They were looking for good writers. They wanted fresh ideas. And they were always interested in new talent.

A creative director at Doyle Dane Bernbach's London office was particularly helpful. He instructed Bell to buy the *London Times*, sit in the park, look at the ads and try to improve them. Which Bell did. He rewrote ads for heating equipment, credit cards, socks, watches—anything. Then he returned to his new friend, spread the ads on the table, and listened to a critique of his work. His friend offered advice on how to improve the ads—and there was plenty of room for improvement.

"I remember one terrible ad I did," recalls Bell. "It was an ad for socks and the headline read, 'Socks Appeal.' I thought it was clever. It had some socks on a clothesline. This guy, rightfully, hated it. He told me it was a cheap pun. He said I wasn't saying anything about the socks—why they're good, what they're made of. Anybody can be clever. Advertising is about much more than being able to come up with a cute turn of a phrase. Or a play on words. It's about finding truly new and fresh ways to *make a sale*."

The ads he created under his friend's direction became the basis for his first portfolio. He didn't present sophisticated renderings—or even the standard three campaigns with three ads each. Instead, his book consisted of very rough drawings, with press type for headlines—all displayed in a green plastic binder. "It was *bad* presentation!" says Bell. "I was starting from scratch and didn't know what I was doing."

Somehow, Bell's talent transcended his rough presentations. Feedback from the creative directors was positive. He was told he had the talent to be a copywriter, but that England's economy was squeezing the job market. And his visa was running out.

Unable to take a U.K. position, he returned to the United States. But with set goals and a tested portfolio, Bell was soon hired as a copywriter by a small agency in Hartford, Connecticut. To Bell, this was a stepping-stone to New York, where talented new creatives were changing the style of advertising. And within two years, he was writing ads at Tinker Dodge & Delano in New York for Smirnoff and British Airways.

But he kept his eye on landing a position at the agency that was leading the creative revolution, Doyle Dane Bernbach (DDB), and eventually he secured an interview with Bob Levenson, probably was one of the greatest advertising writers ever, who was then running DDB's creative department. Bell was hired as a junior copywriter on the Volkswagen account. Of DDB, Bell says, "this was mecca as far as I was concerned."

The environment at Doyle Dane Bernbach was energetic and filled with creative talent. Helmut Krone, Bob Gage, Bob Levenson, and Roy Grace (see Chapter Five) created an environment where everyone learned something every day. The agency operated on the basis of "creative anarchy" with the creatives carrying the standard.

Bell recalls one lesson he learned while writing a Volkswagen ad. Levenson didn't like a sentence and questioned it. Bell rewrote it and brought it back in to Levenson's office. But, again, Levenson didn't like it. So Bell tried it again and again. Finally, Levenson said, "Ted, just because you run over a snake in the road doesn't mean you have to replace it." Bell eliminated the offending sentence. And it's been an editing suggestion that he's followed ever since. Says Bell, "I got a year's education in one afternoon."

Bill Bernbach also had a tremendous influence on Bell. "He taught us all to start with the *concept*. The one thing you want people to take away from the communication. DDB was about *ideas*, not execution. And ideas that *sold* something!"

Bernbach also taught Bell to respect the audience. "Give them some credit for intelligence," explains Bell. "You don't have to pound them over the head with inane or repetitious copy slogans. There can be warmth, humor, wit, and style. That was Bill's battle cry. That there should be some charm and emotion and humanity in advertising. I like to think of it as 'relevant' charm."

The environment at DDB fostered Bell's talents and he soon rose to the level of vice president, copy supervisor.

But, after nearly ten years there, he was itching for a change. In 1982 he moved to Chicago to join Leo Burnett as an associate creative director. It was a step down the corporate ladder, but Burnett wanted new energy in their creative department and Bell recognized this opportunity.

At first, Bell found it difficult to adjust to Burnett's culture. At DDB the energy orbited around the creatives. Creative teams were guided by gut instinct, not market research. At Burnett, however, Bell found that the disciplines were expected to function as a team. The researchers, copywriters, art directors, and account teams all worked as a cohesive, balanced group. Market research, as well as post-production research, was considered valuable in directing a campaign. For Bell, that took some getting used to. He quickly learned that the intrinsic strengths of the Burnett system far outweighed any negative early perceptions. Indeed, at Burnett the idea that "none of us is as smart as all of us" has paid off in some of the biggest, most enduring ideas in advertising history; the Marlboro Man and the Friendly Skies of United are just two examples.

When it comes to post-production research, Bell still doubts its value. Bell believes that up-front research should enlighten the creatives about the realities of the marketplace. Creatives should be provided with as much information as possible *before* they begin working on a project. "I don't need people in the shopping mall telling me they do or don't like my ads. If they're so creative they should be here and I'll go out in the shopping center and offer my opinions," says Bell. "But as far as getting information up front, the more you know, the better off you are. Partnership between disciplines is so important."

One of Bell's first tasks at Burnett was to build his own creative group. He wanted a team of kindred spirits, people who thought the same way he did. So instead of building a group of seasoned veterans, he hired kids right out of school. "I was looking for punks," says Bell. "I wanted kids who had no experience in the business, who didn't have a clue how to create ads. Kids who didn't know the rules and just wanted to do great ads. They had to have talent, excitement, and raw energy about them. And a complete love of great advertising."

And they had to believe that nothing else mattered. Except doing great adverising. Bell didn't care about politics. He didn't care who liked who. If the person came up with great ideas he or she was in his group. If not, that person was out. That was his philosophy: the "get it" factor.

Bell's efforts paid off. He was soon promoted to creative director and then again to group creative director. In 1986, he became president and chief executive officer. Bell attributes much of his success to his mentors for instilling in him a sense of confidence. Says Bell, "I don't know if I'm right or wrong, but I make a gut decision to do something. This is what I think it should be. Not what I think is current, or hip, or politically correct. You may like it or not like it later, but you do it. And, eventually, your career is the sum of those decisions. You are what you make. Bernbach and Burnett helped me figure it out."

What would he be doing if he weren't in advertising? Bell believes he would always be writing something. He has written four screenplays and sold one. The movie was two days away from getting produced when the investors pulled out. Recalls Bell, "It was one of the worst days of my life. I'm still not sure if it was a good thing or a bad thing. I've had a lot of fun making ads."

SELECTIONS FROM BELL'S BOOK

Bank Americard

When Bell was working on a portfolio to show agencies in New York, he ran across an article suggesting that America would soon be a cashless society. The headline came to him and he sketched out this ad for a credit card and included it in his early portfolio.

Yukon Jack

Bell created Yukon Jack in the early seventies. "The creative director told me that the client was always looking for a product that could beat Southern Comfort. All I knew was that the product was going to be Canadian whiskey with honey in it. I liked the idea of a guy who was all by himself. I wanted him to be real macho, a tough guy, a loner. Those ideas lead to the concept, and once I had 'The Black Sheep of Canadian Liquor,' I felt I could write these things forever." Says Bell, "I'm proud of Yukon Jack because I came up with the concept and it turned out to be a huge success." It is still a product today.

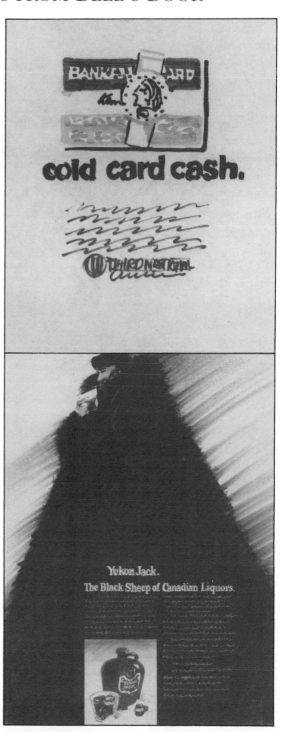

Volkswagen (Thing)

The VW Thing was one of the first assignments that Bell worked on at DDB. "The headline's fun," says
Bell. "But it also tells you something about the Thing, that they're tough cars. They're built to stand up.
It (the headline) is not just a joke. It's cute, but it says something. It has a point. It sells."

Rabbits eat peanuts.

A little friendly advice from Volkswagen for those of you who have to get to work on your own.

Volkswagen (Rabbit)

Here's an example of using current events to create timely, impactful advertising, a technique that was popularized by DDB. Former peanut farmer and president, Jimmy Carter, was well known for his simple lifestyle. Because of gasoline shortages in the late 1970s, Carter decided to discourage the use of limousines by his White House staff. Taking advantage of Volkswagen's economical gas mileage, Bell cranked out this ad over a weekend, and it ran in the New York Times and Washington Post on the Monday that Carter announced the new policy. It won a gold One Show Award, Bell's first. "I always assume that people are smart and will appreciate someone who takes the time to give them a little humor and intelligence," says Bell. "And I always try to give people something back for taking the time to read my ad."

Memorex "Is It Love"

Oddly enough, this is a demo commercial. The girl cries as her hero hops into his Porsche and speeds away, whereupon she hits rewind and watches it yet again. Is it love? Or, is it Memorex? Bell shot this with director Joe Pytka over a Thanksgiving holiday with a very limited budget. But, with a strong, simple concept the story itself delivers.

McDonald's Sound of Summer

This is Bell's Burnett favorite. Each image brings in another sensory experience of summertime. The sounds of early morning birds in the country and egg on a grill, the smell of hot biscuits, and the sun rising all create a warm emotional response in the viewer, making McDonald's a very favorable place to have breakfast. It shows how imagery alone can effectively tell a story. A story with warmth and style instead of with numerous feature/benefit copy points. In fact, there is no copy!

THE PURPOSE OF ADVERTISING, AS WELL AS IMPORTANT ADVICE

BEFORE WE FOCUS ON DEVELOPING A PORTFOLIO, WE MUST FIRST GAIN A BASIC IDEA OF what advertising should do. Bell believes that its purpose is not to show how cute or clever you can be. Rather, its purpose is to communicate the advantages of your particular product or service in a way that makes the audience notice, makes sense and sells, and gives the audience a reason to act.

So what type of work gets his attention? Bell recalled one ad from a creative's portfolio that particularly impressed him. The ad showed two windows. One looked out on clouds in the sky—from above the clouds. Underneath the clouds was the line, "The $599 View."

The other window looked out at rolling hills and the sun setting over a little town. Under that window was the line "The $79 View." At the bottom, it just said "Amtrak" and had some body copy.

"The ad showed an understanding of advertising," says Bell. "Clearly the train ride offered a more scenic and less expensive way to travel than air. That ad showed consumers the benefits of riding the train with a simple, intelligent, and witty message. So I hired him and he's now running our Tokyo office. He 'gets it.'"

In other words, he presented a fresh idea. A new way of looking at an old problem. "The quality of surprise, the freshness, is the trick," says Bell. "You have to hook people emotionally. You've got to give them information and make them see things in a new way."

So once you have these basics down—basics that many experienced creatives forget—how do you proceed? Here are some ideas.

Forget the format

Some schools and many advertising books recommend that your portfolio contain three campaigns—one for package-goods, one for a durable, and one for a service. Bell doesn't buy that. "I believe if you understand advertising, you can work on anything," says Bell. "There's no package-goods guy, no car guy. Really good people can work on anything. And *want* to work on anything. A truly brilliant art director treats a matchbook cover like a two-page spread in *Life*."

Learn the fundamentals

Your book has to show you can think in terms of advertising—that you understand what the job is all about. The right advertising school can help you do this. "It's a real shortcut way to learn the fundamentals," says Bell. "If I had known about these schools when I was trying to get a job, I probably would have gone to one." Leo Burnett primarily recruits out of the Portfolio Center in Atlanta, the Art Center in Los Angeles, the University of Texas in Austin, and the School of Visual Arts in New York. Bell feels these schools have excellent programs.

Read the annuals

It's another way to learn the fundamentals. "Beginners who don't go to a school to create a portfolio still have a chance," says Bell. "A great idea is a great idea even if it's a pencil-drawn stick figure on 8×10 notebook paper." Bell suggests that you find the ads in the annuals that you think are great and discover what they have in common. Says Bell, "Try to figure out what makes the ads fresh." (Look for more about the importance of annuals in later chapters.)

Record interesting images and ideas

"If I'm watching a movie and I see something funny or I see something on the street, I sort of file it away. It's like a novelist who overhears a conversation and jots it down," says Bell. "He doesn't know what he's going to use it for, but somewhere down the line you'll see that conversation in a book. You'd be surprised at how many famous advertising ideas first saw the light of day on a cocktail napkin. In fact, I'd say the cocktail napkin is one of the *essential* tools of the advertising business."

Emphasize the idea

"If a copywriter writes great body copy, that's terrific. But I have to see a great headline concept first. If he's a writer and his art direction is a little weak, I don't get bothered by that. A copywriter can even come to me with an ad scribbled on tissues. As long as I can understand it and it has a great headline, I'll consider him. That's how much I care about fancy presentation," says Bell. As for an art director, Bell says, "If his art direction is weak, obviously I'll get bothered by it. Really good creative people are ambidextrous. Good writers are strong visually and good art directors are strong conceptually."

Improve existing ads

While in London, Bell learned how to create advertising by redoing the advertising in the newspaper and magazines. "Look for ads, tear them out, stick them on a wall and see if you can do them better," says Bell. "That process made me start to think about how to do great work. That was the basis for building my portfolio."

Let it hit you immediately

Bell believes the first ideas are the most valuable. "Most people will tell you that their first idea is what they usually end up doing. When it takes weeks and weeks to come up with a concept, you just ain't doing it. If I keep asking, 'How's it going,' and I keep hearing, 'We're working on it,' I don't hold my breath. We had a game at DDB, 'Blitzkrieg Advertising.' One person says a product name, the other blurts out the first headline that comes to mind. We played all the time. It helped."

Start with print

In agencies like Burnett and DDB, beginners used to work on print, then, after a long time, television. But that's not true today—which Bell believes is a mistake. "Print forces you to have an idea on a page," says Bell. "So you learn the discipline. In television, you have more going on, so you can hide a weak idea."

Stay away from radio scripts in your portfolio

"Nobody has time to read over radio scripts," says Bell. "At least not me. Creative directors want to see your ideas, how you see the world. A strong headline, a visual, a little copy—six to nine truly *new*, great concepts—that will get you hired."

Forget research

When putting a book together, it's difficult to factor in relevant research. Beginners should just figure out a product and come up with a great ad. "What research would have led to the Amtrak ad?" asks Bell. "Everybody knows it costs a lot more to fly than to take the train. Everybody knows when you look out of a plane you see clouds and when you look out of a train you see landscape. The writer didn't need research. He needed common sense and an original point of view."

Team up

If Bell is interviewing a copywriter, he looks at the ideas, the headlines. If he's interviewing an art director, he looks for tasteful art direction *and ideas*. To cover both sides, Bell suggests teaming up. "If you're a writer, find a partner who wants to be an art director and work together," he says. "Look for an art director who is as great a writer as you are. The best art directors are very conceptual. They know how to write their own headlines and come up with their own ideas. And the best copywriters always have a very good visual sense. These disciplines, at their best, are never mutually exclusive."

Don't forget taste

"I think a lot of this business is taste and intelligence," says Bell. "It's a sense of fitness. Style. Of how things should look. There are beautiful ads and there are ugly ads. When in doubt, go with the beautiful."

Go against the grain

Bell learned many lessons while working with art directors like Helmut Krone, Bert Steinhauser, and Charlie Piccirillo. One of those things, says Bell, was "When everybody yells, whisper. When everybody is running, walk. Go against everybody's sense of what's *currently* the right thing to do. People are always talking about trends in advertising. I don't want to know about trends, except to know what to avoid. Trends are what's already been done. I want to start a new trend. And as soon as it becomes a trend, I want to start something else."

Keep it simple

"Just about every ad I've ever been involved with has been very simple," says Bell. "Simple in terms of the idea, the layout, the copy—everything. That was a very good lesson to learn early on. Don't let the art direction get between the consumer and your idea. Don't make the work too hard. We didn't go running around the halls saying, 'Look at this ad. It's really great. It's really complicated.'"

Protect your ideas...

Bell believes that those who succeed in advertising have very strong opinions about what is good. "Great advertising is a very fragile thing," says Bell. "The minute something is created, there are a million people who want to kill it for a variety of reasons." The challenge, according to Bell, is that once you have an idea that you know in your gut is great, you should see it through and get it done. Says Bell, "That's tough to do."

...And fight like hell

Bell believes that the best way to fight for your ideas is to show your unwavering commitment to them. "It's a matter of saying loud enough and long enough that 'This is great!' and sooner or later, people will say, 'All Right. Do it. Maybe you're right.' That's the secret," says Bell. "Fight like hell for your ideas. Because that's all you have to sell."

Move with resolve

Bell recalls a scene from the novel *The Last Tycoon* as an example of the type of focused determination needed to achieve a goal. In it, the Irving Thalborg character is flying from Atlanta to Los Angeles. He's interested in airplanes, so he visits the cockpit. He looks at the mountain ranges and asks the pilots, "If you were to put a road through that mountain range, where would you put it?" The first pilot answers, "I guess I'd put it over there where the valley is, that ravine, and go all the way through." The copilot then answers, "I'd go through the valley." "No," the character says, "If you're going through these mountains, go right through the middle." Says Bell, "This is a guy who understands how to get things done. You just go. This is what we're going to do. Do it."

Don't make excuses for weak work

Bell dislikes hearing a copywriter or art director with a portfolio say, "I have to apologize for some of these ads. They're not what I really wanted to do. The client killed my best stuff." There are millions of stories about what you wanted to do that didn't happen. Bell has heard them all and isn't interested. "What it really comes down to is how you write is how you think. This is you," says Bell. "If your portfolio isn't a representation of your thinking, change it."

Remember, slick don't stick

"Twenty years ago beginning books were very rough. Today, even fresh grads can create tight comps. But if people hiring these kids are smart, they'll look past the glitz," says Bell. High-priced leather portfolios and weird gimmicks turn Bell off. He's seen a lot of slick portfolios that have no fresh ideas. And he suspects a glitzy portfolio may be an attempt to compensate for a lack of creative ideas. Says Bell, "Sometimes a guy knows in his heart that he doesn't have very many good ideas, so he's got to make them look good."

Show your enthusiasm

"If you really have a passion for the business, that comes across and helps you," says Bell. "It comes across as you talk. People sense that you're going to have a certain energy about you. Or you're not. And who would you rather having working for you? The guy who *loves* the work."

Know that everything that sells *is* advertising

"People talking about 'new' advertising are full of it," says Bell. "I recently heard a speaker say, 'We're not even going to call it an ad agency anymore. We're going to call it a sales creation unit.' And I thought, 'What is this guy talking about?' All we do is advertising. Whether we do a 60-second TV commercial with a big budget or a 2-inch ad in the back of the newspaper, or a beer coaster, it's an ad and should be made great. A great direct response ad is a great ad with an 800 number on it. Even a sign in a store showing you where the beer is should be a great sign."

• • • • • • • • • • • • • • •

A Special Postscript
TED BELL'S LOOK AT TWO ADVERTISING GIANTS

THROUGHOUT THIS BOOK, YOU WILL BE HEARING ABOUT THE CONTRIBUTIONS OF LEO Burnett and Bill Bernbach to the field of advertising. Ted Bell was one of the few who was able to work under the influence of both. (Burnett himself had already passed away when Bell joined Leo Burnett, but his influence was still greatly felt.)

In 1987, Ted Bell presented a speech to the Adcrafter Club in Detroit. In it, he described the opposing personal styles, yet parallel advertising philosophies, of Bernbach and Burnett. They both revolutionized the advertising industry. Bell's insights into their ideas help us understand how they created a world of advertising that was big enough for both of them. Let's take a look at excerpts from that speech.

"Leo Burnett and William Bernbach. Any list of advertising giants must include them. Why is that? What did they do? What made them tick? Since I've been fortunate enough to work in both of their shadows, I thought it might be interesting to offer a few comparisons in an effort to discover whether these giants left any tracks of lasting value.

"As I've said, people who met them for the first time were always surprised to discover that each was so short. But then, they never saw either man standing on his wallet!

"Leo grew up a small-town boy, and graduated from the University of Michigan. Bill, born August 13, 1911, under the sign of Leo, oddly enough, graduated from the streets of Brooklyn and then New York University. English major with a smattering of philosophy.

"Leo left his post in Detroit as ad manager of the Old Marmon Company to found his agency in Chicago at the height of the Depression, 1935. I'm sure many of you have heard the story of Mr. Burnett's apples. He was told that anyone crazy enough to open an advertising agency in those times would soon be selling apples on the street.

'Maybe so,' Leo said, 'but first I'll give 'em away.' I'm glad to say we're still giving them away by the bowlful, all around the world.

"Bill Bernbach wrote his first ad while in the mailroom at Schenley, and went on to become creative head of Grey Advertising, New York. In 1949, Bill left Grey to start a new agency with Ned Doyle and Maxwell Dane.

"He opened his doors with this engaging manifesto: 'It will be known as Doyle Dane Bernbach and nothing shall come between them, not even punctuation.'

"I always liked that a lot. As it turned out, nothing ever did come between them...except time.

"In the beginning, and always for that matter, Bill and Leo were copywriters. Both founded their agencies before the flickering dawn of television and both shared a profound and powerful love of the printed word.

"And both men, I would argue, built their agencies and their reputations by simply revolutionizing the way we, as writers and art directors and marketers, talked to people. They felt that to talk to people, or better yet, with them, was far better than talking at them. Both believed fervently in the essential humanity and dignity of their audience. Both were intelligent enough to realize the simple fact that people simply aren't stupid. Give people credit for a little intelligence and they'll pay you back a thousandfold. With trust, and better yet, belief. As Bernbach once said, 'Yes, there is a 12-year-old mentality in this country...every six-year-old has one.'

"Until Bill and Leo, a lot of advertising consisted of jabbering away about this or that product claim, a laundry list of attributes, singing product strategies. Advertising didn't seem to spring from the real world where people lived.

"I think one of the things that made them great was that they were the first to recognize that logic as the basis for advertising is illogical. That the human brain is an organ of survival, and as such it searches not for reason, but for advantage. Everyone yearns for a better life, everyone is in the never-ending pursuit of happiness, everyone longs for freedom from the menial.

"Bernbach and Burnett realized that people make decisions based not on fact, but emotion. It's not how people *think* about you, but how they *feel* about you. As in 'What do you *think* of your new car?' Answer: 'I *like* it.'

"It all sounds simple, now, but Leo and Bill were first. And they were right. As a result, they changed the course of advertising forever, and both men, as you may not know, entered the Copywriters Hall of Fame on the same day!

"Very few people know this, but Leo and Bill were actually friends. They met frequently for lunch in New York during the sixties at Bill's favorite restaurant, the Four Seasons. At a corner table in the Grill Room, where George Lois once went down on his knees to kiss Bernbach's ring, some real power lunches took place. Oh, to be a fly on that wall! Here was a study in contrasts:

"Leo, with the ever-present Marlboro dangling from the lower lip, dusting his lapels with ashes, presenting the rumpled appearance of one who sleeps in his suit to save time…

"Bill, who never smoked or drank, ever dapper in his pale blue English shirts, clearly a man who abhorred any imperfection in dress or manner. A kid from the streets, who'd done all right for himself.

"Leo, shy but gruff in his opinions about the advertising business. On this subject, he threw his body into the discussion.

"Bill, ever attentive, his ice-blue eyes leaping to life as ideas boomed in his mind…smooth, quiet, persuasive.

"On Leo's side of the table, surely a dry martini. Leo was even known to carry his own tumbler of gin and vermouth whenever he traveled by air.

'I just don't trust airplane gin,' he used to say.

"Bernbach, minus a drink or cigarette, but always the teacher, using his hands to try to carve his ideas out of thin air, for Leo to see.

"Two giants, locked in mortal combat, not with each other, but in a mutual rebellion against all that was shoddy or banal or second-rate in a profession they both loved.

"What thought filled the air at those now distant luncheons? What signposts were being hung out to point the way as our business was being moved in new directions, as these two tiny titans pulled the levers?

"I'd like to share a few of their thoughts with you. Here are the thoughts of the man on one side of that long ago table in the Grill Room (Bernbach):

- We must ally ourselves with the great ideas and carry them to the public. We must practice our skills on behalf of society.
- We must not just believe in what we sell, we must sell what we believe in.
- For creative people, rules are a prison.

- Dullness won't sell your product; but, neither will irrelevant brilliance.
- I warn you against believing advertising is a science. Advertising is an art; nothing memorable ever emerged from a formula.
- The product, the product, the product. Stay with the product. Simple.
- The truth isn't the truth until people believe you.
- I don't want scientists, I want people who do the right things. I want people who do inspiring things.
- Let us blaze new trails. Let us prove to the world that good taste, good art and good writing can be good selling.
- The real giants of advertising have always been poets—men who jumped from facts into the realm of imagination and ideas.

"And the thoughts of the trail-blazing gentleman on the other side of the table, Burnett:

- An ad must make no pretense of being anything but an ad. It must not attempt to snare the reader by pretending to be something else. It must say 'I'm an ad and proud of it. I have something important to tell you and here it is.'
- The problem is how to be believable, sincere, and warm but colorful and provocative at the same time, with a good honest ring to our words.
- I have learned that any fool can write a bad ad, but it takes a real genius to keep his hands off a good one.
- I can't give you a formula for success. But I can give you a foolproof formula for failure—just try to please everybody.
- I have learned that the greatest single thing to be achieved in advertising is believability.
- As I have observed it, great advertising is deceptively and disarmingly simple. It has a common touch without being patronizing.
- I don't think you have to be 'off-beat' to be interesting. A truly interesting piece of advertising is 'off-beat' by its very rarity.
- Most writers, when they become sincere, are merely dull.
- A small thought on a slick paper in full color won't live. But a big thought on a scrap of cardboard will live forever.

"If there were arguments long ago in the Grill Room where the giants sat, they may have been about the check, but they certainly weren't about advertising. On that, they seem to have agreed. I wondered earlier about the legacy of Leo and Bill.

"In fact, Leo himself wondered out loud one morning about the same thing. He knew very well what he had built, and, as he was nearing the end of his career, he knew what he would be leaving behind. So, as was Leo's way, he also left very wise instructions on how to keep his spirit and dedication alive. And a warning of what would happen if we don't. (To take his name off the door.)

"It would be fair of you to ask me what these old codgers have to do with now. Not nearly enough, would be my answer. Certainly, the current business of business and the business of advertising bear little resemblance to Leo's world, or Bill's. In the end they left us with this:

- You make a good product.
- You don't take shortcuts.
- You take pride in what you make and you tell the truth.

- You don't allow success to breed arrogance, because you'll never outsmart the American consumer. They'll always find you out, and they are very slow to forgive.
- You recognize the dignity and humanity in people and they'll recognize it in you and believe you."

Susan Gillette

"If you're good, you have a lot more control over your destiny than you think you have," says Susan Gillette, president of DDB Needham's Chicago office. She feels that a lot of creative people waste their talent because they are dreamy types who don't take charge of their lives or their careers.

In this chapter, we'll not only examine more basic ideas for putting together a portfolio and finding a job in advertising, we will look at the career of someone who has taken control of her career and has succeeded because of it.

Susan Gillette moved from copywriter to creative director by the age of 27, and, by 40, was named president. Gillette's dialogue is sprinkled with "reallys," "kindas," and "sortas"—qualifiers that communication workshop professionals instruct women to avoid in order to be taken seriously. Her success, however, proves that who you are and what you deliver are far more important.

Gillette was born in Philadelphia, but her family moved to Villa Park, Illinois, a Chicago suburb, when she was 13. She attended Northern Illinois University and graduated in 1972 with a major in English literature and a minor in psychology.

These days, Gillette, the mother of two, enjoys spending her nights and weekends with her family. Says Gillette, "I don't play golf or tennis or go to a health club and I don't join associations that require evening participation because those activities would take me away from my kids." An avid horsewoman, Gillette waited to get back into her hobby until her daughters were old enough to ride with her. The family now owns a pony and a horse.

A Career on the Fast Track Despite the Mommy Track

Gillette believes all creative people start out with good intuition and a conscious understanding of human nature. "The rest," she says, "is trial and error." In other words, creative people can get more polished over time, but the underlying talent is innate. Says Gillette, "You can nurture talent. You can mature talent. You can improve talent. But you can't develop it. People either have it or they don't."

Gillette had the typical creative personality; dreamy, preoccupied, forgetful, self-critical. As a child, she was a worrier and was always feeling guilty about something. In the fourth grade, for instance, she went through a "save-the-world" period and wanted to give all her birthday money to the church. Says Gillette, "I wanted to be a nun and I wasn't even Catholic. I was a pretty weird kid."

This worrying and guilt gave her a chance to learn how things affect people and, in turn, how to cause that effect. "That's really what the great advertising executive is about," says Gillette. "It's like, I can make you laugh; I can make you cry. Creative people take great pleasure in being able to elicit emotions from others."

Gillette credits an atypical family background for cultivating her talents. Her older brother was incredibly bright, but no one in the family recognized it. When she was four and he was eight, he'd ask her to play chess, explain the rules, beat her, and then tell her that she was stupid. The next day, ("Proving he was quite right," she admits) the same pattern would be repeated. "That sort of set the tone for my early childhood," says Gillette.

Her brother's misdirected mental energy led to tension between him and his mother. At any given time, her brother and mother were not speaking to one another. Says Gillette, "I was a very skinny child because I couldn't eat with all the tension at the dinner table." To relieve the tension, she would tell jokes, stories, anything to divert attention. "Otherwise, you'd want to pick up a steak knife and slit your wrists," says Gillette. "I became quite good at entertaining people." (Note: Despite the turmoil, she describes her family as very loving. Today, she shares a close relationship with her brother, who is now a professor of public policy at Princeton, and her parents, who live a mile from her.)

Gillette, who says she wasn't very goal oriented in college, took her first full-time job because her parents would not let her lie around the house for more than a week. She had tried teaching on a Title I Project and decided it wasn't for her. She considered graduate school.

Since she had always enjoyed writing, she looked up "writer" in the *Chicago Tribune* classifieds. There were two jobs listed. She interviewed for both, lied about being able to type, and was offered a position as a writer/secretary in a small suburban telecommunications firm.

The job was more fun than Gillette had expected it would be. She worked with two young designers from IIT. Her boss was a 30-year-old who drove to work in an orange Corvette. She was soon promoted to assistant advertising director and began writing trade articles and speeches for the vice president, as well as technical materials. But she saw herself getting complacent in her job and she didn't like that. Also, she didn't have an engineering background to truly understand what she was writing about and had no desire to learn the technical side of the telecommunications industry.

Luckily, not long after the restlessness set in, she was asked to write some ads for a trade campaign. She enjoyed writing the ads, which she mentioned to her brother. He, in turn, directed her to a friend of his, Mike Cafferetta, who was a creative director at Leo Burnett.

When she showed Cafferetta the ads she had written, he suggested she put a spec portfolio together. He advised her to begin by studying the *Communications Arts Advertising Annuals.* She got her hands on the annuals from 1968 to 1973— which she thinks were classic years for advertising. She "decoded" the ads in the annuals to figure out what made them great. She took away the headline to see if the visual still worked, she removed the visual to see if the headline still worked.

What she learned was the Doyle Dane Bernbach format: A picture communicates one message, words offer another meaning, and combined they send a third message. For instance, the headline, "You don't have to be Jewish to love Levy's" has one meaning, but accompanied by a visual of an Asian child, the ad makes you smile. Great ads, for Gillette, are this juxtaposition of verbal messages and visual messages. Unless you have an extremely powerful message, she believes words alone rarely make a great ad. (For a fuller description of the DDB format, see Roy Grace's chapter.)

With her book near completion, Gillette quit her job with the telecommunications firm. Her boss reacted by telling her he thought she was making a mistake—that she wouldn't make it in advertising. "But failure wasn't something I was concerned about," says Gillette. "I was a kid and didn't care. I hadn't achieved anything I defined as success, so I wasn't giving up anything. Except a paycheck."

And once her portfolio was complete, Cafferetta provided Gillette with a list of contacts. She called each of them and found that they were very receptive to seeing her. But none had an available position. Some, however, referred her to other people, which generated a second list.

Even with help, she found her job search to be frustrating. On the positive side, however, it gave her an opportunity to see what kind of agency she wanted to work in and what kind of people she wanted to work for. Says Gillette, "Some people I interviewed with were so rude, I said to myself, 'Good, I'm glad you don't like my book. I don't like you either—and I wouldn't want to work here even if you paid me.'"

For instance, at one agency, she was quickly ushered into an office where the interviewer stood with his back to her while he hung awards on the wall. She sat there for over twenty minutes before he turned around and acknowledged her.

This agency had a campaign running for Smile Gum and they had created a slogan that said, "Say Cheese and Smile." Gillette's book contained a campaign for Carefree Sugarless Gum. Her ad showed a dentist sitting in his own chair playing solitaire and had the tagline, "Your dentist will hate you for this." In other words, the gum is so good, dentists will hate you because you will never need them again. Gillette's interviewer told her the ad was terrible. There's no appetite appeal, he explained. "This guy obviously had no sense of humor," Gillette observed. He directed her to look at his campaign for Smile Gum.

Gillette critiqued the creative director's campaign by saying, "Say Cheese? Cheese and gum are the most unappetizing combination. It makes me think the gum tastes like cheese. That's terrible."

She says she feared the guy was going to pick her up by the scruff of her neck and throw her out of the room because of her response, but she was not apologetic for saying it. "Gall is something I've always had," says Gillette. "I had it in the beginning of my career, I have it in the middle, I'll always have it. I've developed a bit more diplomacy than I had at 23, but not much," she laughs.

On the other hand, Gillette offered to work for one prospective employer for free, because he was a great copywriter. The guy turned her down because he said it wouldn't be right. But he promised that he would hire her in two years. She didn't expect to hear from him again, but two years later he called her and offered her a job.

After 30 or 40 interviews over the next three months, Gillette was hired as a copywriter at Stern Walters for the same salary she had been making at the telecommunications company. At this agency, she honed her print writing skills and won some awards for the work she did for the Chicago Transit Authority. One of Gillette's favorites was a 15-second commercial with the headline: "Introducing a new economy model." As the headlights go on, the viewer sees that the vehicle is a bus, not a car. This was the most expensive commercial she worked on at Stern Walters. It cost $7,000, but it had a strong selling idea. She was soon promoted from copywriter to a copy supervisor. But after two years, she decided it was time to move.

When Gillette arrived at the then Needham, Harper & Steers (which merged with Doyle Dane Bernbach in 1985), she had to start over as a copywriter. But she understood that working on national accounts would have a different set of demands. Says Gillette, "I was savvy enough to know that if I was good, it wouldn't take long to be promoted again."

With a strong print book, she was assigned to the print and collateral group. At that time, creative groups were loosely divided by media. It didn't take her long to decide she wanted to do McDonald's commercials, but she was in the wrong group.

She took control when she was asked to write some print materials for a new sandwich called the McFeast, which McDonald's was introducing. When Gillette and her art director did the print and collateral, they also did a television commercial: "I never waited to be asked to do anything. Since no one else was working on the TV spot yet, we sold the entire package. The next time we did it again." After the second time, management promoted her to the television group.

At 31 she turned down the opportunity to become deputy creative director. She was pregnant and was unsure about the demands of motherhood. She didn't know how she would feel after having the baby. But she knew she was going to need more time with her child to be the kind of mother she wanted to be. "I was a psychology minor," says Gillette, "I really understood that there were these couple of years for me to make an impression on my kids." She went from the fast track to the mommy track.

She calls this her proudest moment. "I'd have to say that was the gutsiest thing I ever did," says Gillette. "It really might not have turned out the way it did. It was a risky thing to do. But it was also easy. And it was the only thing I could do emotionally."

Indeed, it was risky. Many corporations still penalize talented employees for taking time off to raise a family. They hold back promotions. They question the person's loyalty. But the fact that her career had come relatively easily helped her decide to take the risk. She figured she could always get work in advertising. "Talent gives you a sense of security," she observes.

Her boss was skeptical of her working part time, but she made a deal with him to work six hours a day, skip lunch, and work at home—for sixty percent of her salary. She was allowed to retain her title as group creative director, but she lost her group.

During her first year as a part-timer, she did everything nobody else wanted to do. "All the garbage," she says. She wrote an in-house Crusade of Mercy campaign, speeches for the then president, posters, and match-book covers. "For one year my biggest media buy was the back of the bathroom door," says Gillette. "But it was okay with me."

Gillette then got involved in pitching new accounts. She helped pitch Sears, which Needham won. She pitched Michelob Lite and won that account. Then she won more work from Sears and some from Kraft. People began asking to be in her group—even though she didn't have one. And after she had helped win the business, the agency knew that she had to be involved with producing the work and servicing the accounts, so they gradually began letting her build another creative group. Over the five years that she worked part time, she estimates she helped win approximately $150 million worth of new business.

"At that point, I think I was the most underpaid person in advertising," she says. "But I didn't care. I still worked part time. I had a real group again." Gillette would get home at two, put her kids to bed at ten, and spend a couple more hours working. Sometimes, she'd go back to an editing suite after her children had gone to bed. Other times, she'd work two weeks straight because they were pitching a new piece of business and then she'd take some time off. When she traveled she took the children with her. "It was flexible," says Gillette. "And that was what I wanted."

During her tenure as a part-timer, Gillette developed the campaign that she is most famous for creating, "The Night Belongs to Michelob." At the time, she was working on Michelob Lite, a brand that lacked a big budget, and she wanted a chance to work on the big-budget Michelob campaign. But because clients are possessive about their creative talent—when a creative assigned to one brand works another brand, the client sometimes feels that his brand is not getting the attention it deserves—she was asked not to work on this account.

Gillette again took control of her career. She did a little research and discovered that there was a product called Michelob Dark. This brand didn't have an advertising budget. It also wasn't taboo for her to work on. She started thinking about the meaning of darkness and night imagery. While walking across the Michigan Avenue bridge in Chicago, she came up with the line, "Nothing's the same after dark." And she knew she had it. Recalls Gillette, "I started laughing because I knew it would sell the moment I thought of it."

The next morning, she talked with her art director about the imagery she had envisioned. They put together a commercial knowing that they were actually trying to sell a Michelob campaign and sent a cassette of it to the client saying, "We know you don't have a budget for Michelob Dark, but isn't this kind of provocative?" Ten minutes after the client saw the cassette, Gillette received a phone call from them telling her they loved it, but that they didn't have a budget for the product.

Gillette suggested that maybe, with a little rewriting, they could use it for Michelob. With the client's interest in her campaign, Gillette was able to obtain permission to work on its creative development. Says Gillette, "It ticked off a few people who were working on it creatively. But we proceeded to do ten commercials."

It took nine months for Gillette to sell the campaign, which was developed around a very simple idea. Consumer sales were sluggish because Michelob was perceived as a "special occasion beer." Gillette's ad attacked that perception and said that every night is a special night. So, says Gillette, "It was for a special occasion that came every night of the week."

After five years of part-time work, her boss, who was becoming president of the agency, asked her to return to a full-time schedule and become creative director. It was difficult for Gillette to turn down the offer. She doubted that another agency would offer her a similar position after five years of working part time. Says Gillette, "You are most valuable in a place where the clients trust you." Since this might be a once-in-a-lifetime opportunity, she decided to try it.

"It was like going from 0 to 60," she says. "As involved in my group as I was, it was different running the agency's entire creative department." She believes that once you rise to the position of creative director, your biggest challenge is to control the creative process by making people feel good about their work while keeping them out of trouble. Creative people, she claims, love to hear themselves talk; they always think they have the right solution. Gillette's role was to make sure the work was not only artful, but strategically sound and could be sold to the client. "Sometimes," she says, "you get work that is none of the above."

Gillette feels that getting promoted early helped her career; she quickly learned that she'd be responsible for everything. She was going to get credit for work that was successful and suffer humiliation when it was not.

"I'm still not sure I was ever a great creative director because being a creative person, I would always come up with my own solutions to problems," she says. "It's human nature. You see a problem and your mind looks for a solution. I'd ask myself, 'Do I suggest the solution or do I let them get there themselves? Do I tell them what I would do and then let them figure out what they would do?'"

Gillette's answer depended on the deadline. "If we had to go to the client the next day with inferior work, you have to push for a solution. Hopefully, I can say, 'Boy, this seems off to me. Here's why. Here's what I think you need to do. You guys go back and figure out how to do it.'"

In 1991, Gillette was promoted again, this time to president. "I loved being a writer—and I still do. I could be very happy as a copywriter," says Gillette. "But as a creative person, your ultimate fantasy is to be in control of everything."

She says that being president of an agency is just a different kind of pressure, a different level of problem solving. She compares her promotion to going from composer to conductor. "You step up and you're just as concerned about the solo that night and the excellence of the performance," she says. "But you tend to have a different perspective. You worry about more things. You know if you can't keep the house full, you can't pay these people—and if you can't pay these people, you lose your best soloists."

As president, Gillette's philosophy is much the same as it has been throughout her career: Every piece of work should be as good as it can be. That includes the idea, the words, the pictures, the music, the film, the nuances—everything. When a copywriter writes a couple of headlines and thinks she has written an ad, she is disappointed. "I probably went through a pad a day," says Gillette. "I'd write a hundred headlines before I'd be happy and I'd rewrite the body copy fifteen times."

She says that each problem sets her mind off in many different directions. She believes this is not a result of talent, but of mindset. Gillette uses herself as an example. "I always hated to lose. They could keep rejecting my work but I would keep coming back with another great idea." She feels this kind of competitiveness is ultimately good for her clients. "I want my clients to win in the marketplace. I want them to beat the heck out of their competition. I'm very goal-directed. Win the business. Build the sales. Win the awards. Focus on the work. My success has been a result of that focus."

A FEW SAMPLES FROM THE DREAM PORTFOLIO

Feminine Protection

Students of advertising are often told to avoid public service ads in their portfolios. There's a perception that public service ads are easy to do. But Gillette believes that to write a great public service ad is to write a great ad. "Besides," she says, "it gets to people and it's more fun to do than toothpaste."

Gillette's early portfolio included this public service spec ad which presented a different kind of "feminine protection." Body copy told women that they had a right to carry condoms to prevent venereal diseases.

Ironically, her public service work for preventing sexually transmitted diseases didn't end with her spec book. Eighteen years later, Gillette is creating ads to inspire people to protect themselves from AIDS. "They do not have the same kind of headlines or executions," says Gillette. "They are not as flip. VD is curable; AIDS is not."

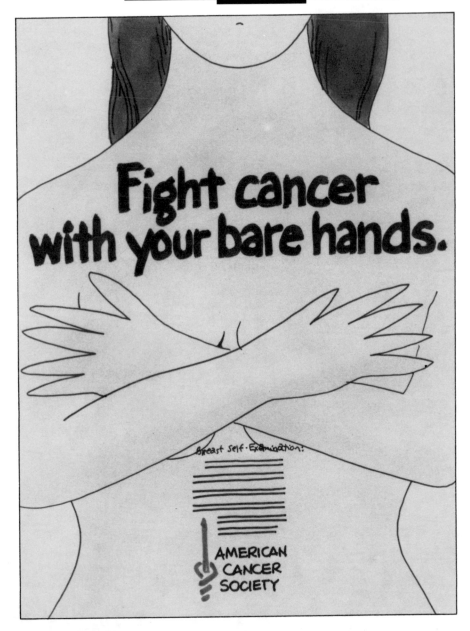

Cancer Advertising

Gillette chose the American Cancer Society for public service work because her grandmother died of breast cancer. One public service campaign Gillette included in her early portfolio was this ad to encourage women to examine their breasts. The copy included simple instructions on how to conduct the exam. Gillette wrote this in 1973, long before mammograms.

    Then, in 1984, she wrote this ad, which is still running. It is a good example of juxtapositioning in advertising because the headline, "Fry Now, Pay Later," means nothing by itself. Is it talking about cookware? A sunny vacation on credit? And the visual, without the headline, sends a pro-sun message. But together, the words and visual clearly communicate a different message. "I look for a strong under- standing that words alone—and pictures alone—do one thing, but when pictures and words come together, they do a third thing," says Gillette. "When I see someone who understands that, then I know that person understands the power of print advertising."

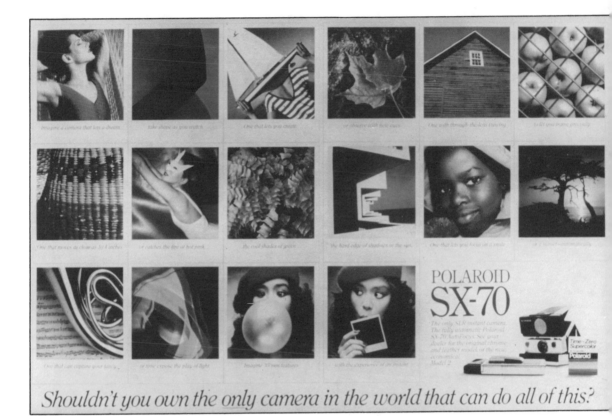

Polaroid

Although Needham had the Polaroid account for only two years, Gillette is proud of the work she and her group produced. At that time, the account was out of New York and split between the pre-merged Needham, Harper & Steers and Doyle Dane Bernbach, which made it difficult to service. This work for the SX70 camera was award-winning. The ads didn't have headlines—only poetry under the photos. But the pictures told the entire story and were best complemented by an unconventional format. "There is no formula for good advertising," says Gillette. "An innate consciousness of the power of words and pictures and an ability to put the two together in a magical way is what makes somebody a good print writer."

First Kiss for McDonalds

"I'm proud to be able to make commercials I like with or without big budgets," says Gillette. Except for the talent, this McDonald's commercial was produced on a very low production budget. Copy credits also go to Jim Glover, who I coached through his first dialogue spot. It was shot by my former art director, Jan Yarbrough.

McDonald's did so many commercials in a year that Gillette was able to experiment with writing dialogue, humor, or anything else she wanted to do. It gave her a great training ground with instant gratification and national exposure.

Gillette worked on McDonald's for seven years until the account moved to another agency. "I went from being a copywriter to a group creative director on McDonald's. I worked on new products—everything that McDonald's sold, and I was heartbroken when we lost that account. I was so upset, but then the client called and assured me it wasn't the creative," says Gillette. "But that only made me feel worse, because that was all I had control over. The week I was made president we got back part of the national McDonald's ad account. That was a great promotion gift."

BASIC ADVICE FOR CREATING SOPHISTICATED ADVERTISING

"A LOT OF ADVERTISING IS LIKE CHINESE FOOD; IT'S OKAY, IT TASTES GOOD, BUT IT JUST goes away," says Gillette. She believes that good advertising should make people say, "Oh, I never thought of it that way. It should have impact and it should stick with you."

But what makes substantial advertising? "Going for the kill is an instinct that good creative people have," says Gillette. "They have a laser-like ability to pull everything together, to harness all the elements and give them power." Gillette looks for ads that look different, sound different, or take something from a slightly different perspective and then "nail you" with their relevance.

She says great ads stop you when you first look at them; then you stop and enjoy them for a while. A young copywriter once told her that the best ad research would be to put a bunch of ads in a room and let people walk around and see which ones they stopped at. Says Gillette, "First it's stopping power. Then it's staying power. It's that little insight that makes the ad speak to you and helps the product fill a void the reader may never even have known he or she had."

Here are some ideas to help you create ads that speak to your audience.

Embrace the joy of discovery

"I think somebody could have tried to teach me how to make ads but I'm not sure it can be 'taught' to everyone," says Gillette. "There are a lot of kids taking communications courses. Few of them will be great copywriters or art directors." Gillette suggests you decode award-winning ads to see why they work. Question the visual, the headlines, the words. See what excites you about these ads and see if you can apply the theories to your own advertising.

Set deadlines

"There are two great creative stimuli," says Gillette. "One is the noose, which means we either have to come up with the solution by tomorrow or we all die. And the other one is—and (sometimes related, sometimes not) they're polar opposites—problem solving by thinking around the problem. You think about other things, sometimes related things, and always have the problem in the back of your mind." Gillette believes both methods are effective. "If you're having trouble finishing your portfolio because you have all the time in the world, try the 'noose' method. You just might surprise yourself. Sometimes sorting through too many options just gives you a headache."

Find a great boss

"It makes a big difference who you work for—how smart they are; how nice they are; whether or not they're going to nurture your talent—or try to squelch it," says Gillette. "Some advertising people are jealous of the talent and intelligence of the young people under them. When that happens, a brilliant young copywriter can begin to think he or she is untalented. When you take your first job, you can't be picky. After that, try to get to a place where you can work for somebody you respect who cares about you personally. You have so much to learn, especially in those early years. You can't do it completely by yourself. And you can't *sell* ads without somebody's support. Especially at the beginning."

Look at your own life

"Write ads for products you have a lot of familiarity with," says Gillette. "Don't try to do Porche advertising if you don't know cars or have one. Do something that hits close to home. Breast cancer was something I wanted to work on because my grandmother died from it."

Have a notion of sales

"A lot of kids coming out of school think that they're getting jobs at the Art Institute. But they're not. You really have to sell products," says Gillette. "You can't just be a clever writer or be able to compose a stunning layout or visual—you have to communicate a sales message. A talented advertising person creates a selling idea people can't dismiss. The reader has to read it, relate to it, and be moved by it."

Develop a new product

Gillette finds new product ideas intriguing. "It shows me the art director or writer is someone who not only knows how to draw or write, but also thinks about consumer activity." In Gillette's beginning book, she included an ad for a cordless hairsetter—which became a real product ten years later. "When I was in college, it was a pain to have all these small electrical appliances, blow dryers and hot rollers, plugged into the same outlet. The idea for the cordless hairsetter came from my own experience," says Gillette. The ad's headline read, "Isn't it time you cut the cord?" Says Gillette, "The ad wasn't that great but the idea for the product was smart. It was solving a problem that existed in real life."

Turn up the "provoco meter"

"I was really trying to get people to pay attention to me," says Gillette of her portfolio, which she describes as being very sassy, sexy, and irreverent, but very well written. She believes that the world is not waiting for a new ad. She says, "Advertising should continuously strive to surprise, delight, and move people."

Put the in-house work in the "outhouse"

When Gillette began her job search she included in her portfolio some poetry she wrote in college: product letters, a company newspaper, and trade ads from the telecommunications firm. One interviewer handed Gillette the poetry and said, "Save these for your boyfriend." He handed her the product letters and said, "These prove you can spell. Don't show them to anybody." It was the kind of blunt assessment that is worth a lot to a beginner.

Look at an idea inside out

At DDB, an elaborate lifestyle study is used, along with data from focus groups, to guide creative direction and determine strategy. But, for beginners, market research is difficult to find and incorporate into a campaign. To compensate, Gillette suggests you simply look at your own reactions to advertising. "I did this when I wrote my Carefree Gum campaign for my spec portfolio," says Gillette. "I hated the original campaign. I didn't believe dentists recommended sugarless gum because I figured everybody's basically a mercenary. So I tried to look at the ad and take the flip side of it. Look at a campaign that's running and turn it inside out. See if you can argue the other side of the case. I don't expect young creatives to understand marketing. I expect them to understand ideas and logic and the power of the unexpected."

Show your work to everybody

"Give your ads to normal consumers, your mother, your dad, your peers, and see if they get it. See if they understand the ad and if it makes them respond," says Gillette. Showing it around also keeps you from humiliating yourself by presenting a concept that's already been done. "You might have written something that was actually written by somebody else—which happens a lot," says Gillette. "If people feel your ad is vaguely reminiscent, leave it out of your book. Of course, telling a successful creative director who's critiquing your book that your Mom 'just loved that one' probably won't turn the tide."

Develop advertising strategies

"I don't expect creative people to be market researchers," says Gillette. "I don't expect them to have marketing degrees. Fortunately, at advertising agencies, we have entire departments to do the strategizing. But I do expect creatives to have a working strategy for the products in their portfolios. You really can't develop an ad without one. A good book on advertising strategy is *Planning for R.O.I.* by Dr. Bill Wells. Read a couple of the case histories and you'll get the drift."

Identify the agencies where you want to work

Gillette recommends that you try to get a working knowledge of what agencies are producing which ads. "There might be an agency that has a famous name, but its Chicago or Detroit office is not in the same league," says Gillette. And, target agencies that produce work that is compatible with yours. Are you a Chiat/Day type or more a Hal Riney type? There are different styles of good creative approaches. You'll go farther in an agency whose philosophy and approach resembles your own. If you can't assess your style yet just choose an agency whose work you like."

Make them feel it

"At some point, a copywriter and art director cross over from wanting to tell you everything or show you everything to wanting to make you feel something," says Gillette. "When you cross over, you are no longer an art director or a writer. You're an advertising person."

Start small

Unless you can get into a formal training program at a large agency, Gillette advises beginners to start at a small shop. At Needham in her first round of interviews, Gillette was told that she didn't want to start there because the agency wasn't good for beginners—they'd probably ignore her and leave her thinking she was not good. This was advice Gillette did not want to hear. (She admits she would have taken a job from Jack-the-Ripper.) "Kids out of school can be extremely talented and not very useful at a big agency like DDB Needham," Gillette says. "We expect a lot of self-sufficiency. We would fully admit that you either sink or swim if you come in the door here as a beginner. I'm not sure I would have ended up president of this agency if I'd started here."

Learn print first

"This focuses your thinking on the core idea because you're forced to reduce it to a simple thought," says Gillette. "People who learn this discipline and then become television writers write simpler advertising. They don't overwrite. And that's the best advertising. Reversing the process is difficult, especially if you start on big television accounts with ongoing campaigns because then you're not trained as an idea writer, but as an executional writer."

Keep interviewing

"Persistence is something a lot of young kids don't have," says Gillette. "It's like they think they're going to go on two or three interviews and get a job." Gillette claims to have gone on more than 30 interviews before she found her first job in advertising. "If you believe in yourself and you're good, you will get a job eventually. Don't be too proud to take a job in a promotional or direct-marketing agency. Just don't stay too long or you'll be pigeonholed as a specialist."

Move on

Staying in unrewarding positions for a long time strikes Gillette as odd. "I have had people come in at age thirty and say, 'I've been at this terrible in-house agency for eight years.' Why? Unless you have an amazing tale like you've been supporting two blind maiden aunts, you'd have quit," says Gillette. "I know of no one who has created garbage for nine years and gone on to be an award-winning copywriter. How can you survive nine years of garbage and have the soul of a great copywriter? That logic does not apply to someone doing *good* small-market advertising and then coming to a big national shop. All these people have usually lacked media exposure. A small regional agency is a great place to start."

Cheat

"Anything you can do to get attention is okay as far as I'm concerned—as long as it's not stupid or illegal," says Gillette. Gillette broke many "rules" in her quest to find a job in advertising. "Use all of your creativity and your sense of humor. You're not just selling your book, you're selling yourself."

• • • • • • • • • • • • • • • •

Postscript
YOU AND THE FUTURE OF ADVERTISING

THE FIELD OF ADVERTISING IS QUICKLY CHANGING. HERE'S WHAT SUSAN GILLETTE HAS TO say about the future of advertising. It may help you decide where you fit in.

"My theory is that selling is an art. To create a good ad requires a combination of a strong consciousness of the essence of the product and the person you're selling to. Never forget that the first person you have to 'sell' is the client.

"People who think advertising is about writing good ads will be disappointed. Advertising is about solving problems for clients. It now requires thinking beyond the page. Some copywriters and art directors can do that. And some cannot. Those who can't really don't want to solve a client's problem; they don't want to sell product; they don't want to be involved in the "dirty" part. They just want to create art. But it's not about selling art. It's about the art of selling.

"The reality is, with the business having changed as much as it has in the last fifteen or twenty years and with media changing as much as it has—going from four major magazines in 1956 to 11,000 magazines and to forty-five television channels—we may have to start doing great matchbook covers again. The notion of what advertising is is going to change many times within the next ten to fifteen years. What isn't going to change is the need for creativity and a powerful selling idea.

"Advertising is going to be an exciting field for people who love change. It's going to be depressing for people who just want to go back to the '60s and write a great headline and a great ad.

"Artfulness, entertainment value, and simplicity have never been more important. If the media keeps changing as exponentially as it has in the last couple of years, and I believe it will, how will we reach people? How will we talk to them? We have to find even more remarkable ways to stop people. They can already hide from us like never before. They can zap us into oblivion.

"You'll have to be an expert at the traditional form—the world's best headlines, the world's most stunning layouts—but you'll also have to go beyond what is traditionally known as advertising. There may be a new form of advertising that combines promotion and advertising, or it may be interactive like a computer program.

"The people who will really make a name for themselves in the nineties will be people who go beyond the page. Not just great copywriters. Not just great art directors. But the people who see beyond the barriers, the visionaries. The people with the next generation of big ideas."

CHAPTER THREE

Mike Koelker

"Too many people try to back into an ad," says Mike Koelker, corporate director of creative development for Foote Cone & Belding/USA. "They try to apologize for it being an ad. That doesn't mean that you can't be clever. But it does mean you have to get at it."

Koelker's success comes in part from his willingness to approach advertising—as well as his career—head on. Always with directness, honesty, and humility. He created one of the greatest "lifestyle" campaigns ever for Levi's 501 jeans, winning numerous awards in the process. It was even selected by the Smithsonian Institute for their permanent collection of landmark American advertising.

He has also created campaigns for such products and companies as California raisins, Agree shampoo, Clorox, Supercuts, Tone soap, Epson computers, and Italian Swiss Colony wines. "I didn't like doing wine advertising very much," he says, "because I don't like vineyards. They're boring and they're hot."

Prior to joining FCB/San Francisco, Koelker spent ten years in a variety of copywriting positions—he wrote for a department store, a daily newspaper, and several agencies.

A native midwesterner, Koelker has lived in San Francisco since the mid sixties, but does not claim to enjoy the relaxed California lifestyle. He earned a bachelor's degree in social casework from Augustana College in Rock Island, Illinois.

ONE SMALL STORY WITH VERY BIG RESULTS

MOST—IF NOT ALL—BEGINNING CREATIVE PEOPLE HAVE DREAMS OF STARTING AT A BIG agency, working on glamorous accounts, creating big-budget television commercials and glossy print ads. In this chapter, we're going to look at a more realistic approach to succeeding in advertising: the "humble, but confident" approach, an approach that extends from job search techniques and strategies to the actual creation of a piece of advertising.

From the very beginning of his career, Koelker was in a position to know that this approach can work. Born in Omaha and raised in Chicago and Shenandoah, Iowa, he is one of the few people featured in this book who became familiar with advertising as a child. That's because his mother was a copywriter and art director for Bozell & Jacobs in the 1940s.

An average student, he dropped out of college for a year and worked in a number of unusual positions. He drove an ambulance, worked in road construction, and embalmed people in a mortuary, as well as holding an assortment of other jobs just to get by. Then he returned to college in Sioux City, Iowa, and became interested in sociology. "I got fascinated with the way society plays on a person's mind," he recalls. "So much of what we, as a society, value and believe is actually learned." In addition, Koelker took a basic advertising class and was fascinated by it.

With these two interests, he decided to transfer to Augustana College in Illinois, only to discover that while this school offered sociology courses, there were no advertising courses.

Since he was interested in advertising, he decided to apply for a job in the advertising department of Davenport, Iowa's daily newspaper. At first, they wouldn't interview him. Every day for two weeks he went to the office wearing the same inexpensive suit. Finally, his perseverance paid off and he was given an interview. He said he wanted to write advertising, pulling that goal out of the air because he couldn't draw and was too shy to be a salesperson. And they hired him. The pay was low, but he didn't care. He was proud to have been offered the opportunity. And he loved it. To manage, Koelker worked part time and attended school part time.

Upon receiving his undergraduate degree, he applied to the University of Omaha, in his hometown. He had decided to become a clinical psychologist. At the same time, he applied through the mail for a job as a copywriter for Brandies, an Omaha department store. The retailer liked the young writer's letter and samples from the newspaper and immediately hired him.

Koelker credits his letter for getting him the offer. "I didn't want to appear to be a smart ass," he says, "because I was young and there was a lot I didn't know. But I wanted to appear very confident in my ability to meet challenges. That sounds like a lot of MBA hogwash, but it's really true. If you write the letter correctly—it comes across. You just have to find the right tone of voice."

Koelker planned to again work part time, go to school part time, and use advertising to support himself through graduate school. After one semester, however, he realized that his interest in clinical psychology, social casework, and everything else related to sociology had faded. He loved writing ads. "I don't know any way to say it other than I just loved sitting down at a typewriter with a blank sheet of paper and making something happen," he recalls. "I got to the point where I took internal pride at being able to start a sentence with any word, finish the sentence, and make it work. The volume of work I did was just tremendous. Some days, I'd literally write all day long just as fast as I could."

The variety was just as tremendous. He wrote ads for hardware, women's lingerie, women's clothes, men's suits, men's sportswear, baby clothing—every department. And he wrote image ads and seasonal ads.

After two years, Koelker wanted to experiment. He had only done print ads, and he thought that by moving to an agency he'd have the opportunity to write for radio. Writing for television was inconceivable to him.

Again he sent his samples and a letter saying something like, "I have never worked for an advertising agency. I know it's different. I know it has to be infinitely more difficult. But I think I can do it." This "humble, but confident" approach again worked. And he was hired by a small agency in Omaha.

From there, he moved to a larger agency in Omaha and, under the direction of a coworker, refined his talents. "Throughout my life I have been able to identify people I could learn from," says Koelker. "I'd attach myself uncompromisingly to those people. They'd help me write better copy. And they'd look at my headlines and say, 'This is stupid, this is crap, why are you doing it,' and then coach me into creating something better."

One day, the agency lost a big piece of business and had to trim the staff. "They cut the guy who had always helped me, but kept me because I got a lot of work done and was cheap," says Koelker. "When they let him go, I was crushed. I worked there another three months and realized I hadn't grown so much as a quarter of an inch since the day he left."

Not long after, Koelker's mentor phoned from Kalamazoo, Michigan. He'd landed a job as creative director and wanted Koelker to come work for him. Without hesitation, he accepted and headed for Michigan. Once there, he discovered the power of art direction.

"In my excruciatingly painful manner, I did my copywriter's rough and went to the art director with it. He was out of Chicago, which was big time, and he looked at it and replied, 'What is this? I don't want to see these roughs. If you have an idea for an ad, let's sit down. We'll talk about it. You'll talk about what you think. I'll talk about what I think. And we'll see where we go from there.'"

It was an enriching experience. Koelker learned the value of leaning on the talents of someone else 50% of the time. He felt that learning to work as a team to find solutions was the most wonderful thing that had happened to him in his business career to that point. For the first time, he was working in a partnership. He learned that two people can work as one and be very productive. "I learned that, sometimes, you may have to give in, even if you think you're right, for the sake of the partnership," he says. "No ad is worth destroying a partnership. I also learned to contribute in a unforceful way."

After two years, Koelker felt he had learned all he could and was ready to move on. "By then, I was conscious of the need to grow and learn," he says. "You have to work for people who are far more talented than you are, so they can teach you how to do things."

He applied for copywriting jobs at three agencies: Tracy-Locke in Dallas; McCann-Erickson in Portland; and an agency called Meltzer, Aaron & Lemen in San Francisco. "I thought, what's to lose?" says Koelker. "I didn't know anything about San Francisco. California was like a rumor to me. I had always lived in the Midwest and had never gone anywhere. I'd never even seen an ocean."

Koelker's inquiries were met with interest. Tracy-Locke flew him to Dallas and offered him a job. They seemed nice and the atmosphere seemed fun. McCann-Erickson flew him to Portland and came close to offering him a job, too. Meltzer, Aaron & Lemen (MAL) met him in the Detroit airport to talk. Koelker liked the opportunities, but decided against them. He wrote MAL a letter saying he had decided on Tracy-Locke instead.

A letter came back from MAL's creative director. "It was the cleverest, best-written letter I'd ever read," recalls Koelker. "I phoned him the next morning and said, 'I have to work for anybody who can write that well.' It was probably the best decision I've ever made because, of all the people I worked for, this guy was the best. He was brilliant and insightful. He was able to look down a long piece of copy and find the headline. And he was right every time. It was a killer."

The creative director also helped him perfect his ad writing style. "I learned to look at a piece of copy as a visual element, not just words. I started looking for balance in my copy—short sentences, long sentences, short paragraphs, long paragraphs."

From there, Koelker went to Honing, Cooper and Harrington (HCH), giving him an opportunity to create for television. It was a Levi's commercial and he was terrified. "I thought I had to speak some special language to do TV ads," he recalls. "I thought I had to know about zooms, cuts, dissolves, and reveals and how to write the visual directions." But then Koelker's art director told him to let the film director take care of all that, and he became comfortable with the medium.

Five years later the agency merged with FCB—a merger that Koelker compares to Jonah merging with the whale. But it suited both parties well. While FCB was huge, their office in San Francisco was small. Likewise, while HCH was the largest independent agency on the West Coast, they were nationally small. The merger strengthened FCB's position and gave the San Francisco office the global capabilities that major clients had come to expect.

After the merger, Koelker was promoted to associate creative director, then to executive creative director, in the mid-eighties. During this period, he created his most famous campaign—the 501 "Blues" for Levi's (see portfolio section).

Today, Koelker is still involved with the Levi's account, but as North American Director of Creative Development, his days are also occupied with agency business. "Now my job is to try to help creative people in all of FCB's offices do their best work," he says.

To do so, he writes long memos addressed to a person named "Al," exploring his feelings about strategy development and about how creative people and account people can best work together. "Account people don't normally work in partnership," he says. "But once they start working on a creative project, they become vital to the partnership. This takes sensitivity on everybody's part. It also means that there can't be rulers. A person can't pull out all the stops and win by position or title."

Within the San Francisco office, he uses a laissez-faire style of management in supervising his staff. "I manage by hiring," he says. "If you hire good people, not necessarily award winners, provide them with an open climate (it brings out the best in them), be available to help at any time and with anything—you don't have to spend much time managing anyone."

Why does Koelker manage this way? His answer is simple: "Every now and then, I have to feel like I'm doing something useful. I can't let that change. Whether I work on 501s or Dockers, my work is important to me. To do that work takes time. I have to be able to trust people to carry on without me."

A VERY REAL PORTFOLIO

Early Levi's Print

Here's an example of an early Koelker print ad for Levi's, as well as an example of how to charm people without apologizing for it being an ad. "Consumers do not want to sit around and fumble their way through word games to get to the point," he says. "You can be clever, you can be seductive, charming, romantic, image-oriented. You can do all that—but you have to give people some idea of what you want from them...what they're supposed to be thinking. Give them some clues as to where you're going. Don't just dance around or play word games. Don't apologize."

Chances are, they're not talking about our jeans.

Nor is it likely they're discussing how Levi's' 501' jeans are made of a special denim that shrinks in the wash to fit only you. Your waist, your thighs, you.

Indeed, they probably don't even care that it's like having your jeans custom tailored. For a personal fit ordinary jeans can't match.

But they *are* wearing Levi's 501 jeans. And they do appear to be enjoying themselves.

And that's good enough for us.

Levi's

501 Print

Prior to 1984, Levi's wasn't advertising specific products because no particular item had wide enough distribution to justify national advertising. Consequently, their advertising focused on the variety of products they made—cords, denims, skirts, and the variety of colors. But they were willing to gamble with single-product advertising.

Since 501s (button fly jeans) had the widest distribution, Levi's decided to experiment with them. But people didn't know about 501s. Button fly jeans were barely available on the East Coast. And the public had difficulty accepting buttons in place of zippers.

To address these problems and build awareness, Levi's management favored the fun and upbeat lifestyle approach Coke and Pepsi were using in their advertising. Koelker felt, however, that most lifestyle advertising rarely reflected the average lifestyle. "I'd walk down the street and none of the people were that blond, that happy, that handsome or beautiful as lifestyle ads suggested. And young people didn't spend their lives playing volleyball on the sands of Malibu. They'd just hang out."

What Koelker created was a campaign capturing real people doing real things. "After we ran the campaign for three years, we went around the country asking kids to imagine a door to the Levi's world—what's behind that door? They didn't say that's a world where everybody wears Levi's. Instead, they said there's a world where I'd be welcome no matter if I were short, thin, fat, tall, a different color, or in a wheelchair. It didn't matter. I'd be welcome in that world. That's the world we wanted to build. Kids got it, even though we never explicitly said it."

And the results of his work can be seen in one very important statistic: Within 36 months, sales jumped from 9 million to more than 30 million pairs of jeans a year.

501 TV

Here is a sample from the television component of the 501 Blues campaign. In most commercials, according to Koelker, agencies take a jingle and work it into many different musical styles. Instead, he wanted every commercial to have a completely different piece of blues music from different musicians, yet all with the same upbeat feel and attitude.

He also wanted to find a director who could capture real life, a task he found frustrating. He and his partner went through close to a hundred reels. They all looked alike. "After four weeks, I suggested we just pick a reel out of that stack," he recalls. But then, a producer told Koelker to look at a documentary on black street musicians a director had done in South Africa. It was soulful and honest—exactly what he wanted.

With the right director signed to the project, the next step was to decide what would be shot. At this stage, most agencies do storyboards. But Koelker didn't want that. "If we did storyboards, it wouldn't have reflected life. It would have been a Marin County copywriter and art director imitating life," he says. "And we decided to shoot in New York because we wanted to shoot strong people. California kids were not particularly strong. They are handsome, nice, and into tofu, but it isn't hard to grow up in California. It's hard growing up in New York. You've got to be tough to survive."

Once in New York, their plan was to avoid using commercial actors. They used some struggling stage actors. But most were real people the casting director found around town. And during the casting sessions, instead of asking them to do something particular, the young people were told to do whatever they wanted to do. One young woman said, "OK, I'm going to serve you coffee." She went out, got coffee, brought it in and served it to the group. She was hired.

The team gathered the events they thought charming from the casting session and structured them. Then they decided on locations and a general scenario that would best reflect them. And the 501 campaign was born.

Surely, she is not telling him about our jeans.

It's also likely she's not saying that Levi's 501 jeans are made of a special denim that shrinks in the wash to fit only you. Your waist, your hips, you.

In fact, she's probably forgotten that while button-fly 501 jeans used to be made just for men, they're now also cut especially for a woman's figure. For a fit so personal, it's like having them custom tailored.

But she *is* wearing 501 jeans. And it *does* look like she's about to have a very special day.

And that's good enough for us.

Women's 501s

Initially women were buying men's Levi's. So the company saw an opportunity and decided to gamble on the female market. They brought out a 501 cut for women. Their goal was to achieve the same kind of cult status that men's jeans had achieved.

The result was a commercial with a woman sitting in the back of an open car. And then, in the distance, she sees a guy walk out of a house. She stands up, turns her back to the camera and yells, "Travis, you're a year too late." That was it.

Research found that women absolutely despised it. It made them angry. Everyone wanted to know who he was and why he was a year too late. People even discussed it on radio talk shows. "It sold more jeans than any other single Levi's commercial," Koelker says. "It worked because everybody thought about it, talked about it, and wondered who Travis was. So it added a sense of mystery to the jeans. And the whole idea behind a cult item is that there's a sense of mystery."

Once the jeans were introduced, Koelker created the print ad above. In addition to showing how he captured the attitude of the 501 Blues campaign in print, it shows how words and sentences create a visual element. "The eye needs relief from long sentences," he says, "But every once in a while the mind hungers for a long sentence filled with information. It can't be fact, fact, fact. But it can be fact, charm, charm, fact, charm, charm."

Levi's Dockers

Here is another example of how Koelker uses reality as a creative resource. "I'm fascinated by reality,"
he says, "because I think it can be filmed in really interesting ways and can be very persuasive. We take
it for granted. We never look at it. It's fun once in a while to let the camera look at life and we go, yeah,
that's the way it is. Ain't it happy, ain't it sad, ain't it something!"

A Realistic Approach for Putting Together a Career

Koelker recognizes that beginners are in a bind: They need samples to get experience. But they don't get samples until they have experience. To make a beginning spec book, he suggests you start with print. "That's something tangible," he says. "Television is a committee job."

He suggests taking a magazine, tearing out twelve ads that you find interesting, studying them and finding the basic point they're trying to communicate about the product. "Every ad starts with a problem," he says. "Around here we say the word 'strategy,' but it's really a problem. Maybe people don't know about the product. Maybe there are misconceptions about the product. Maybe people think it costs too much. Maybe the world just needs to be told that the client is a good, friendly, big-hearted company."

Then he suggests that you try to figure out the problem from the ad. "What are they trying to communicate. That it lasts longer? That it's beautifully designed? Take Geo. It's positioned as an inexpensive and slightly counter-culture vehicle. It's for people who do not take cars too seriously, don't want to spend much money, but still want their money's worth. They still want satisfaction. It's the Volkswagen of the nineties without as much emphasis on reliability.

Once you have the ads figured out, find a new way of communicating the message without violating the tenor—or attitude—of the campaign. "Do that 12 times and you've got the foundation for a portfolio," says Koelker. "And you've got enough to talk to somebody. And say, 'I don't have any inflated value of what I'm going to be doing when I walk through the door with absolutely no experience. You're going to ask me to do the grunt work. The backups. So I have a portfolio of backups.' That would be so refreshing in this business.

"Realistically, a beginner is going to be asked to continue a campaign someone else started. No one is going to ask you to come up with the next great campaign for Chevrolet. They're going to ask you to continue some advertising campaign that's been proven."

If you want to take a realistic approach to breaking in and succeeding, here's some more advice:

Dump the school samples

"I will not look at people who come in with portfolios of newspaper articles they wrote in college, short stories, poems, any of that stuff," says Koelker. "It's all well and good, but what's the point? That's not this business. This business is a lot crueler than that."

Learn how agencies work

Koelker suggests studying advertising for one semester just to learn how agencies work and how they're organized. "I talk to kids in colleges every once in a while and they don't even know how a commercial happens," he says. "They think the client says what to do. But they should know that the assignment goes to an agency, to writers, and art directors. They present it to the client. It gets changed and finally a director gets it. Beginners should also know what the 15% commission is all about. And they should know how agencies make money."

Work hard before breaking in

Sometimes beginners take Koelker's advice and put together a book based on existing ads. And sometimes they don't. "A lot of them don't come back because it's work to sit down and do that. So they give up. But, hell, writing one ad is work. It's work once you get here so it doesn't hurt to do a week's worth of work before you come here."

Find the strategy in existing campaigns

"Anyone can look at an ad and figure out the strategy," says Koelker. "Write that down as a presumed strategy statement. That's your analysis of what they're trying to do and shows you can work within a strategy. Then show how you'd extend the campaign. Show how you'd do it differently. Enhance it and make it live longer in the marketplace. That's not to discredit the previous execution; it's to demonstrate you'll be able to understand your first assignments."

Team up

"As early as you can, team up and start building a portfolio. You're both going to need it," says Koelker. "Ideally, a would-be copywriter should team up with the would-be art director to put together a sample portfolio." Without an art director, Koelker believes that copywriters shouldn't try to draw. Instead, they should just draw a rectangle on the page and describe the visual. If that's uncomfortable, he suggests cutting pictures out of a magazine for the visual. Likewise, art directors shouldn't try to write. "Even if you're not interviewing as a team, you can talk about the working relationship," he says. "The creative director will realize you have an idea of what the business is all about."

Cultivate varied styles

Beginners should be able to create advertising using varied styles—aloof, factual, warm but always with an attitude that says, "This is really important and now listen carefully." Art directors should also have varied styles—rich, whimsical, or dynamic, yet always engaging. Koelker looks for that ability to be different depending on the situation. "I like to see variety in a portfolio. I like to see work that's straight, buttoned down, and work that's loose. I don't like to see headlines that are all puns. I also want to see headlines that are brutally direct and give an unexpected view of the product."

Avoid humor

Despite the fact that humor is so prevalent at awards shows, Koelker advises beginners to avoid it. "You might want to try a little bit of it to show that you have an amusing streak, but don't dwell on it," says Koelker. "Humor tends to fall flat in print. Very few print ads are really hysterically funny. And without the benefit of somebody professional reading a radio script, very few radio scripts are funny. Most creative directors look for the 'solid stuff' in a portfolio."

Do the unexpected...

"I like to see people try the unexpected," says Koelker. "And that's the biggest thing I look for. And clarity. People in advertising are usually more experimental than clients and clients are usually a little more experimental than consumers, who tend to be very comfortable with Madge, Marge, and Harry out in the kitchen. People say they hate it—and they probably do—but it's far more comfortable."

...And be rationally outrageous

"People with portfolios shouldn't worry about being rejected because their work is unusual, but they should have good reasons for having done what they did," says Koelker. "If you sense your work is perceived as a little too off the wall, have a good rationale and defend it. You can say something like, 'Maybe I'm reaching a little far, but it seemed like a legitimate shot at it.' It's easier to pull back than it is to stretch."

Be likeable

"I don't know if I've ever looked at a portfolio and said, 'We have to hire that person.' I really base the hiring decision on what kind of person he or she is," says Koelker. "Do I like this person? Is he or she nice? Would this person be pleasant to be around? Can I talk to him or her? Do I feel comfortable with them? It's very subjective and it's very narrow. When I'm interviewing, all I have are my own opinions. If I like the person, and I think the person's work is good enough, I'd really try and hire him or her."

Start small

Unless an agency has a formal training program, Koelker suggests starting at a small agency where they need help with non-critical assignments and have enough time to help you learn the business. Although FCB has hired graduates from The Art Center who have worked out well, the agency prefers hiring people with experience. "We tried hiring beginners, but without a full-time manager, they don't get the coaching they need. They end up sitting here and rotting. It's not fair to them. It's horrible. Unfortunately, we're an agency full of people who want to *do* the work, not manage the staff," says Koelker. "I came up from the smaller agencies. I was lucky. I had good people every step of the way to help."

Don't whine

Koelker has noticed that many beginners often want their work to be considered "hip and cool" and are discouraged when clients suggest changes that detract from this "coolness." Then, he says, beginners whine. Clients don't want to hear that their own comments aren't hip and cool. He suggests that beginners pause and say something like, "That's an interesting point. Let me give it some thought." Then look at what the ad is trying to accomplish. Maybe your approach isn't consistent with what you were trying to do or what you agreed to try to do. If you still believe in your approach, be able to support it with a logical rationale that supports the agreed upon strategy.

Respectfully submit your ideas to your partner

"I've learned you can hurt someone's feelings when you step on their ideas. You have to be careful. You have to be sensitive or you won't have a long-term partnership. No ad is worth jeopardizing the partnership. When somebody tosses out an idea, don't trample all over it," suggests Koelker. "You nod, even if your first reaction is horror at the stupidity of it. You try to build on it. You go, 'Gee, that makes me think we could do this, too.' Maybe it will go nowhere. Because

as you extend it, it gets even worse and then it becomes apparent to both of you."

Give in to your partner once in a while

"Even if you're absolutely convinced you're right, it's important to occasionally let your partner win," says Koelker. "Maybe you've won three in a row. Winning four in a row could destroy the partnership. Your partner won't contribute like he or she used to."

Rise and fall with your partner

"In an ideal partnership," says Koelker, "both partners think, 'Gee, I hardly did anything, the other one did it all.' Even if you get talked into doing something that you don't think is entirely right, you go along with it. At the next level, if it's rejected you bail out your partner. You came up with it together by whatever route you got there. That's where you are and that's what you show and defend."

Draw the client into the partnership

Koelker suggests that you don't look at the client as an adversary either. "They're giving us a tremendous amount of money and entrusting us with the fate of their company," he says. "They have their company to run. We have advertising to do. We need each other. And I want to work in partnership with my client. I do my thing and he does his, but that doesn't mean we don't meet on our little lifecycles. There are lots of little meetings and suddenly you find the job has been approved and you can't even remember when. So everything you can do to draw the client into the creative mix is great."

Don't get stuck, get information

You have to know everything about the product in order to say something significant about it. Someone Koelker once worked for told him that if he couldn't come up with an idea, he probably didn't have enough information. "It's really true," he says. "And you may have a pile of information, but there's nothing in it that leads anywhere but to the conventional and ordinary. If you're trying for something new, you need some sparkling pieces of information that haven't occurred to the competition."

Brainstorm without paper

"To come up with an idea, I keep thinking about the problem," says Koelker. "My partner and I work differently than most creative people. We never kick around ideas. We always kick around the problem. We talk about it. We ask ourselves why we think the client said what he did. Why they want what they want. We never have a scrap of paper in front of us. We just keep talking until we have eliminated a thousand possibilities and

then we start to work. And the ideas just come out of what sounds almost like business school talk."

Ignore post-production research

Like many of the creative people in this book, Koelker puts little value on post-production research. "At its best, this is a pedestrian and pretty mediocre gauge of an ad's potential. If you have a lot of money in your advertising budget, then I suppose it helps. But it's probably better suited to packaged goods than to anything that really wants to break through the clutter of television. If you need to make a small budget work like a big one, then you need creativity. You need the unexpected and the unexpected never tests very well in the beginning."

Recognize the absurdity of awards

"I don't care much for awards," says Koelker. "Or entering contests. They're silly. If you have ever judged an advertising show, you'd understand why the humor spots always win. By the eighteenth spot, you're a zombie and so bored that anything that illicits a response from your brain makes you say to yourself, 'I'll vote for that.' It isn't necessarily good because it sells the most product or is even the most creative. It's just that you're so bored looking at a reel of a 100 commercials. So if you laugh, you give it a check mark and with enough check marks, it wins."

Prepare yourself for the tension between business and art

"When you run a business, you attempt to make everything 'win/win.' But creative work is unfortunately not 'win/win,' but 'win/lose.' Either your idea gets sold or it doesn't," says Koelker. "There's really no in between, except appalling mutations, which sometimes happen. That's when a piece of work evolves to a point where it has no integrity anymore; it has no soul. It's just more advertising on television. And, God knows, that's the last thing we need in this world."

• • • • • • • • • • • • • •

Postscript
INTEGRATED MARKETING COMMUNICATIONS

THROUGHOUT THIS BOOK, YOU'RE GOING TO HEAR THAT ADVERTISING IS CHANGING, THAT it's evolving into what is called integrated marketing communications. But what is integrated marketing communications? And why is it growing in importance? What Koelker has to say in this area may give you a clue.

"Doing nationally renowned television commercials is still a great way to advance. But there isn't really all that much room for advancement in this business. This industry isn't that large. So beginners had better get out of their minds that only broadcast advertising is important.

"And I can tell you that integrated marketing communications is the way it's going. The wave of the future. The key is to do it with top flight creative people so it doesn't look like typical promotional advertising.

"With integrated marketing communications, everything a client does speaks with the same level of creativity—and with a single voice. We're doing that with Levi's right now. We're setting up a design group within our creative department. It's not a separate department like at most agencies. We're bringing in the best designers we can find to do outrageous point-of-sale. We're even helping our clients do hang tags.

"We're putting the same creative horsepower against that as we're putting against network TV. I know that because I'm working on it myself. I'm doing network TV and I'm doing hang tags. And I'm having a ball! It's fun to do.

"The client loves it because it's all important. Clients are saying that they intend to spend less and less in broadcast. They're not going to cut it out completely because it's still a great way to reach people fast and with high impact. But they're saying that they're going to spend more on integrated marketing communications—if we can make it work for them. And they want it to work for them because their dollar goes further.

"In the case of Levi's, they want all of their communications to retailers to have the same voice, the same look and feel as their network advertising. Then everything pulls together. So beginners should think more along those lines. The times really are changing."

You ... to be making at least
twent. five? Yes?

Thir..

Are yo. .a. .... Te.. me.

Thirty, ...

Well...what've .... besides the car?

Inves.ments? ....insurance?

No?

When are you .o...... ... .hing?

You're not eight.... ...y.a..

Don Easdon

"Most people who are creative are dyslexic," says Don Easdon, executive vice president/executive creative director at Backer Spielvogel Bates* and an admitted dyslexic (his son is, too). "If you think black, I think white. And, I'm always surprised you're thinking black. A lot of creative people are like that—creatives normally think a little off center—and that's an asset. Good artists and writers have a unique point of view."

True or not, one thing is for sure: Easdon's ability to convey life in a way that is subtle, yet attention-getting. He's always looking for fresh images and messages. In this chapter, we'll look at how you too can create unique work by drawing on a unique source—yourself.

In his twenty years in advertising, Easdon has created hundreds of commercials for such clients as John Hancock Financial Services, Wang, Gillette, Dr. Pepper, and AT&T. His efforts have won him much industry recognition: seven awards at Cannes including three Gold Lions and the Grand Prix; six Clios; four One Show awards; and twelve Andy's—to name a few.

But Easdon's career has had low points as well. Only dogged determination seems to propel him. "You get to the point where you'd die for your work. Nothing is more important," says Easdon calmly. "I'll be trying to make a certain thing happen. And, I'll make it happen even though others don't think I will. You have to be naive enough to keep positive; But if you lose that, you're dead."

*Easdon has since formed Heater/Easdon.

CREATING A BIG BANG WITH A WHISPER

EASDON BELIEVES THAT THERE'S A CERTAIN SAMENESS TO MOST ADVERTISING, A RESULT OF creatives following an accepted methodology of the industry. "There's a certain way to do headlines," he says, "and a certain way to do layouts." But how does one learn to break away from this and create truly unique advertising? Easdon believes you do this by looking inward. "It really does come out of your personality," he says. "As soon as you put away the award books, you usually do great work. And you really stand out."

To fully understand this, let's look at Easdon's career. His big bang began with a chirp—his fourth grade teacher asked the class to draw spring birds and her reaction to his bird was so positive he was inspired to become an artist.

Fearing that he wouldn't make money, however, he soon directed his attention toward architecture. But while studying at the University of Connecticut, he got a job working in the school's promotion department. He enjoyed this and changed his career plans again, this time deciding to become a designer. He put together a portfolio of mostly design work, though he included a campaign for Webster's Dictionary. He designed the ads with plenty of white space, a small picture of a dictionary in the corner, and an enlarged definition from the book. Since the editor had taken a progressive approach and included the word "ain't" in the dictionary, Easdon showed an enlarged definition of the word "ain't," with the headline, "Dictionaries ain't what they used to be." Says Easdon, "My very first book was really naive."

But he never had to use his book because in 1970—his senior year—one of the promotion pieces he created for the university caught the eye of someone in New England's largest agency, Wilson, Haight & Welch in Hartford. He was hired as assistant art director and was teamed with the then-assistant copywriter Ted Bell (Chapter One), also in his first job.

"I worked on all those horrible projects no one else wanted," recalls Easdon. "I did ads for crutch tips—those little rubber tips on the bottom of crutches—and ostomy bags." Those ads gave Easdon a chance to learn production and type. "You don't get the glamorous assignments when you start."

Easdon's career developed quickly. After a year at this agency, he was hired away by an agency in Providence, Rhode Island, because—like his first job offer—someone there had seen his work. "Like so many agencies," muses Easdon, "you had to work at the place to be able to remember the name."

But he yearned to be in New York, where advertising was booming. And, from the shop in Providence, he did get his chance. He moved to what he calls the "Korean War of advertising"—a small New York agency. He should have suspected the job wouldn't be easy when the man who hired him quit on Easdon's first day. Easdon felt as if he'd been left to the wolves. Working on GAF film, Maidenform, Jean Naté, and a host of antiperspirants for Bristol Meyers, Easdon functioned as an "idea factory" in a "workaholic" environment. "It was creative direction through intimidation," he recalls. "Management tore boards up in front of you."

With tight deadlines and with the bulk of his work being for television, Easdon was forced to learn how to draw boards quickly. Since one art director there was able to produce storyboards with very little effort, Easdon studied his technique. "He'd draw cartoon figures and put a couple of dots down for eyes," says Easdon. "Then he'd draw a nose, go on to the tie, and maybe sketch in the hands." This disconnected way of drawing worked for Easdon. "I started drawing this way and now I can crank out a storyboard in a few minutes—and draw it pretty well—where it would have originally taken me half a day to draw it."

He tried hard to make this job a success. He tried to build his book in an environment where it was hard to get great advertising accepted by the principals. "It was awful," says Easdon. "I never did anything that was quality."

To maintain his sanity, Easdon did a tremendous amount of freelancing. "It's the only thing that keeps you sane while you're doing junk," he says. "It gives you the control that creative people want out of life." Meanwhile, Easdon learned like crazy, perfecting his graphic design and production skills. Says Easdon, "People today don't put in their time to learn the basic skills."

Easdon left this shop to take on a short-term job at another agency and, after three months, he sent his book to Young & Rubicam/New York, where he was hired as a junior art director. Eager to do great work, Easdon went to his creative director three times a day and said he'd be happy to work on anything. The creative director respected Easdon's initiative and rewarded him with a choice assignment—a double-page print ad promoting Puerto Rican tourism. Almost immediately, he and a photographer headed for Puerto Rico.

But Easdon was apprehensive. The shoot was very expensive and, like Koelker with the 501 campaign, he was unclear about what he'd need. He planned to crop the shots into narrow vertical strips of images no deeper than an inch. Easdon had the photographer shoot and crossed his fingers. Then he planned to take the pictures, blow them up, and arrange them into the vertical scheme. Since he was using a 35mm format, he could only go by instinct to know if the format was working or not. If it didn't work, Easdon would be looking for a new job. But he found wonderful slices, put them together and created an innovative, provocative ad. It won "Ad of the Month" at Y & R. Ironically, the prize was a trip to Puerto Rico—where he'd been every week since he started his job.

As a result of his work on Puerto Rican tourism and his success on several other ads, Y & R promoted Easdon to associate creative director. He worked on Eastern Airlines, Right Guard and other Gillette products, and won his first Clio for Dr. Pepper. Gillette management encouraged Easdon to work with research people and he began to understand the consumer. That process helped him see that his own feelings weren't entirely unique. "I realized that if I followed my feelings, I could anticipate trends," he says.

After 12 years at Y & R, the lack of advancement opportunity dictated that he move on. The highest position he felt he could achieve there was group creative director. "I decided to be a big fish in a small pond. I'd gotten divorced and wanted a different kind of lifestyle away from New York." Hill, Holliday, Connors, Cosmopulos (HHCC), a small, but significant agency in Boston, offered a position as an executive vice president, creative director which Easdon understood to imply hands-off, high-level decision making. But the long title didn't accurately portray the level of direction the position entailed. HHCC gave everybody big creative director titles and put emphasis on creating ideas, not managing other creatives. And the creatives lived and died by their work.

Easdon's first assignment was to pitch John Hancock. "I killed for that category because my father had been assistant chairman of the board, executive vice president at Equitable Life Insurance. He died young as a white collar grunt. In my mind, I was doing the campaign for him," he says.

"I remember when the idea for Hancock clicked," recalls Easdon. "I was watching a TV documentary about a women's band. But I was thinking about Hancock and realized I was stimulated by the style of the documentary. I thought, 'why can't we do that.' At that point, 'slice-of-life' advertising had bad connotations. But I thought commercials could be done in a documentary style."

The instincts Easdon was learning to trust began to come out through his Hancock work, but his creative partner presented a stumbling block. "He was an ex-DDB guy and when I presented ideas, he'd play back something from the awards books. Everything was within the confines of that box. It had to be from the awards books. So I couldn't do anything fresh with the guy," says Easdon. Frustrated, he started working by himself. But he needed to work with a copywriter.

One day when he was particularly frustrated, Easdon wandered into Bill Heater's office. Heater was working as a technical writer. "He stood about 6'5", wore a big lumberjack shirt and a full scraggly beard and never said a word," says Easdon. "Secretaries would walk into the elevator and take one look at Heater and walk out, but he wouldn't hurt a flea." Heater listened to Easdon's complaints and then asked about his idea. Easdon started talking but then walked away after Heater's phone rang.

Four hours later, Heater came into Easdon's office and threw down a piece of green paper. "Green was his trademark," says Easdon. "Everyone has their little affectations." On the paper was a rough of how the copy might work.

It was the beginning of the campaign. Easdon realized he could do the kind of work he wanted to do if he could work with Heater. So, he went to management to ask to change partners. They listened and things started clicking. "That's the difference between having a bad and a good partner," says Easdon. "You really need someone who listens and you in turn can listen to. A good partnership is 80% chemistry and 120% respect."

When the Hancock ads came out, Easdon's friends, who had no idea he was working on the campaign, asked him if it was his. Says Easdon, "It was the beginning of my creating what I felt was me. It was quiet, a bit intense and, hopefully, intelligent. A more respectful brand of advertising. And, I tried to make everything fresh—every element."

The Hancock account gave Easdon the credibility he wanted. He won the Cannes Film Festival, Grand Prix, as well as many other awards. The agency built off that success and doubled their billings. It was his first big success, but he also became apprehensive about being able to do work that would surpass it.

Easdon's new-found status—he followed up the Hancock campaign with a groundbreaking campaign for Wang—and HHCC's committed strategic team attracted Nissan's Infiniti business. The Japanese car maker was ready to introduce a new luxury car to America. Instead of introducing the car with an attitude of arrogance typical of the category, Easdon wanted to create "specialness." Together, the team looked at every element of traditional car advertising. "It's zero-based advertising," says Easdon. "Instead of us just sitting down to design ads and write headlines—that's the methodology of the business—we asked ourselves: 'Why is a car beyond styling?' and 'What is a luxury car experience?' In other words, we started at the beginning and even questioned the concept of luxury. What is luxury?"

Easdon wasn't allowed to look at the car before he created the campaign. Yet everything he heard about the experience of the new car sold him. He decided to use the same approach. To do that, Easdon compared the Infiniti's experience to nature. "I never looked at it as a teaser campaign like the rest of the world did," he says. "I'm very happy with the Infiniti campaign. It created a car with a personality that was the first car true to the Japanese spirit—yet the personality was relevant to Americans. And several polls reported it to be the most well-known campaign of the eighties."

In his four and a half years at HHCC, Easdon did exactly 156 commercials. After HHCC, he freelanced, thinking of creating his own company. But then in 1991, Easdon joined Backer Spielvogel Bates (BSB) in New York as executive vice president, executive creative director. He was asked to join BSB to help turn around their fortunes. They had lost several accounts before he came on board, and many more were on their way out. After his arrival, the exodus of accounts stopped, and they won a few major new ones.

"What annoys me about the advertising business is its negative image—that we're just hucksters," says Easdon. "There are some bad people in every profession. Advertising is a profession that allows you to meet people. And it's a profession where, if you're honest, people listen; if you're dishonest, people know it."

A Different Portfolio

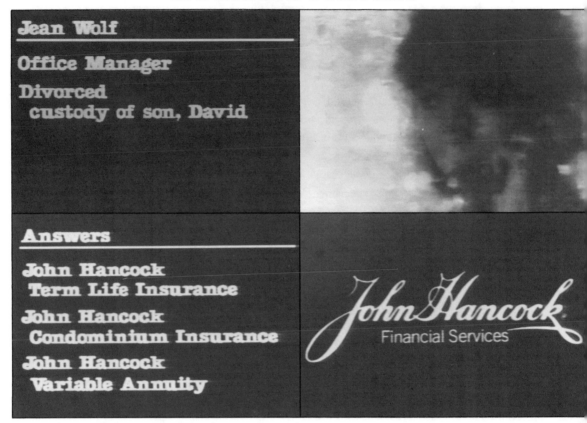

Jean Wolf

Office Manager

Divorced
 custody of son, David

Answers

John Hancock
 Term Life Insurance

John Hancock
 Condominium Insurance

John Hancock
 Variable Annuity

John Hancock Financial Services

John Hancock Financial Services

Hancock wanted a product-oriented campaign. Most creatives would have been turned off by this request, but Easdon took it as a challenge. He felt he could market the products if he presented them in a very low key manner and thought "slice-of-life" could be a successful technique—if it had a fresh approach. Until that point, slice-of-life advertising seldom was interesting. And "good" advertising people avoided it.

But Easdon knew it could actually be wonderful if he controlled the feel, making it more like a movie or a documentary. The creative team decided on the look and feel of the ad and established a format that communicated the concept with an understated feel. Decisions concerning the type, film texture, pacing, pauses, and lights were all filtered through the concept.

The ads were intentionally quiet, so people wouldn't feel they were being sold. The first viewing of a commercial stops you because of its fresh structure (see p. 66). The next time you see it, you are paying a lot of attention. "Oddly enough, by then, people paid so much attention," recalls Easdon, "that tests showed they could repeat the copy verbatim." He knew he'd tried to make the campaign's quietness draw attention, but he never expected it to have the impact it did. "It was like a nice painting you put on a wall," he says. "Each time, you see something a little different."

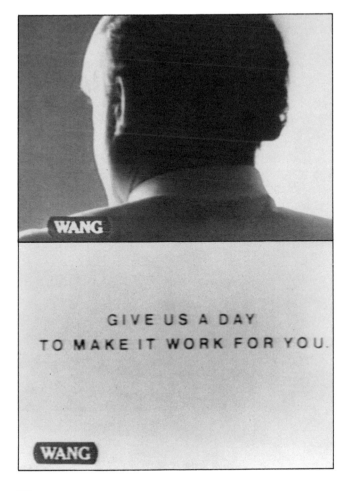

Wang

By the time Easdon began working on Wang, he was trusting his instincts. This was at a time when MIS (Managment Information Systems) professionals were fond of talking in jargon. "I had no idea what the hell they were saying. It was like being in the army and hearing conversation that was all acronyms. And it was pretty consistent. I recognized I could use this 'techno-jargon' to do a campaign."

The campaign targeted MIS people in companies who were already inundated with computer industry magazines and direct mail pieces. Easdon felt that although television would reach a much broader audience than necessary, it would have greater impact on the MIS directors.

For Wang, television commercials were unorthodox. "That was good for Wang," says Easdon, "because they were looked at as being not as high-tech as other companies. The aim was to show how high-tech they actually were."

As predicted, the language turned some people off, but it created instant empathy with MIS directors and was very successful at evolving Wang's image.

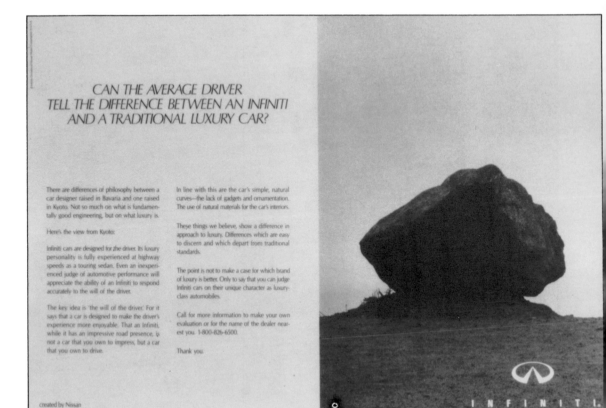

CAN THE AVERAGE DRIVER
TELL THE DIFFERENCE BETWEEN AN INFINITI
AND A TRADITIONAL LUXURY CAR?

There are differences of philosophy between a car designer raised in Bavaria and one raised in Kyoto. Not so much on what is fundamentally good engineering, but on what luxury is.

Here's the view from Kyoto:

Infiniti cars are designed for the driver. Its luxury personality is fully experienced at highway speeds as a touring sedan. Even an inexperienced judge of automotive performance will appreciate the ability of an Infiniti to respond accurately to the will of the driver.

The key idea is 'the will of the driver.' For it says that a car is designed to make the driver's experience more enjoyable. That an Infiniti, while it has an impressive road presence, is not a car that you own to impress, but a car that you own to drive.

In line with this are the car's simple, natural curves—the lack of gadgets and ornamentation. The use of natural materials for the car's interiors.

These things we believe, show a difference in approach to luxury. Differences which are easy to discern and which depart from traditional standards.

The point is not to make a case for which brand of luxury is better. Only to say that you can judge Infiniti cars on their unique character as luxury-class automobiles.

Call for more information to make your own evaluation or for the name of the dealer nearest you. 1-800-826-6500.

Thank you.

created by Nissan

INFINITI.

Infiniti

Easdon and Heater began working on Infiniti advertising in a Japanese garden in Kyoto. "We were trying to figure out why the Japanese garden was so intriguing," Easdon recalls.

"It was beautiful. Simple. But after a few minutes, I realized I wasn't looking at the garden. It's just a place that makes you feel very comfortable. The garden lacked visual information. After a while, your thoughts wandered. The simplicity and familiarity of the Japanese garden make you very comfortable." Easdon says, "Try staring out the window for 30 seconds. Be aware of what goes through your mind. You see a building—the building doesn't change—and your thoughts start to wander. By using one nature scene (no cuts), you bring greater focus to the announcer. The scene becomes a frame, if you will, for the message." That's where the executional element of nature came from. Creating an analogy between the Japanese experience and nature was designed to make consumers feel very comfortable with an alien concept.

"People knock subtle advertising," says Easdon. "They say it doesn't sell hard enough. Give me a break. If there is something in the concept that articulates a feeling the consumer has felt, but has not been able to articulate yet, then the ad has done you a service. Empathy has been created, a bridge between the service and the consumer has been created. And that is an accomplishment."

Budweiser

Together with Heater and the director, Joe Pytka, Easdon did a Budweiser commercial. The commer-
cial showed two policemen, soon to go off duty, in conversation. One tells the other of his brother-in-law's
lucrative position selling municipal bonds and his own frustration at not making a lot of money.

The other officer responds, "You wouldn't want a Yuppie job like that; it's not going to make you
happy. Why would you want to do that? What it comes down to is, you wouldn't want to have a Bud
with a guy like that, would you?" Then the other officer looks down at his shoes and says, "Nah." And
they go off.

The only mention of Budweiser in the entire commercial is the reference to "have a Bud...." Only a
market leader could have run that commercial, and it shows Easdon's style of trying to create a more re-
spectful form of advertising.

SOME ADVICE FOR CREATING UNIQUE ADVERTISING

EASDON LOOKS FOR "IDEA PEOPLE." AT BSB, NEW HIRES DON'T NECESSARILY HAVE THE most polished portfolios—or all the skills. "There's a sameness among a lot of creative people. They come in for interviews with incredibly similar executions. But I rarely see new ideas or innovative executions. In the group of fifty art directors and copywriters who work for me, there are only about five or six people who excite me with their ideas and problem solving. They're hard to find. They're rare.

"Those people follow their instincts, which is what enables them to be confident—and their personalities are so strong that they can't help but put themselves into their work," says Easdon. "And they're immediately successful. They just scream ahead."

To follow their example, Easdon suggests that you use your instincts to figure out the feelings that people can't articulate and translate it into a campaign; you have communication and the consumer feels a bond. "The real trick is to be able to integrate the message in a non-selling way so people can feel comfortable about it," suggests Easdon.

Easdon has mastered an ability to create impact with a whisper. "I think the type of work I've done," says Easdon, "especially over the last five or six years, has been intelligent, and very simple. It doesn't intrude into people's lives. It's advertising that shows respect for the viewer."

Here's some advice from someone who looks at things differently.

Don't get into the business

"The advertising industry is probably worse now that it ever was," warns Easdon. "It's hard. It's rewarding as hell, but it's competitive. It's like being a baseball player. You'll either be a real star or you'll end up with an antique store in New England. Emotionally, that's very difficult. Every campaign I've ever worked on has taken a couple of years off my life." I will say 20th century advertising structure is dying. The agency of the 21st century is being created right now. If you follow the tried and true ways, you will not fit in this new 21st century creative environment."

Ignore awards books

Unlike so many other creatives, Easdon says that, to do your best work, you should ignore the awards books. "People who look to awards books and are directly influenced by them are doing work that is probably not as good as the originator had done," he says. "I judge a lot of shows and they're so disappointing. The fresh work is rare—usually, one, maybe two pieces in an entire show. Easdon explains that some creatives have built their careers on a certain type of advertising style, and they vote for the work that represents that style, even though it may not be right for the particular client. He does admit, however, that the awards books are a valuable tool for learning the basics of advertising and for keeping current. "You have to stay current," he says, "but these are not any more important than picking up a copy of *Vogue* or *Details* or watching the newest hot movie."

Use yourself as a resource

Rather than looking to awards books as an idea resource, Easdon encourages creatives to look into themselves. "As people put their personalities into their work, their work becomes more unique. If you're brash, you'll do brash work. If you're sophisticated, you'll do sophisticated work," says Easdon. "So, you should have the confidence to let your work reflect yourself. The last executions of the John Hancock campaign, which I didn't work on, showed a woman who suffered from stuttering. She worked on a computer, which helped her feel very eloquent and articulate. It was a wonderful commercial. The reason I believe it was so good is because the person who wrote it also stutters. He put himself into his work."

Explore new approaches

In his search for havens of fresh executions, Easdon finds American awards books dull. "But I pore over Japanese magazines and films. They approach things differently. Their current trend in advertising is to put down their own products. They'll trash their own product! I find that intriguing. So, I'm drawn in," says Easdon.

Trust your instincts

One quality that separates outstanding creatives from others is not necessarily their talent, but the ability to recognize instincts and trust them. "I trust my instincts. Creatives will come with work for me to review and I always have a visceral reaction," says Easdon. "You have to listen to your instincts and even though you feel inarticulate, just start talking about it, and try to find the words for what you feel. After a while, you get used to articulating what your gut is telling you. I know that sounds basic, but that's it."

Recognize you need others

"Nobody does great work by themselves," says Easdon. "If you succeed and think you've done it yourself, you're either egotistical or you don't recognize reality. It's impossible to do it yourself."

Find a good partner

Easdon credits much of the success of his work to having a great partner. For many years, that partner was Bill Heater. "You need somebody who listens and someone whose ideas are worth listening to. Bill and I had our differences. But we'd talk them through. Where copy was concerned, he had the final say. But where art direction was concerned, I had the final say. It was just a wonderful relationship and it helped create a lot of good work."

Make fear your friend

For Easdon, fear is a big motivator. Fear of not being successful drove him to create his best work. And when he finally won recognition with his Hancock work, fear of having had his career peak motivated him to work harder for his next major success.

Be confident

Easdon is very sensitive to the insecurities every creative feels. "Everyone is intimidated by the blank page. The blank page makes you feel like every day is your first day. That feeling never goes away. You don't know how it's going to happen, where the ideas will come from, but they come."

Respect the client

Unlike many advertising people who believe clients are naive and uncreative about advertising, Easdon sees them as a valuable resource. "Clients know the brand and have the responsibility of policing the brand." Today, many agency people move to the client side, so they are more sophisticated about both sides of advertising.

Be positive

"Good advertising people have to be confident and brash enough to come out with something different," says Easdon. "You're naked when you come up with something totally brand new—that can make you nervous. A fresh thought is easily killed. Anything new doesn't thrive in an environment of negative thinking. Think positive and surround yourself with positive people."

Understand the product's most basic value

"For instance, basically a car is just transportation," says Easdon. "If you're writing an ad for a car, also understand why it's styled the way it is and the other emotional factors that motivate the consumer. So it's best to start at zero and question everything before you start to develop approaches.

Don't impose your personal style on your client's products

"Use only the parts of your personality that match your client's personality," advises Easdon. "You certainly communicate through your personality, which is the only way to work instinctively anyway. And sometimes there's just a good match-up."

Preserve fresh ideas

"Nobody's idea is great at first. Learn to build on it. It's like playing with a little tinker toy, a puzzle, or Lincoln Logs; fiddle with it until it works. Even bad ideas can foster brilliant campaigns. The other day, I was reviewing an atrocious campaign. It was so bad, I smiled and tried to find something nice to say about it. But in trying to find something nice to say, a great idea came up."

Reach for the audience with visuals

Easdon feels that, like the target audience, an ad must stop him to gain his interest. "I want to be startled. I look for things I haven't seen before. At award shows, I'll only put my glasses on to read the copy if the ad works on a visual level. If it's not interestingly designed, I won't even look at it. If it is, then I read it."

Make terrible assignments terrific

"Most people think that the only way to create great work is by working on flashy products like jeans or perfume. The Hancock campaign, before I worked on the account, showed a scale of justice with a miniature family on one side and on the other side a hand putting weights on the scale. It suggested term insurance to balance out the family's needs. It was awful—the challenge was to create something fresh. Any product or service has the potential for fresh ideas!"

Keep it consistent

Easdon usually looks for a unique yet consistent approach in a beginning portfolio. "I can learn something from that," he says. "The more people put themselves—their personalities—into their work, the more uniqueness you can see. And if his or her personality is fairly consistent, that uniqueness should be seen throughout the portfolio. I only put the work in my book that I believe is fresh. Good executions aren't good enough."

Look at limitations as assets

Easdon has learned to look at the advertising specifications that clients make as assets instead of as limitations. For example, Avis requires that 20% of an Avis print ad's space and 20% of commercial air time be devoted to the car. That's because General Motors supplies the cars as well as finances their advertising. An employee at Avis is even paid to figure out the exact percentage of space and time on each ad or commercial. Rather than look at that as a limitation, look at it as an asset and work to discover ways of using the car much more creatively, making it a much more integral part of the communications, rather than just being an add-on. Similarly, Hancock wanted to mention numerous products in each communication. Rather than just tack a list of products on at the end of each piece, Easdon found a way to employ the product orientation in his creation of a breakthrough campaign. (See portfolio section.)

Work in all media

All media lend themselves to great creative work. "Most creatives think the only way to make it is by doing fashionable, hip TV campaigns. I thought so. The truth of the matter is, it's the other media that give you an opportunity to be really creative," says Easdon. "And doing a billboard is as important as doing an entire campaign."

Consider the ad's content

People look at advertising in the context of the other ads on the air or on a page. Keep that in mind when you're coming up with ideas and deciding on an execution. The context may affect how the commercial will be received; if it will be toned down or jump out.

Make your boss look good

"If you make your boss look good, you go farther. No one is going to hire anybody who's not going to make them look good," Easdon reminds us.

Freelance

At some agencies Easdon worked in, employees caught doing freelance were fired on the spot. But Easdon realizes that most beginners need freelance work to survive. "I tell people that they can freelance, if it's not for a conflicting account. It makes you better," he says. "It's also very fulfilling because you don't have all the management layers. I still freelance."

Avoid tantrums

"I've quit a number of jobs," says Easdon. "I quit on Wang. I quit on Infiniti. That works against you in the long run because people think you're some kind of prima donna. At this point, I should be mature enough to convince people of my point of view without a tantrum," says Easdon.

Reflect society

"Advertising doesn't drive society. Society drives advertising. And good advertising people are a barometer of what's happening. The better ones can articulate what's happening in society before society articulates it. If you don't do it, someone else will. If I didn't do the Hancock campaign, it would have been done six months later by Prudential," says Eas-

don. "I just had the right opportunity and the luck to be able to execute it first."

Keep your hands on

Easdon believes creative directors get out of touch when they're promoted up and no longer do the work. "I'm a working creative director," he says. "This is a billion-dollar agency. I have every right not to work on specific projects, but I've found I lose my edge and confidence when I'm not involved. And I found I lost interest in the business when I stopped working myself. That's not good for a career. I know I have a pretty decent portfolio, but that doesn't matter. It's what you did last week that counts."

Stay involved with the culture around you

Although the advertising industry is filled with young people, Easdon doesn't think age is a factor. However, the experiences and knowledge that creatives input *are* big factors. "You can only output what you input from your experiences," says Easdon. "People dry up fast when they don't get involved in the culture around them and instead just work. You have to constantly get yourself excited about things. One of my three creative directors has worked here for years and created the classic Anacin spot with the hammers in the head graphic. I'm absolutely fascinated by this guy. I always learn something from him. He's a vault of information."

Postscript
Ads Easdon Would Like to Create

Easdon has proven that low-key, respectful, reserved advertising can work. He credits his advertising's effectiveness to being able to be provocative yet inviting, and being able to communicate a new consumer insight—an insight that automatically creates a bond between the advertising and the consumer.

To do this, he suggests you look for the idea first. Then think of that idea as a pair of glasses. "Then put on a pair of glasses," he says, "and look through those glasses at the type, the visuals, the sound, every element. Make sure everything is filtered through the idea."

In addition to his style, he has shown in television commercials for such companies as Wang that using media in unexpected ways can be provocative as an unexpected message. Easdon has some unexecuted ideas that demonstrate both of these principles—ideas that should inspire you. Here are a couple of them.

Easdon had the idea for a television commercial for a women's fragrance showing a close-up of a beautiful woman's eye, or maybe even a man's eye, on half the screen. During the 30-second spot, the eye starts to tear and the camera follows the tear down the cheek into "nothing." No supers. Nothing—just a provocative image. It would be seemingly meaningless to everybody. Then, in women's magazines, an ad would show the same imagery, with the tear dropping into the fragrance bottle. Next time the women would see the TV spot, they'd know what it was about and they'd be part of an "inside" secret.

In 1986, Easdon wanted to do two sixty-second commercials for RC Cola during the Super Bowl. He wanted to show a group of people breaking into the game carrying RC Cola and trying to climb up the scoreboard for a nice view. Just when the viewer thinks they may be caught by security, the commercial ends. Then, on the screen, the question is asked, "Should they go ahead or retreat?" The audience gets to make that judgment by calling a 900 number and in the fourth quarter, RC Cola would report the results of the voting in a super at the bottom of the screen. The ad would associate the drink with "choice," a choice where consumers have the control.

CHAPTER FIVE

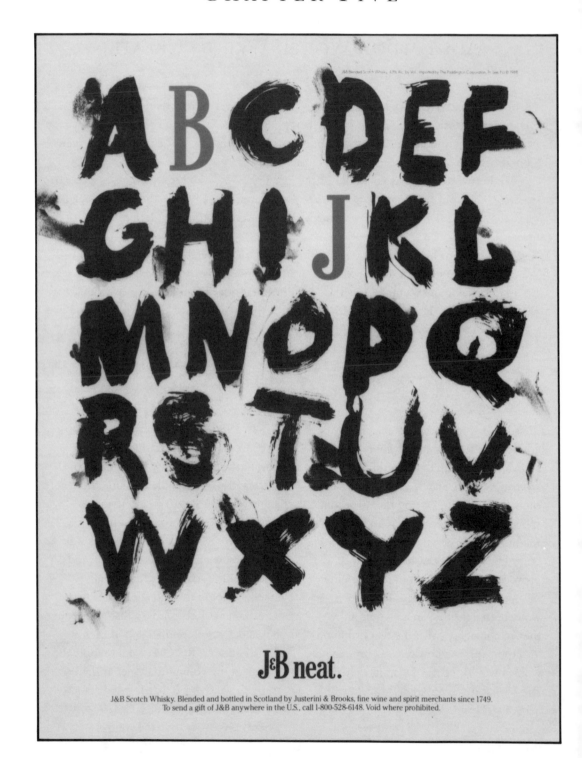

Roy Grace

"A lot of kids come out of school today and all they've learned to do is think. They can't execute their ideas. They can't even communicate them visually on a piece of paper," says Roy Grace, Chairman of Grace and Rothschild. "It's like a surgeon who knows all the techniques, but is unable to use all the instruments."

Roy Grace is surely a "surgeon" who knows how to use all the tools. He has art directed some of the most groundbreaking ads ever to come out of Doyle Dane Bernbach. He has won numerous Clios, One Show awards, and Cannes Lions, as well as many others.

In this chapter, we will investigate one aspect of creating a groundbreaking ad—graphic invention—as well as other "tools" you may need. In addition, we will become familiar with a very original and important player in the history of advertising.

Before he started his current shop with former DDB copywriter Diane Rothschild, Grace worked his way up to the positions of chairman of Doyle Dane Bernbach-U.S. and vice chairman of the board of The Doyle Dane Bernbach Group. Says Grace, "I doubt if these were titles you could really put on a business card."

THE GREATEST 14TH CENTURY TALENT IN THE 20TH CENTURY

IF YOU HAVE TALENT, YOU CAN SUCCEED. IT MAY TAKE MANY INTERVIEWS AT MANY AD shops. It may even take many jobs. But once you find your home, you'll know it. You'll thrive. And you'll create the type of advertising you've always wanted to create. That's one major lesson you should learn by looking at Roy Grace's career. But that's not all. You'll also learn about a truly original creative personality.

Roy Grace was always interested in doing creative things. His passion was ignited for what he calls a very shallow reason: It stole attention away from his older and very bright sister. "When I was very young—about five—I drew Donald Duck and my mother and father oohed and ahhed," says Grace. "From that moment on, I knew art was for me."

His schooling reinforced this interest in art. In grammar school, he was bored by the academic subjects. And like any bored but bright child, he got into a lot of trouble. School officials constantly sent for his parents. The only subject he excelled in was art. This prompted his teachers to recommend he apply to the High School of Art and Design (then known as the School of Industrial Art).

It was not something he had ever considered. But it seemed interesting. So he applied and to his astonishment—he felt that the others taking the entrance exam were much more talented—he was accepted by the school.

However, again bored by the academics and teachers, he became the class clown. He constantly made wisecracks and acted inappropriately. Once, for instance, he covered his entire face with loose-leaf paper reinforcements. "Let's put it this way," says Grace, "I certainly wasn't voted the most likely to succeed."

What Grace did learn was "craft" from a very young age. Throughout his education, he constantly worked with his hands, learning many different techniques and, more important, learning how to visualize. He studied printing, photography, three-dimensional design, and paper sculpturing. He learned chiseling, point lettering, retouching, drafting, cartooning—every subject aligned with the commercial arts.

"It gave me a sampling of what was in the real world," says Grace. In addition, by gaining a knowledge of these things, as well as by physically practicing them, he learned other forms of visual communication.

"I really prepared for the 14th Century," says Grace, something he sees as a plus. He explains: "Kids aren't prepared for the 20th Century or the 21st Century. There are certain things to know, and I'm not talking about the concrete production of an ad. I'm talking about knowing how to approach problems on an intellectual level. They don't seem able to do this."

At 17, when he graduated from high school, he was ready to work and interested in making money. He didn't know what he wanted to do, outside of the fact that it should be something to do with art or illustration. His job search strategy consisted of looking at building directories to find the advertising agencies and studios and then going up to the receptionists and announcing he wanted a job. "It was awful," says Grace. "That entire summer of 1954, I remember literally walking the streets, getting depressed, and being discouraged by employment agencies because they said I needed this and that."

Finally, through his father's friend, he learned about Famous Studios, Paramount Studios' East Coast division. They produced all the animation for the Paramount cartoons—Popeye, Tubby, Baby Huey, Tom and Jerry, Little Lulu, Casper the Friendly Ghost—and ran it like an assembly line: First, an animator made the initial drawings. Then an in-betweener drew the rest. Next, an inker took these drawings and, after following a series of preparatory steps, traced them with a fine quill pen. Finally, an opaquer painted the figures. The studio gave Grace a job as an apprentice inker.

At first, he thought he could never do the job, but he turned out to be a natural. An inker had to produce 60 to 80 frames a day. Grace could produce nearly 120 frames a day. He learned to be very precise with a pen. And, more importantly, he learned that often a task that looks impossible, with enough practice and determination, becomes a piece of cake. "It taught me that there's no challenge too great," he says. "You just have to make up your mind you're going to do it. And not run but attack."

It wasn't long before he grew bored and restless, so he quit. "I was never good at finding another job before leaving one," says Grace. "I was very impulsive."

At that point, Grace wanted to become an illustrator. He realized that he needed more education, so he began taking night classes at the School of Visual Arts. But these courses did not put him any closer to developing a career goal. Instead, Grace learned that illustration might not be the best thing for him.

At the same time, he had begun working at studios as a messenger. He thought this was a great way to learn key lining and paste-up. He planned to work his way into a bullpen. "Sometimes they gave me a break and let me clean the rubber cement off the mechanicals," says Grace. "But nobody would ever teach me."

His career stalled and with people being drafted, Grace and a group of his friends decided to enlist. Ironically, he became an illustrator in the army, drawing tactical equipment in a little Washington, D.C. spy unit. He'd get blurred photographs taken from a moving car along with sketches of machines and weapons. He was supposed to interpret them, but he didn't. Without an engineering or military background to understand the photos and sketches, he'd make things up. "I'd put a bolt on it if it looked good," says Grace. "I wish I had those drawings. They were really nice. Again, I kind of taught myself and had 18 months of practice. So I got pretty good at it."

When Grace was discharged from the army, he landed his first big job. The studio made packaging mechanicals, the most precise and thus most difficult kind of mechanicals because dies were cast from them. Since he had never done them before, he lied to get the job. "I was heading into deep, deep trouble," says Grace.

Within a few months, Grace was fired. "I felt awful," he says. "I was devastated. Nobody likes to be told they're inadequate. But I couldn't do it. It was really more than I could manage at that point." (Note: This happened in 1958 and the studio was still in existence when Grace was voted into the Art Director's Hall of Fame in 1986. At the induction ceremony a man came up to Grace and said, "You're not the same Roy Grace that..." and Grace said, "You fired over 20 years ago." The man responded, "We should have kept you.")

Not to be discouraged down, Grace went to another studio, one where the work wasn't as precise. The new skills he had learned in his previous job made him a star. He liked that. But after two months, he asked for a raise because of his rise in status. When they said no, he quit. From there followed jobs at studio after studio, as well as at a printer—they offered a layout, mechanical, and printing for the price of printing alone anywhere else—and at a now-defunct trade publisher.

At the same time, he went back to school—Cooper Union—studying at night. "This really opened up the world for me," says Grace. "It all came together. Everything just kind of lit up for me and I began to understand about thinking and concepts."

One teacher, an art director/supervisor at Benton & Bowles, offered Grace a job as an apprentice. This was approximately his twenty-fifth job. "I knew nothing about advertising at all," says Grace. "It wasn't my goal. In fact, I fought it for years. It felt kind of crass to me. And I really wanted to become a graphic designer. I wanted to design posters, book jackets, record albums. I liked the feeling of graphic design. The two dimensionality of it. The elegance and aloofness of it."

But the creative revolution was just beginning. People were doing things that felt exciting and interesting to Grace, and he wanted to be part of it.

At this point, Grace had much more of an advertising portfolio, containing more advertising ideas than completed ads. "What I really wanted to do," says Grace, "was demonstrate my thinking and my ability to be graphically inventive, which, by the way, is what's missing from art directors' books today." Grace defines graphic invention as "finding a new page." It's laying out the ad a little differently, doing something that's never been done before. And it's finding a way to graphically communicate the idea, rather than having to verbally express it.

Grace took to advertising very quickly. Within six months, he went from apprentice to working on national campaigns. He was a "star" again. But then a photo rep suggested he send his portfolio to Grey Advertising. He did and doubled his salary.

At Grey, he got very frustrated. Immediately, they had him working on television commercials. He had never art directed television before and he was in over his head. But he hung in there and forced himself to understand it. He learned, for example, that with print, you work in space, and with television, you work in time.

"You learn by doing," says Grace of his floundering. "That's the best teacher in the world. Also, you learn by failing. Nobody does anything that's an immediate success."

The first commercials he art directed were for Pampers. Says Grace, "Thank God, I blotted them from my mind. From Procter and Gamble's point of view, they were a resounding success. From my point of view, they were a resounding failure. These were the old style of commercial. It was babies in diapers and side-by-side faucets. You know, one diaper absorbs. And the other doesn't."

After more than 27 jobs—quite a lot for a 26-year-old—Grace went to Doyle Dane Bernbach, where he stayed for 23 years. His portfolio was filled with roughs for ads he wanted to do that had been killed at either Grey or Benton & Bowles. "I had produced some ads," said Grace. "But in my book, I basically had spec. They (DDB) wanted to see how I thought."

Grace had wanted to work at DDB "for a long time." But he was afraid to apply because he thought they wouldn't hire him. He didn't want his fears confirmed. As he explains it, "I didn't know what I would do if I couldn't work there because I felt there was no place else for me to work."

To avoid rejection, he kept stalling. He'd promise himself to do one more ad to make his portfolio better. "I probably stalled for six months, which is an eternity for me," says Grace. "I usually do things pretty quickly. Finally, I took a deep breath and sent the book. I didn't present it. They wouldn't see people. Books were lined up by the thousands. Everybody wanted to work there. And, amazingly, they called me."

DDB offered him a job at less than what he was earning. "Everybody who went to work there at that time had to take a cut," says Grace. "That was part of it. But I refused. And they hired me anyway. I couldn't have been happier. It was as if I had died and gone to heaven. To be working at Doyle Dane Bernbach was like being on the 1927 Yankees. They were hot. There was no other place at that point."

Grace was nervous about refusing to take a pay cut, but he had already begun to understand a hiring pattern at the agencies. "When I went to Benton & Bowles, they asked me to step into a room, figure out my expenses, and tell them the least amount I could possibly live on," says Grace. "I did a very honest evaluation and they offered me less. Then when I went to Grey, they offered me a certain amount, but the day I started, they tried to give me a pay cut because they just lost an account. I decided to be obstinate. And it worked."

After bouncing through so many jobs, what kept Grace at DDB? Simple. His ideas were produced. "All the stuff I had been trying to do at the other agencies found a life there," says Grace. "I was allowed an enormous amount of freedom from virtually the first day I walked in. They let me be on my own. It was very loose and I liked that."

Grace's 23 years at DDB were not always smooth sailing. And he did stray twice from the fold. The first and most instructive time was shortly after DDB opened their first office in Germany. They asked Grace to create some Volkswagen ads for the German market. He did and they were so well received by Bernbach, DDB decided to run some of them in the States and offered him the job of co-creative director of the German office.

To Grace, it seemed like a great opportunity—here was a chance to be a creative director just 2½ years after beginning as an apprentice. So he jumped at the chance and went to Germany. He agreed to go for three years, but after less than 6 months, he knew he had to return. "I just felt I was out of the business," says Grace. "The creative revolution was happening in the States and I was in a backwater. And with DDB growing, I was afraid they wouldn't take me back."

Around that time, Wells, Rich, Greene was becoming a hot agency, and Grace had gotten an offer from them. So he figured he'd work there and went back to New York without telling anyone. "I was still a little crazy," says Grace. "I had a girlfriend (who is now his wife) and I holed up in her apartment. And Bill Bernbach called me there and said he wanted to talk. I was shocked he would call. He said, 'Look, we want you. If you don't like it there, we understand, just go back and stay there a little longer until we can find a replacement.' I was so floored by the generosity, in view of the fact that I did not fulfill my agreement, that I felt incredibly obligated to him."

Even though the job at WRG was for considerably more money, Grace returned to Germany for a few more months. Then when he came back to the States, he went back to being an art director/group supervisor at DDB/New York.

What did Bernbach do to instill this loyalty? Grace says it's because he loved advertising. "With most agencies back then, management was crusty, cynical, and narrow minded. You'd have to bludgeon, sneak, and manipulate an ad into existence. Bernbach was open, exuberant, and encouraging. And he loved what you loved. The work coming out of the agency showed that."

Of his working relationship with Bernbach, Grace says, "I always wanted to please him. There was no doubt about that. When you brought an ad or commercial to him and he liked it, his level of enthusiasm was intoxicating. I was five years old again, drawing Donald Duck and my mother and father were 'oohing' and 'ahhing.' There was that same elixir. I was getting respect and admiration from the best. What could be better than that? That seductive brew."

Ultimately, Grace worked his way up to chairman. But this didn't mean much to him. "You know what it meant?" he asks. "It meant the same thing it meant when you were a kid: that somebody else didn't get it. It pulled me away from what I really liked to do, which was the advertising. It got me more and more involved in the management and that's one of the reasons I quit. I just wanted to get back to advertising."

Grace also quit because he felt that the agency changed when it went public. "Instead of wanting to be the best," says Grace, "DDB wanted to be the biggest." He says this change in emphasis took place slowly.

A final reason—and the driving force behind his leaving all his previous jobs—he felt he no longer could do his best work. "I just felt very frustrated," he says. "And that same feeling led me to quit every single job I've ever had."

Grace formed his new agency with writer Diane Rothschild, who was a creative director at DDB. One day, after a particularly frustrating meeting, he asked her if she'd like to go into business with him. She said, "Sure." They opened their doors without a client because Grace felt he shouldn't solicit any of DDB's clients. "Because of my position as chairman," says Grace, "I didn't think it was ethical."

In addition, he wanted a clean slate. His last year at DDB had been a difficult one. He didn't want to carry any of that baggage with him. "I really wanted to let the scar tissue heal as much as possible," says Grace. "And take a fresh new look at things."

Grace and Rothschild began with five people and a willingness to "wait and see what happened." Today, the company consists of 45 employees and billings around $85 million.

Outside of advertising, Grace spends his time sculpturing, carving, painting, playing tennis, and reading. "I'm into doing a lot of stuff with my hands," he says. In advertising, he likes learning about new businesses. "You can find yourself in the middle of the desert in the Southwest, in a factory in Moravia, Yugoslavia, in a balloon in Morocco," says Grace. "And you're studying some esoteric part of something you didn't even know existed six months before."

A PORTFOLIO FILLED WITH GRACE

After we paint the car we paint the paint.

Every now and then a VW runs into a little trouble at the factory.

Early Volkswagen

Grace worked on Volkswagen advertising for 20 years. The overriding strategy was that Volkswagen was a smart buy—aren't you smart to buy one? Says Grace, "Look at those dummies. They have to put a lot more money in the gas tank and they get stuck in the snow. It was really a smart buy."

He doesn't know if anyone ever wrote out that strategy. "But that's what it turned out to be," he says. "We just did it unconsciously."

The first ads in the campaign were done by legendary art director Helmut Krone. Both "After We Paint the Car, We Paint the Paint" and "This Car Ran Into a Little Trouble at the Factory" were among the ads that caught Bernbach's attention, prompting Grace's promotion and transfer to Germany.

For a later example of Volkswagen advertising, look back to Ted Bell's portfolio in Chapter One. You'll also find more Volkswagen ads in Appendix 1 of this book.

IBM Can You Spot the Copycat? and AT Fabulous Jack

Grace spends a lot of time talking about the lack of—and the need for—graphic invention in a beginner's portfolio. These ads may help you understand what he means by that term.

That's because the visuals express the idea. And the headlines simply comment on it. For example, with American Tourister, the visual communicates the suitcase's strength much more than any headline can. What's more, when they were first produced, the layouts were new and fresh.

Of graphic invention, Grace says, "You can see it in virtually any good ad. But I can't show something new to explain it because, by definition, it hasn't been done yet."

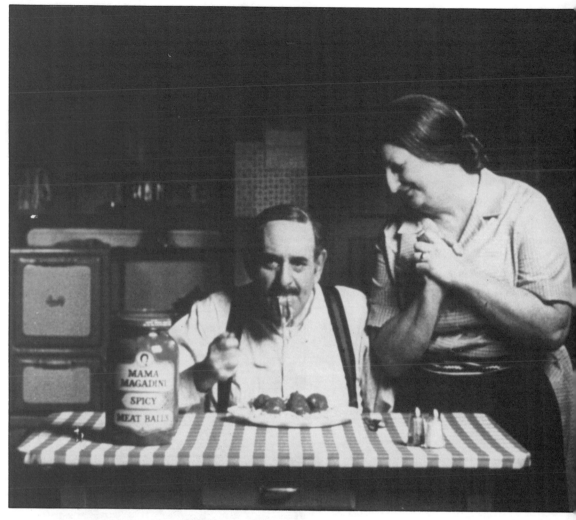

Alka Seltzer Spicy Meatball

"It's amazing, wherever I go, this one comes up and it begins to become something I want to escape from," says Grace of this commercial. It was one of the first to break the taboo against using humor in advertising and many argue that (just like most humorous advertising) it didn't help sell the product (see Chapter 3). Now, however, this spot is in the Museum of Modern Art and the Clio Hall of Fame, and was voted the best commercial of the last 25 years.

Of its creation, Grace says, *"We were looking for situations where you're forced to overeat. We were working under the rule that you could not show a glutton in a commercial. Our own experience in food shoots—where you're forced to eat stuff for hours—was a funny, interesting idea."*

J&B on the rocks.

J&B Scotch Whisky. Blended and bottled in Scotland by Justerini & Brooks, fine wine and spirit merchants since 1749. To send a gift of J&B anywhere in the U.S. call 1-800-238-4373. Void where prohibited.

J & B on the Rocks

"We were looking for something young and contemporary so we could shed J & B's old fuddy-duddy image," says Grace. "We were to replace a campaign that featured a bottle of J & B, a sword, a dragoon helmet, and some lead soldiers. We knew we wanted it to be fresh, a little bit disarming, and a little bit wacky. We were looking for something that had a lot of legs so we could do a lot of ads from it (which is critical to Grace in his approval of a campaign). So we put it through all those filters and we thought along very precise lines."

Despite the success of this campaign, Grace says he tries to stay away from puns in headlines. "I do visual puns," says Grace. "I hate puns and I've always stayed away from them. For me, they're a cheap shot. But J & B seemed so wacky, so over done, and so excessive that it seemed appropriate for the audience we were trying to reach. The frightening thing is, visual puns seemed to have caught on, and I see more and more campaigns based on them."

The oil that saves you gas.

Mobil One

"Here was a five-dollar can of oil, about four times the price of the competition," Grace says, "but it was the oil that saved you gas." This campaign evolved during the energy crisis of the early seventies and is an example of a product's positioning containing a benefit. "The solution was relatively simple," says Grace. "It had a real, factual benefit."

Range Rover (Precisely How Sturdy is a Range Rover?)

You typically buy a jeep for about $16,000 or $18,000. So how do you justify buying what is essentially a $40,000 jeep? And how do you communicate that justification on a very small budget?

"We had to create an aura of something really special," says Grace. "There was a slow hammering out of the strategy with the client."

The first ad—which 4½ years later now looks tame to Grace—consisted of a big, white Range Rover covered in mud on a white page with the headline, "Introducing the most beautiful vehicle in the world."

"Nobody had ever introduced a new car with a speck of dust on it, let alone dripping with dirt," says Grace. "I thought it was really revolutionary for the client to accept it and encourage it."

The ad communicates that a Range Rover is a very sturdy automobile. To sum up this campaign, Grace says, "We just looked for dramatic ways to express the strategy to show that Range Rover was the best off-road vehicle in the world and was also a luxury car."

Precisely how sturdy is a Range Rover?

Not *this* sturdy.
Ten tons of careening boulder would undoubtedly turn even a Range Rover into a convertible.
Short of such an inconvenience, however, you can reasonably expect a Range Rover to bear up under some considerably unreasonable conditions.
In fact, with features like a 14-gauge steel chassis and welded frame, Range Rovers routinely survive not merely for decades, but for decades in jungles, deserts and the odd tundra.
So it's hardly surprising that Range Rovers here hold up so well they retain their value better than a host of comparable cars. Including some with names like BMW and Mercedes.
And even at a starting price just under $39,000, that makes Range Rover one of the smartest investments on the road. Or off it.
Why not call 1-800-FINE 4WD for a dealer near you?
After all, when it comes to building an uncommonly strong vehicle, we leave no stone unturned.

RANGE ROVER

ADVICE BASED ON THIRTY YEARS OF ADVERTISING EXPERIENCE

WHERE DOES GRACE SEE THE ADVERTISING INDUSTRY GOING? NOWHERE. AT LEAST, nowhere fast. "The basic engine of this business is ideas, and that doesn't change," says Grace. "I've seen little nuances, technological changes. But it hasn't changed much in the 30 years I've been doing it."

At the same time, Grace realizes a new idea now will be an old one by tomorrow. "When anybody really has a new idea, it's co-opted and becomes common," he says.

This should make it easier for you to break in because you're not continually having to play catch-up. In reality, however, this makes it harder. Grace says he looks for fresh solutions to fresh problems, as well as originality in thought. "Anybody can do another Range Rover ad," he says. So in an industry that's hardly moving, how do you come up with something fresh? While Grace can't tell you exactly how (if he could, it wouldn't be fresh), he can give you some ideas to start your thinking. Here they are:

Forget advertising schools

Some schools are just factories, Grace believes. "You see the same ads from book to book and you don't know who did what," he says. "It's a very hard job (teaching) not to fall into a rut and I think these people have. One of the reasons I never taught is that I never felt qualified to be inventive enough to challenge students in a fresh way." And don't think that your portfolio will be lost in the shuffle because of your lack of school credentials. Grace says he will look at anybody's book.

Pick your teachers carefully

"Most graduates from advertising programs are barely adequate," says Grace, which he thinks is a result of poor instruction. "The advertising problems are ordinary and the direction is ordinary," he says. "When you see a group of students from one place all excelling, it's because of the teachers." There are a couple of schools he thinks are doing a good job of preparing students, including the Art Center in L.A. and the Portfolio Center in Atlanta. So if you feel you must go to a school to prepare your book, pick it carefully. It could make the difference.

Be bold

Grace looks for a sense of adventure and a broadness in thinking. He looks for people who are not afraid to take chances. He would rather hire people who are in danger of being absolutely wrong than being timidly right. "There are so many ads that are okay and nice and it's hard to find something wrong to say about them," says Grace, "but the ads that are exceptional are usually a little irreverent, foolish, or dangerous. Some even cross the line and get the creative in trouble with a client. Exceptional advertising is like walking a very delicate tightrope, but if you don't have the courage to take a chance, you'll be doing mundane work forever."

Don't suffer for your craft

Grace doesn't believe in enduring miserable working conditions or long hours. "I believe in working hard," says Grace, "but doing it in a normal lifestyle. I like being home with my kids. I think I can count every weekend I've worked on one hand. Keep everything in perspective and have fun while working. And if it stops being fun, get out."

Run with your first idea

Grace believes the first idea is usually the best. "I've never been one to dwell on a problem," he says. "If it takes three seconds to have an idea, it's too long. If it takes 30 seconds, I panic. I go, 'Oh my God; I'll never solve this.' I'm a student of the school that the solution should become apparent in one big explosion with-

in the first few seconds. Once you understand the problem, the answer should be there."

Redefine the problem

"Sometimes this is the hardest, but the most important thing to do," says Grace. "Often, if you have difficulty solving a problem," he says. "The way the problem is defined creates the difficulty. By redefining it, you can understand it."

Research before you create

Grace encourages research before production. "Research helps you paint a perfect target or, at least, a near perfect one," he says. But after production, Grace avoids it. "You're measuring, in essence, the unmeasurable," he says. "There are just too many variables, too many unknowns. It's a waste of money and a waste of time. If it worked, I'd be the first to subscribe to it. There would be no failures in the marketplace."

Go to the library

You need information before you start. But beginners don't have the resources of an agency. So what do you do? Grace thinks you should look to your neighborhood library. "This is the best kind of research a beginner could do," he says. "In a library you can get an amazing amount of information. It's the best source. You can also call the company that manufactures the product you're going to use in a spec ad. If you get through to the right people, they generally help."

Work in a fantasy world

"No person in his right mind is going to look at a beginner's solution and expect him or her to know the absolute, exact temperature of the marketplace," says Grace. "I see many, many books where solutions didn't make sense because beginners didn't know the marketplace. But I didn't hold that against them. There was no way for them to really know. Within their defined world, their view made sense and I accepted it."

Show it with attitude

Nowadays you'll hear a lot about attitude. Grace thinks attitude is probably the latest version of the word image or even position. And he defines it as the tonality you want to convey in an ad, the point of view. "Attitude is maybe a little snottier than tonality, but essentially it comes down to the same thing," says Grace. "You have to have one voice—one tone—in a campaign. That voice has to be appropriate to the product. What's right for a J & B is certainly wrong for a Mount Sinai Hospital."

Learn to "dance"

"Very few ads that come out and make a direct statement are good," says Grace. He believes direct headlines are good when you have something concrete to say, like announcing a cure for cancer. "You wouldn't want to play around with that," he says. "Because you really have something to say." The rest of the time,

Grace believes you have to entertain. "With the vast majority of advertising, you don't have product superiority or real news," he says. "What you have to do is dance a little bit. Part of what you're selling is a good feeling about the product and a positive image of it."

Take calligraphy

Grace took years of calligraphy and found it forced him to think visually. "It teaches you about negative and positive shapes in a way that nothing else can," he says. "That's critical in designing a page. It helps you know how big a headline should be and how small the body copy could be."

Try humor

Grace feels a commercial should be entertaining while conveying its message, which is why he uses humor. "I think it really helps. I remember when I first started in the business, humor was a negative. People said funny advertising didn't work. Now, everybody tries to do it. But it's hard to do."

Believe in yourself

"I was fired three or four times in the beginning—once for turning over a pot of ink on my boss," says Grace. "If there's any message here, it's that if there's something you really want to do, and you really believe in it, persevere and it will happen. It really will. You've just got to keep hanging in there."

Postscript 1
How to Tell a Good Idea from a Bad One

There's no easy way to tell a good idea from a bad one. However, Grace has developed a checklist that may help. He goes through this list automatically and unconsciously. You may wish to eventually develop your own criteria; his offer a great start. Here they are and what he has to say about them.

"One, is it relevant to the product? Does it bear some relationship to the product?

"Two, is it the kind of idea that's never, ever been done before by anybody else for this category?

"Three, is it an idea you can do many variations of? Could it last for many years?

"Four, is it not only informative, but entertaining? People don't come home at night to watch commercials. And they don't open a magazine to read the ads. Does the message move you? Is it dramatic? Is it impactful? Will it attract somebody's attention?

"Five, does it make people think? That's critical. Do people participate in the ad? Do the little motors in their brain start running, so they're actually involved in the premise? And is it motivating and persuasive?

"Six, do I like it? If you like the advertising, there's a good chance the audience will like the product.

"Finally, when I first see it, do I get a tiny tingling in my stomach? Does it make me nervous? I like ads that make me nervous because they're a little dangerous and new. You don't get nervous when you're seeing something you've seen before.

"No doubt there's something you get from experience. When I was far less experienced, how did I know? It felt right. I could not articulate it, but it felt right. And I was prepared to logically defend every part of the ad. I asked myself: Why am I doing this? Why is the type so big? Why am I choosing this type? Why am I choosing this picture? Why is the headline expressed this way? Why is the copy like this?

"Feeling great is only the beginning. It's important that you're also able to logically justify your feelings. You know, it would feel great—probably—to walk out of the window of my office right now and fly down 20 stories. But when you hit bottom, it's not going to feel so good. That same process is in place when you create something.

"What I do is create the ad and then try to analyze why it works. You come up with something that just feels good to you and then you investigate your premise. You check to see if it's right. Sometimes you go back and say this won't work. It doesn't make sense. Then you find a way to make it make sense."

• • • • • • • • • • • • • • • • •

Postscript 2
MORE THOUGHTS ON GRAPHIC INVENTION

THROUGHOUT THIS CHAPTER, WE'VE TALKED ABOUT THE NEED FOR GRAPHIC INVENTION and that it is missing from most beginners' books. To help you understand graphic invention more fully, here are more thoughts from Roy Grace.

"The solution to most advertising problems today is verbal. If you can come up with an arresting visual idea, you've got a leg up on the competition. However, most art directors come out of schools more as writers than art directors. That's because, in school, they're forced to think conceptually, which is fine. And they're forced to think verbally rather than visually, which I think is horrible.

"Art directors also have to think executionally. Art direction is like running a little factory: you work with the writer to come up with the headline, you may come up with the idea, or you may even come up with all of it. But then you have to manufacture the product. To produce the ad. And that requires a lot of knowledge.

"Now, I've hired scores of young art directors out of school and, believe me, it's astonishing to see how ill prepared they are to be art directors. They're good at thinking, but they're not able to put something down on a piece of paper that helps sell an idea. That's because they don't think visually any more. They think verbally. The whole revolution of the sixties was a revolution in thought. Art directors and writers sitting together and thinking has dominated so much that it's swept everything else aside.

"The other way of approaching it is to come up with the visual idea first. With the right visual idea, the headline writes itself. Take a look at the Range Rover ads.

"Or take a look at the J & B ads. They're not exactly the same as what I'm talking about. But they're close. Virtually every ad has a visual invention in it. They're pictorial creations, little visual puzzles. Not blatant black-and-white concrete, absolute statements. You're forced to participate in them, to come up with your own conclusions."

Steve Hayden

"I think all advertising people come from dysfunctional families," says Steve Hayden, chairman and chief creative officer of BBDO West. He believes creative people have an ingrained need to receive extra attention and a need to please people—traits that are often developed as a result of an unhealthy family environment. "I probably had them very early on."

A similar observation was voiced in Susan Gillette's chapter. In Tom McElligott's chapter, we will hear a theory about why children of dysfunctional families make great creatives. In this chapter, we will see the results of someone who grew up in a dysfunctional family—grew up to create some of America's most noticed and *pleasing* advertising.

Over the course of his career, Hayden has worked on top accounts such as Apple Computer, Porsche, Pizza Hut, Nike, and Home Savings of America. He has received some of advertising's most prestigious awards, including the Cannes Gold Lion award, the New York Art Directors Club award, the One Show award, the Clio award, and the British D&AD award.

Hayden attributes much of his success to his collaborative nature. He believes that it's better to own 20% of a great idea than 100% of a so-so idea.

FROM MUSIC TO ENGLISH TO INDUSTRIAL TO CONSUMER ADVERTISING

IF THERE'S ONE LESSON TO BE LEARNED BY LOOKING AT STEVE HAYDEN'S CAREER, IT'S THAT your goals can shift and change and you can still come out on top. Hayden originally wanted to become a professional musician. He then became a writer, went back and forth between big and small agencies, and even explored the option of writing for television. It wasn't until almost ten years into his advertising career that he decided to dedicate himself to advertising as a lifelong profession.

Hayden's career shifts may at first seem to have served no purpose. But, in fact, his later success was a direct result of his varied background. Studying his career shifts may also help you along.

A budding cellist, Hayden enrolled in the University of Southern California in Los Angeles to study with Gregor Piatigorsky. He claims he was the worst cellist in the class. Out of a class of twelve, says Hayden, ten went to Moscow, four of whom placed first through fourth in the Tchaikovsky Competition. He says he was left behind playing bar mitzvahs.

At the same time, Hayden started writing and his work came to the attention of the English department; they asked him to join an experimental honors program. The reward for joining: guaranteed A's and a limited number of hours in class. This was more than enough of an incentive to get him to become an English major. He kept music as a minor. He then went on to publish a "hippie humor magazine" at USC, which was his first semi-commercial writing experience.

After college, Hayden married and moved to Michigan, where his wife was working on her master's degree. He initially supported himself by playing cello. But when his money ran out, he began looking for full-time work. His reasoning for applying for jobs in advertising: "It sounded like more fun than being a trainee salesman with Xerox."

To have something to show during job interviews, Hayden created a spec portfolio using the Campbell-Ewald Creative Test. In the test, he was asked to solve a series of advertising problems. For instance, he developed a campaign for oatmeal and another one for a coffee maker. His book was more rudimentary than those developed today. He had stick figure illustrations and his headlines were hand written.

Hayden's portfolio—as he readily admits—might not be strong enough to land him a job today, but back in the sixties it did the trick. MacManus, Johns & Adams/Bloomfield Hills hired him as a junior copywriter to work on industrial accounts, a position that helped him change his attitude toward the morality of advertising. Says Hayden, "I went into advertising with this sixties sensibility that all advertising was a manipulation and that it was created by horrible, criminal people who put property rights above human rights—

and that all of them probably should be killed—but I was going to do this anyway, just to make a few dollars."

By working on industrial accounts, Hayden learned that a copywriter really can't lie. In industrial advertising, you are writing to engineers and other people who know a great deal more about vitrified grinding wheels or centrifugal vacuum pumps than you do. So if you lie, they will find out. This holds true for consumer advertising as well.

Starting in industrial advertising also gave Hayden the foundation for later success for two very basic reasons. First, he was forced to produce a very high volume of work. Because profit margins are typically much higher in consumer advertising, the amount of work creatives need to produce is usually much lower than in industrial advertising. Second, he had to cope with vast amounts of source material and to delve into technical areas he didn't know anything about, which taught him how to learn new areas very quickly.

As we've seen in earlier chapters, careers are sometimes shaped by events outside of an individual's control or professional life. We find this here, too. Despite his initial success, Hayden quit his job and moved back to Los Angeles. His parents had become ill and they asked him to live closer to them.

Back home with a portfolio of published industrial work and some unpublished samples for Pontiac, which was a client of his former employer, he started looking for work. Despite being well received at Doyle Dane Bernbach, he took a job at a little industrial shop.

Hayden worked at a series of these small shops before the next major twist in his career, a position with Clinton E. Frank. At that time, Clinton E. Frank was one of the largest and most creative agencies in Los Angeles. They'd won the Belding Sweepstakes two years in a row, and they had Toyota among a number of other major accounts. "Going from working at a little industrial agency to working for Clinton E. Frank was a big jump," says Hayden. "A major leap up. At Clinton E. Frank, Hayden worked as a liaison between the account and creative areas doing strategic planning for Toyota.

Satisfied at being allowed to write at least some ads along with his strategy papers, Hayden continued to work as a liaison until he was asked to become an account executive. But Hayden wanted to stay on the creative side of advertising. Says Hayden, "While the strategy side is very interesting, it's a much colder endeavor. It's much more removed from people. It doesn't allow you to be quite as silly. It seemed like a choice between working for an insurance company or a film company. I'd much rather work for a film company."

Since he didn't want the promotion, Hayden went to the creative director and asked for a shot at staying in the creative department. With this simple request, Hayden became a full-time copywriter.

Within a year and a half, he was promoted again, this time to group supervisor on the Toyota account. Then in 1975, two major events changed Hayden's career. First, his father passed away, prompting him to reevaluate his life and career goals. Second, Toyota fired Clinton E. Frank.

"The firing was ironic," says Hayden. "Three months before, Toyota had thrown a big party for us because they had passed Volkswagen in sales for the first time. They said they were on their way to becoming a dominant force in the world automotive industry and they thanked us for our contribution. When they fired us, they said that we were too small for them now that they were bigger than Volkswagen."

In response to the firing, Clinton E. Frank laid off more than 100 employees. Fewer than 20 people remained at the agency. Says Hayden, "I thought, advertising certainly is a horrible, disreputable, terrible way to make a living because these things can happen to you and there's absolutely no security.

To revive the agency, they tried bringing in new clients, but without success. Their last hope was getting the Kawasaki motorcycle account. For the pitch, they brought up motorcycles in the elevator and put them in their lobby. And they were confident about showing their reel of award-winning spots. Unfortunately, when the prospective client came in for a tour of the offices, someone opened a door off the conference room and exposed an incredibly long hallway of empty offices. "It was unbelievable," says Hayden. "All we needed was tumbleweed blowing through." Of course, Clinton E. Frank did not win the Kawasaki account and, a few months later, the agency was closed.

Luckily, Hayden wasn't out in the cold. He had decided to write for television and had just sold a script to "Welcome Back Kotter," a popular show at the time. Since the script was produced and aired, he thought he was on his way to having a successful second career. He wrote for other television shows. He discovered that writing episodic television was not that much different from writing commercials. It's a collaborative effort. The producer is, in effect, the creative director. And it's much more of a commercial form than an art form. Many formulas have to be followed. The difference? Hayden found the people in advertising to be a little more pleasant.

Since he still needed a way to pay the rent while launching his television writing career, Hayden accepted a part-time freelance job at yet another small industrial agency. He planned to work only four hours a day. But, while at the agency, he wrote several ads that attracted a lot of attention within the advertising community and brought assignments from major advertisers, including *Time* magazine and Universal Pictures. Consequently the agency grew and Hayden's role expanded.

One of the ads he wrote even won a Belding Award (see KFAC ad in the portfolio section). Suddenly, he was attracting the attention of very senior creative people and was recognized as somebody who had done something very special. So he decided to give up television writing and get serious about advertising. He felt he needed to work for a larger agency, where he could get the training and experience he needed to develop his skills.

Hayden first took a writing position at Foote, Cone & Belding. He got the job because he had worked on Toyota and they wanted him to work on Mazda. In addition, he was given some National Semiconductor ads to write because of his business-to-business experience. Says Hayden, "Obviously, I wasn't getting the kind of training I needed." Hayden stayed for three months.

Jay Chiat also noticed the KFAC ad and subsequently hired Hayden. "For my first five months, I thought I was going to get fired every day," says Hayden. "The level of competition was so intense, and the people so hip-swanking cool. It was a very intimidating environment to be in."

But Hayden also had a solid reputation. He was known as someone who could produce good long-copy ads, a rarity even back in the early eighties.

After a little over a year at Chiat/Day, Hayden was asked to help Jay Chiat open a New York office. But New York was not the only city targeted in Chiat's expansion plans (Chiat once purportedly said he wanted to see how big the agency could get while still doing good work). Eight months after opening this office, Chiat bought Regis McKenna Advertising in San Francisco, acquiring the Apple Computer account in the process. Since Hayden had a technical/industrial background, Chiat had him write for this account while the San Francisco office was being assembled. But Chiat wanted to keep it a secret because he didn't want Hayden leaving New York.

When Chiat/Day acquired Regis McKenna Advertising, they also acquired Dick Cavett as Apple's spokesperson. Hayden's task was to figure out how to use him. He wrote some spots where Cavett interviewed the computer. Hayden claims these spots were very simple-minded and not very good, but they were noticed. Because of this success, Hayden was kept as Apple's copywriter and eventually moved to the San Francisco office.

The success of Apple is legendary, changing the makeup of the entire computer industry and, more importantly, increasing the accessibility of computers. Much of this success was due to the personalities involved with Apple as well as to its advertising.

First of all, Jay Chiat was constantly dissatisfied with the work and the people. "He was like General Patton," says Hayden. "Every couple of weeks, he'd fly into town, fire the creative director, and put someone else into place."

Secondly, Apple boss Steven Jobs was very demanding. Jobs didn't just want the best advertising in the computer category. He wanted the best advertising ever.

Since Chiat felt that the San Francisco office wasn't working well enough and since Jobs felt that he needed more from the agency, the Apple account, along with Hayden, was moved to the Los Angeles office in 1982, enabling Chiat/Day to draw from a bigger creative department. It also enabled Lee Clow, creative director at Chiat/Day's L.A. office (see Chapter Twelve), to help develop approaches.

Apple was also going through many changes. "Every week we'd have somebody new to deal with," says Hayden. "Our working environment was abusive, threatening, and impossible." Finally, the creative group was so fed up that in 1983, they asked Jay Chiat to resign the account. Chiat's advice was to be patient and to "hang in there." In retrospect, this approach paid off. "Subsequently, all of us got ground-breaking work in our portfolios," says Hayden. "But it took a lot of endurance to get there."

When the environment is bad but the work is good, you too may want to "hang in there." It could pay off in an improved portfolio of published work.

In the fall of 1984, after Apple sales had stalled-out completely, Jobs wanted to introduce a whole new suite of office products to enhance work-group productivity. Hayden came up with a name for it, "The Macintosh Office."

"But one little problem came up," says Hayden. "A lot of the things that were to make up 'The Macintosh Office' didn't exist or wouldn't be ready for a long, long time. At that point, I came up with the phrases, 'Don't bite the karmic weenie,' which means if you lie in advertising, people have a way of finding out, and 'Never write a check with your advertising that your product can't cash.' Some people hold that against you, especially if you're a very high profile company." Both of these phrases directly relate back to Hayden's experience as a writer on industrial accounts.

Because of his beliefs, Hayden got into a number of more or less public arguments with the Macintosh group around the time of 'Lemmings' (see portfolio section) airing during the Super Bowl. "I think the people at Chiat/Day felt I was not being a team player," says Hayden. "The agency position was that we wanted to run 'Lemmings,' that we wanted to run all these other ads." Hayden had more of a strategic concern. He believed that Macintosh sales should go up gradually as the product was able to deliver more functionality. He thought that Apple should be putting resources toward the Apple II family, which was still the cash cow of the company. "I was kind of vocal about this at a couple of meetings and I used the phrase, 'The caboose is trying to blow up the locomotive,'" says Hayden. "In other words, Macintosh was being dragged along by the Apple II, and yet we were trying everything possible to destroy Apple II sales."

As a result of his public arguments, Hayden was asked off the Macintosh portion of the account. Normally, that would have been enough of a blow to get anybody to quit. But Hayden didn't. He stuck around and wrote more commercials for the Apple II.

But then a huge offer came in from Tracy-Locke. They wanted Hayden to start their Los Angeles office and run the $50 million Taco Bell account. And they promised to double his salary. "Being essentially unhappy—I felt I had made a contribution to Macintosh and that I was unfairly banished—I took the offer," says Hayden.

Hayden claims he developed one of the best creative departments in Los Angeles in only a month. "We had won the Princess Cruises account and it looked like we were going to have a very successful new agency," says Hayden. "But I was not the kind of guy to get along with Tracy-Locke's culture."

Selling tacos was also new to Hayden. He didn't know how to make taco meat look good. Strategically, he thought Taco Bell was an alternative to McDonald's and Burger King. So he developed a theme line, "Burgers? We don't want no stinking burgers!" and got Cheech Moran to be their spokesperson. Says Hayden, "The object of the game was to get every 10-year-old in America to say this line whenever they were asked to go to McDonald's or Burger King."

When Hayden presented the campaign to Taco Bell's marketing people, they were horrified. At Chiat/Day, you'd be forgiven if the client was horrified if you believed in the campaign," says Hayden. "But, with Tracy-Locke, the agency was equally horrified."

Consequently, the relationship between Hayden's creative department and the rest of Tracy-Locke began deteriorating. "The body had rejected the transplant," says Hayden. "They came to me with 19 demands on how I and the creative department had to change our behavior." Instead of trying to meet these demands, Hayden and his staff quit. "Subsequently, most went on to freelance and I was home for a while," says Hayden.

Meanwhile, Chiat/Day had some very unfortunate luck with Apple Computer and the account went into review. "Here's where the story gets rather kinky," says Hayden. "They were going to have a two-agency review between BBDO and Chiat/Day. I was at home after Tracy-Locke. BBDO contacted me and wanted to hire me. Apple Computer called up—they were speaking in some weird diplomatic code—but were essentially saying, 'We're not so sure you should go to Chiat/Day. If we were you, we wouldn't go to work for Chiat/Day.'"

But Hayden went back to Chiat/Day. He met with Jay Chiat and Lee Clow, the two people who were his only real mentors in terms of teaching him how to do good advertising. At the same time, he claims to have had a semi-abusive relationship with them. Says Hayden, "It's like if you went to a strict boarding school where they made you take cold showers every morning and beat you with paddles, but if the school were to burn down, it would still touch a soft spot in your heart."

Chiat and Clow made Hayden the creative director of the Los Angeles office. But that didn't work out. Says Hayden, "As a rule, never ride into an ad agency on a white horse because people will try to get mud on you right away. I ended up being blamed for the loss of Apple by Chiat/Day."

Even though Hayden returned to Chiat/Day, BBDO/New York kept trying to recruit him to work on the Apple account now that they had taken it over. "I didn't want to change agencies again," says Hayden. "I wanted to be at the same place for a while and be able to stay there. And being creative director of Chiat/Day even under the worst of circumstances is still one of the best jobs in Los Angeles. It was very hard to walk away from."

Finally, in August of 1986, Hayden did walk. He hired two former Chiat/Day staffers and within two weeks developed an entire print campaign for Apple. Although Hayden worked in Los Angeles, he was not made part of BBDO West because they did not have a good creative reputation.

The presence of another agency in Los Angeles named BBDO, however, caused the original one to disintegrate. According to Hayden, BBDO West's creative people were unhappy and there was all sorts of jealousy and dissension. To put an end to this strife, Hayden was asked to take over all of the Los Angeles and San Francisco operations.

Hayden claims to have approached the merger with a little more humility than he did when starting Tracy-Locke's Los Angeles office. He wanted to integrate the agencies without making it an us-against-them situation. To do so, Hayden personally worked on some of the more difficult accounts and spent hours meeting with the clients. For instance, with Sizzler, he learned their market system and the level of creative they needed to do their business. This time he didn't automatically assume they were going to want something like "Burgers? We don't want no stinking burgers."

"This time I wasn't going to be this creative firebrand who is not going to tolerate any deviation from the highest possible standard," says Hayden. "Because there are different standards. One is, how many dinners did you sell last night?"

Today, Hayden says he is just trying to be supportive of his staff. "I'm giving them headlines. I'm helping them get unstuck, suggesting other approaches. I'm trying to have a congenial atmosphere here, one where people aren't shredding their concepts and putting them in the waste basket because they're afraid someone else will steal them."

Here's an example of how Hayden works: He has a senior art director who is very talented and has been in *Communications Arts* many times. When he came up with an Apple ad that Hayden didn't think looked right, they worked back and forth on it. He did it Hayden's way and he did it his own way. Hayden vastly preferred it his way, but gave the art director the choice by saying, "We pay you a lot of money for your talent and expertise. I want you to go away and think about it and tell me if that's what you want to do." Of course, the art director wanted to run it his way. And Hayden was willing to live with that.

Hayden says he runs a totally open office. "We try to cut down on politics as much as we can," says Hayden. "We also try to give young people a shot. We welcome geniuses here and give them a real opportunity to do ads instead of run errands. I work at mentoring people. I guess that's where I now fit in."

A LOOK AT HAYDEN'S PORTFOLIO

Bendix Corporation

Hayden claims he probably wouldn't hire himself. "In my early years, I wasn't really trying to reach people," says Hayden. He says he looks for creatives who can reach people in an emotional way, not just in an intellectual way.

Although he claims that this piece does not show the humanity he'd later express, this period enabled him to develop his style. Says Hayden, "It seemed to me that if I could do something that, at its core, was very rational and plausible, but look irrational, I'd attract more attention."

What prompted Hayden to come to this discovery? Basically, he says, it came from his need to keep things interesting and from the freedom of small budgets. Says Hayden, "I often find that you get your best work from accounts that are too small for anybody else to screw up. Some of the worst work comes out of the biggest budgets because it's really too important to do a good job. It's kind of a backwards thing, but there's just too much resting on it."

Baked Apple

This ad was written in Chiat/Day's San Francisco office, but was produced in Los Angeles under Lee Clow's supervision. Recalls Hayden, "Lee had his own comeuppance with Steve Jobs and Jay Chiat. So we were caught in this meat grinder between these very extreme personalities. But the work got better and better under this pressure.

"Meanwhile, John Sculley came in from Pepsi to take over Apple. And that was yet another personality, one who was much more used to disciplined advertising and less to the kind of piratical advertising representing Jobs and company.

"I can't emphasize enough how painful this period was, because Jay would sort of beat everybody up and he'd leave the room. Then Jobs would come in and he'd do the same. And this continued. And every three months—or maybe every two months—Jobs would threaten to fire the agency. 'You guys aren't keeping up with us,' he'd say. Yet, under those circumstances, we produced some very fine work."

Welcome, IBM.

Seriously.

Welcome to the most exciting and important marketplace since the computer revolution began 35 years ago.

And congratulations on your first personal computer.

Putting real computer power in the hands of the individual is already improving the way people work, think, learn, communicate and spend their leisure hours.

Computer literacy is fast becoming as fundamental a skill as reading or writing.

When we invented the first personal computer system, we estimated that over 140,000,000 people worldwide could justify the purchase of one, if only they understood its benefits.

Next year alone, we project that well over 1,000,000 will come to that understanding. Over the next decade, the growth of the personal computer will continue in logarithmic leaps.

We look forward to responsible competition in the massive effort to distribute this American technology to the world.

And we appreciate the magnitude of your commitment.

Because what we are doing is increasing social capital by enhancing individual productivity.

Welcome to the task **apple**

Apple Welcomes IBM

Although there's a great deal of content here, it's presented in an emotional context, making it seem exciting and worth reading. "Most copy," according to Hayden, "reads as if it's the most boring thing in the world to get into. You know, clients like that. Clients drive copywriters to a grinding level of dullness. To get around that, you need a tremendous amount of stamina, resilience, and pleading—a certain amount of 'trust me'—but also I think you can demonstrate that you get better readership with ads that have some personality—that have some surprises and rewards for the reader."

KFAC

This is one of Hayden's first ads to gain recognition. Says Hayden, "The ad was very, very successful. It was reprinted by classical stations all over the country. And it got a tremendous amount of attention in town. All these studios and advertising agencies noticed it and it wound up pinned up over many desks."

A classical music listener himself, Hayden wrote the ad based on his knowledge of typical listeners as opposed to typical advertising for classical music stations. "The ads that I'd seen usually had a violin with a rose next to it or a French horn with a glass of wine or something like that, but classical music listeners don't particularly think of themselves that way."

Hayden believed there must be a different way to attract attention. "Radio stations are not very interesting to advertise. However, it doesn't cost the reader anything to sample the product. It's totally free."

Based on that thinking, it occurred to Hayden to do something similar to a direct response ad. "I thought of it as something like an ad for, oh, a Dale Carnegie course or some kind of a snake oil. I took that approach and made it humorous and somewhat absurd. Obviously the man in the before picture is not the same as in the after picture. I then had the copy come out of that—it's pretty funny. It rattles on in a very L.A. style. And it ends with this absolutely free offer. You can try the station with absolutely no obligation whatsoever."

Hayden says of the ad's appeal, "Rationally, classical music is not going to change you from being a fat slob into a rich, trim, and sexy person. But in terms of how classical music people feel about themselves and their relationship to the music—and as a broader statement of their cultural wardrobe—it does get at that. There is a kernel of truth under the irrational presentation."

BEFORE
*This is me before I started listening to
KFAC. Overweight, poor, unhappy and alone.*

AFTER
*This is I after 16 short years as a
KFAC listener. Rich, trim and sexy.*

How classical music changed my life.

The other day at Ma Maison, as I was waiting for the attendant to retrieve my chocolate brown 450 SLC, the Saudi prince I'd been noshing with said, "Say, Bill, how did an unassuming guy like yourself come to be so rich, so trim, so... sexy?"

My eyes grew misty. "It wasn't always this way, Ahmed, old buddy..."

My mind raced back to the Bad Time, before the investment tips, the real estate empire, before Dino bought my screenplay and I bought my Columbia 50.

Once I was a lot like you.

Working at a nowhere job, hitting the singles bars, watching situation comedies in my free time. I tipped the scales at a hefty 232, but my bank balance couldn't have tipped the bus boy at the Midnight Mission.

Finally, I hit bottom... picked up by the Castaic police for barreling my old heap the wrong way over some parking lot spikes.

My last friend in this lonely world, Hardy Gustavsen, set me straight while he was driving me back to L.A.

"Bill, get hold of yourself! Start listening to KFAC!"

"Gosh, Hardy, don't they play classical music? I'm not sure I cotton to that high brow stuff!"

Aside from a couple of summers at Tanglewood and Aspen, and one semester in Casals' Master Class, **I knew absolutely nothing about classical music.**

"Bill, who would be wrong if you got better?"

Looking into his steely blue eyes, I realized Hardy was right. I resolved to give KFAC a shot.

At first, it was quite painful. Listening to all those 100-piece groups was confusing—I was used to having the drums on the right and the bass on the left and the singer in the middle. All those semidemihemiquavers made my head spin.

But I started to feel the beneficial effects of classical music listening in just one short week.

In no time, I was using napkins with every meal. I switched from Bourbon to an unpretentious Montrachet and I became able to hear sirens even with my car windows rolled up.

Soon I was spending every night with KFAC and a good book, like Aquinas' *Summa Theologica.*

I realized that some of the wealthiest, most famous people in this world listened to classical music—Napoleon, Bismark, George Washington, Beethoven... and many others who are yet alive today.

Then I met Marlene. The first girl who knew there was more to *Also Sprach Zarathustra* than the theme from *2001.* And I fell in love.

Today, I'm on top of the world with a wonderful wife, close friends in high places and a promising career in foreign currency manipulation.

Can classical music do for you what it did for me?

A few years back, scientific studies showed that when dairy cows are played classical music the quantity and quality of their milk dramatically improves.

Now if it can do that for plain old moo cows, imagine what it can do for you!

You might use it to control disgusting personal habits and make fun new friends. The possibilities are endless!

Can you afford KFAC?

Is lox kosher?

Even though marketing surveys show that KFAC's audience is the most affluent assemblage of nice people in Southern California, yes, you can afford KFAC! Thanks to their Special Introductory Offer, you can listen FREE OF CHARGE for as many hours as you like without obligation!

Begin the KFAC habit today.

Remember, the longest journey begins by getting dressed. Don't let this opportunity slip through your fingers. Tune to KFAC right NOW, while you're thinking about it.

And get ready for a spectacular improvement in your life.

Warn your family and friends that you may start dressing for dinner.

You may lose your taste for beer nuts.

And the next time you're on the freeway thinking about playing with your nose, you'll find yourself asking:

"Really. Would a KFAC listener do this?"

1984

Jobs's objective was not just to have the best work in the computer category, it was to have one of the best campaigns of all time. And according to many critics, Hayden achieved that feat with this commercial. It was one of the most remembered commercials of 1984.

Although "1984" looks elaborate because of its sophisticated production, the thinking behind it was very simple. "To me, the secret of advertising is to make an irrational presentation of a rational argument," says Hayden. "The rational argument is that we're making computers accessible to everyone. So, theoretically, you should show a farmer with a computer, a fireman with a computer, a nurse with a computer, a little kid with a computer, or something like that.

"Indeed, commercials like that have been done. But why not try to come at it in an irrational way, creating something that's interesting and yet still gets to the idea that we're democratizing technology?" Hayden clearly found a way with this commercial.

Lemmings

While "1984" received a lot of praise, "Lemmings," according to Hayden, "was totally reviled." Part of the problem was the lack of redemption, says Hayden. "It had a threatening ending, as opposed to a hopeful one. We were showing customers walking off a cliff.

"It's interesting though. John Sculley played 'Lemmings' at MacWorld and it received a standing ovation. And it was the most remembered commercial of 1985...but then the Hindenburg was the most remembered event of 1938. Or was it '36?"

ADVICE AND OBSERVATIONS OF CHAIRMAN HAYDEN

WHAT TURNS STEVE HAYDEN ON ABOUT ADVERTISING? HE SAYS IT ALL BOILS DOWN TO THE old Alexander Pope saying, "True wit is nature to advantage dressed, is often thought but ne'er so well expressed." Hayden explains, "When there is a commercial concept that shows up on television that seems so absolutely natural and yet riveting that it causes a re-action of delight and intrigue—and on top of that, everything works—that's what I find exciting."

Hayden is also excited by advertising that makes life seem truly "interesting." Says Hayden, "Anything that hints that we're not a brain-dead culture makes me very happy. I think that most people are kind of in a rut, just going along. You look through a maga-zine and all the ads are pretty much expected and you're watching a sitcom and you've sort of heard a version of all the jokes before. Life is grinding on. And you're just living somewhere. Then, all of a sudden, something strikes you as delightful. And you think, 'maybe life is not so bad; maybe life is interesting after all.'

"What I like is that certain stuff that we can all come together and say, 'God. That's great. That's great stuff'— whatever quality 'that' is. It can be as simple as a prune com-mercial that says, 'Today the pits, tomorrow the wrinkles,' and leaves you with a smile. Or it can be as elaborate as the 1984 commercial.

"For me personally, Doyle Dane Bernbach's Volkswagen ads certainly turned me on a lot. I thought there was something neat there. It showed that human beings do have a sense of humor, that they can be outrageous, that there's a never-ending flow of original-ity. Also, I love the Fallon, McElligott stuff, their Episcopal Church ads and the other wonderful things that they've done."

To help you along in creating your portfolio, Steve Hayden has the following suggestions.

Be aware of your natural tendency to edit

"I think that the measure of a great cre-ative idea is when you laugh out loud at the thought. And yet, it's not necessarily funny, it's just the idea may have such power that you take delight in it. If there's sort of a spontaneous reaction of joy, then you know you're on to some-thing. Much of the time we are so self-critical and self-filtering that we walk away from an idea that makes us laugh, thinking we can never possibly do that idea. And yet some of the best things we've done are those ideas brought to life."

Give your copy some personality

"I look for body copy that's written with care, for copy that strikes the imagination. I look for phrases like, 'Most people come back from vacation with little more to show for it than tiny bars of stolen soap.' You know, how did that get into the ad? But it's that occasional application of wit that lets you know you're still alive. I look for surprises that say there's a human being behind this, as opposed to a corporation. And I look for that ability to project a human quality. To communicate one-on-one."

Study the advertising that strikes you

"The annuals are a great place to start. Emulate or even imitate what you admire—learn by doing that. Many times I've written down a headline by somebody else and tried to figure out what gives it power."

Attach yourself to a mentor

"I've had very little mentoring in my career, which I feel in some ways has been a tremendous handicap. I know a number of people who were taught early on a certain way of doing things. A way of problem solving. By not having a mentor, I had to work in a series of small shops. I had to struggle. I did a lot of retail advertising. I spent a lot of time writing, 'Boat Oxfords, $2.99.' Things like that."

Hayden thinks that mentorships for art directors are especially important: "Just in terms of the technicals skills, there are a lot of things you must learn about art direction that you are not going to get out of a book or a class."

On the positive side, Hayden feels his lack of mentorship helped him evolve a separate style—it forced him to discover what works on his own.

Play up your gift

"Every person I've met in advertising has a particular kind of gift. Some people are great at writing dialogue. Some copywriters are masters of strategic thought. Others are masters of a clever phrase. Some art directors are great at shooting objects. Others are great at shooting people. My style, if there is one, is the long-copy argument that combines a certain amount of technical information with a certain amount of emotional appeal. You should figure out what your gift is and work from there."

Work where there's work, but strive

Hayden believes there's nothing wrong with working for a department store or for a small agency or an industrial account as long as you're able to keep striving. Says Hayden, "Every time you're given an opportunity to do something good, do it. Our most successful team was hired away from an industrial agency here in Los Angeles."

Make sure the agency is culturally suited to your personality

"No matter how much money they give you, if you don't fit into the agency's culture, it's not going to work out," says Hayden. "The other side of that is: you can't make an uncreative agency creative by hanging a couple of good reputations on it. It's like putting ornaments on a barren tree."

Please, your portfolio should be your own

Honesty is the best policy. If you steal ads, chances are you'll get caught. "Once I interviewed someone who had some of my work in his book. He came to interview with me at Chiat/Day and he showed me these terrible ads that I had done. He never dreamed that I had worked at the very agency that he was at. He wasn't aware of the fact that I'm actually a small agency scrapper." So remember, you never know the background of the person reviewing your portfolio.

• • • • • • • • • • • • • •

Postscript
OVERCOMING PRECONCEPTIONS ABOUT IN-HOUSE AND INDUSTRIAL ADVERTISING WORK

THERE'S A PRECONCEPTION AMONG MANY CREATIVE DIRECTORS THAT ONCE YOU SPENT some time in an in-house or industrial agency, you're washed up. But, as Hayden proved with his career, you can move from doing low-budget industrial work to doing big-budget consumer work. Here's what Steve Hayden has to say about the subject.

"There are many people who are very fortunate to start their careers at prosperous agencies or big agencies or very creative agencies and motor on happily from there. When you're working hand-to-mouth at poor, small agencies, you feel like you're a second-class citizen...that you could not hope to aspire to work for one of these great, creative agencies...that it's just so far above what you're doing. We felt we were ahead of the game if we didn't run coupons in reverse.

"I suppose there's a point to the argument that if you haven't gotten out of that environment there's cause for concern—people generally do work themselves out and go on to something new—but I wouldn't say you're absolutely finished if you don't.

"But you must also be lucky enough to come across a creative director who recognizes your ability. I guess I was lucky enough.

"Similarly, Chris Wall and Susan Westre work here. Most creative directors in the city wouldn't give them the time of day because they were from a small industrial agency that had crappy accounts. I think many people are totally dazzled when they see the right set of logos in a book. Usually, they're the same logos that have appeared in award books recently.

"One of the fortunate things for me is that Chris and Susan have evolved into real stars and now these same creative directors are calling them and begging for interviews. But since they weren't given a chance in the first place, they're not going to go over now. That's great.

"I suppose in an art director's book, I do look at the execution. The value of an art director is unsurpassed: an art director can make so-so headlines award-winners while the brightest copywriter in the world cannot survive bad art direction. I look for taste levels, and I want to get a feeling from the ads. I think that I could look at an art director's roughs and get a feeling of how his or her ad is going to look.

"I also look for the quality of ideas, the ability to turn a phrase and to take the unexpected approach. I'm looking for someone who does something arresting, but not just for shock value.

"In evaluating work from in-house and from industrial agencies, I probably have an internal point system, the same way you'd judge award shows. The lowest level is that the work is not embarrassing, the next level is it's pretty good, and the highest level is, gee, I wish I'd done that; I wonder if I can steal it?

"Overcoming people's perceptions is ultimately contingent on the quality of your work. If all your headlines say '.0035 perimeters in a z-spec thurester,' you're not going to get many people offers. On the other hand, if you get people reading about stuff they don't want to know—or care—about, then you're on to something.

"You can be doing things for the weirdest, oddest product and have a certain bent of mind or put a certain power in your communication. Take that and apply it to something else and good things happen."

CHAPTER SEVEN

Always There! The most important job in the world has long hours, little recognition and no salary. But the fringe benefits are great for fathers who make the time to be there. Always There.

Tom Burrell

"Anybody who's getting into advertising today needs to understand that the mass market is dead," says Thomas Burrell, chairman of Burrell Communications Group, Inc., an organization consisting of advertising, public relations, and consumer promotions arms—all specializing in creating programs to reach special market segments.

In this chapter, we're going to explore ways to create effective communications in a post–mass market era. Burrell was one of the first to bring big agency experiences and sophisticated tactics to segmented marketing. He founded his agency in 1971 and has provided such clients as Coca-Cola, Ford Motor Company, McDonald's, Brown-Forman, and Procter & Gamble with advertising targeted to the African-American population. The firm also has provided general market advertising for top brands such as Schlitz Malt Liquor.

Prior to forming his agency, Burrell worked for general market advertising power-houses—Needham, Harper & Steers; Foote, Cone & Belding; and Leo Burnett U.S.A., among others. He started his advertising career with the now defunct Wade Advertising and earned his undergraduate degree from Roosevelt University in Chicago.

Today, Burrell lives in Chicago and is active in numerous community organizations outside of his work. "My involvement has nothing to do with what I do for a living. I'm really crazy about Chicago. So as a citizen, I'm involved. I volunteer."

THE TEST OF AN INDUSTRY LEADER

How do you know you have talent? Sometimes, it means painful years of struggling. And sometimes it is as simple as taking an aptitude test in school.

A product of Chicago's south side, Burrell wandered through his first two years of high school not knowing what he wanted to do with his life. "As a matter of fact, I was at a school that was not conducive to making any decision," he says. Yet he became a highly influential industry leader—all because of the results of an aptitude test. A look at his life after he took the test—as well as slightly before it—can be highly instructive to anyone interested in a career in advertising.

Knowing that he wanted to make something of his life, he engineered a transfer to a better school and started hanging out with students who wanted to be doctors, lawyers, and engineers. He also enrolled in a course called Careers, a class with the sole purpose of helping kids determine what they ought to pursue, and he took a test to measure his areas of interest and aptitude. The results? He scored highly in two areas: "artistic" and "persuasive."

Burrell had no idea what to make of these results. So he took them to his teacher. She suggested he become an advertising copywriter because it required both abilities. "Whether I believed it or not, I now had something to tell people," he says. "And not only was it something definite, it was something unique. Something that made me special. My friends didn't know what an advertising copywriter was either. So the lunchroom conversation now focused on me."

Eventually, he had to back up his claim by becoming more knowledgeable about what he was telling people. So he started studying ads and trying to figure out how they were written. And when he graduated from high school, he went to college as an English major and an advertising minor, enabling him to take copywriting courses.

"At this time (1960), there were no black people working in Chicago advertising agencies in any capacity," says Burrell. "I mean, no secretaries, no mailroom people, no receptionists. Nobody."

Burrell remembers his copywriting instructor at his college asking him, "What do you think you're doing? There's nobody hiring black people in the advertising business. What are you going to do with it?" Burrell's reply? "Well, I'm going to do it."

To help himself along, Burrell found a job in a related area. "I not only worked for free, I worked for a struggling company whose owner was strapped for cash himself," he says. "On a couple of occasions, I wound up loaning him fifty cents." But the job did offer him much-needed experience.

Through a network of friends, Burrell learned that Wade Advertising, then the third largest advertising agency in Chicago, was looking to hire a black youth to work in the mailroom. Says Burrell, "That was revolutionary." He interviewed for the position and found he wasn't what they wanted. "I was too old," he says. "They were looking for an

18 year old who was going to night school. I was 22 and going to day school. And they wanted a marketing major. I was majoring in English with a minor in advertising."

Burrell believes they set up that criteria because they were hoping to take a longer time to move that person into a professional area. Says Burrell, "An 18 year old in night school would have given them maybe eight years." And they wanted someone studying marketing so they could move that person to an account services position. "But I was the only guy looking for that job because, for the most part, black kids didn't know anything about advertising and the agency business," he says. "So they didn't find any other candidates."

Wade hired him. Burrell promised he'd switch to night school. "I lied," he now admits, "I convinced my mailroom supervisor to allow me to take my lunch break at various times during the week. So I continued to go to day school and continued to go pretty much full-time." Within six months, he graduated. "They thought I would take a year or two," he says.

When working, Burrell always conducted himself as if he was above the mailroom job. "I wanted people to look at me and say, 'Doesn't he look ridiculous pushing that wagon around?' That was a visual message I wanted to convey. I wanted them to realize that they were holding me back by having me do that work. I wore white shirts and ties. I was neat even while I was changing towels in the men's washroom or working with that messy mimeograph machine (this was before Xerox)."

Even though he wanted to communicate that he was being held back, he found many opportunities to use his job to help him along. "One of the great things about being in the mailroom is that it gives you a chance to find out what's going on. I was collating memos and running the mimeograph machine, so I'd make copies for myself. I had quite a file. I also got a chance to see everybody. I got into the habit of going past secretaries and putting the memos right in the executives' offices."

While collecting the agency material, Burrell also started working on some projects of his own. He was aware that the creative director was having some problems with Alka-Seltzer. So he conducted research, going house to house in his free time.

And once his research was completed, he pushed the mail wagon to the creative director's office and asked if he could have a minute. He told the creative director about the research he had done. He emphasized that he had some ideas that would be helpful.

What was the problem? Alka-Seltzer was an all-purpose medicine—for upset stomachs, headaches, hangovers. But at that time, specialized remedies were coming out. You have a stomach ache, you take something for the stomach. You have a headache? Why take Alka-Seltzer, when you can take a headache remedy? Alka-Seltzer was like an old patent medicine."

Unfortunately, Burrell doesn't remember the creative solution he presented. "I was so focused on getting the job," he explains. "But my ideas came out of my research. And frankly, these ideas did not become part of the solution. They were just for talking. The important thing was that I demonstrated that I was thinking and talking about the problem in an intelligent way."

Burrell then made his pitch. He explained that it didn't make any sense for him to be in the mailroom when he could be helping solve problems. They talked, and within three weeks, Burrell was transferred to the creative department as a copy trainee.

As mentioned, the strategy never changed. Burrell's first Alka-Seltzer commercial involved a family at the monkey cage of a zoo. The father wasn't feeling well, and the chimp was mimicking how he felt. Then the father took Alka-Seltzer and was a totally different person. And reflecting the change, the monkey acted totally different toward him.

At the start of the creative revolution, Wade lost the Alka-Seltzer account—and ultimately went out of business. "Wade was doing work for this account for 34 years and basically doing the same Speedy* Alka-Seltzer stuff," says Burrell. They got complacent and here come these hotshots and they get the Alka-Seltzer business and then, quickly, the rest of Miles's business. Since Wade allowed Miles to constitute about 85% of their total billings, when that account went, they went."

Burrell sees two lessons in this. First, you shouldn't let one client dominate your business. Second, always make sure you don't become complacent. Instead, you must continually test the work and see if it is still fresh. Wade's work did not adapt to the changing marketplace. After 34 years of doing Speedy, Alka-Seltzer started becoming more sophisticated.

While at Wade, Burrell enrolled in the initial course of the Institute for Advanced Advertising Studies, an intensive one-year program set up by the American Association of Advertising Agencies in conjunction with Northwestern University. This exposed Burrell to other agency people, and helped him get an offer from Leo Burnett. "I went there in '64 and worked on Pillsbury cake and frosting mixes," he says. "I became a cake and frosting guy."

Unlike his later jobs, Burrell found that Burnett did not provide the greatest learning experience for him. "Part of that was due to my own immaturity," he says, "and my failure to really take advantage of the situation." He claims he spent too much time shooting darts. "There was not enough pressure put on me." Consequently, Burrell believes in putting pressure on his employees. He sets deadlines and gives employees as much work as they can handle. "I make sure they understand I'm counting on them to do it," he says.

Burrell also found the competition at Burnett to be discouraging. "The person supervising your work was competing with you," he says. "If I give you an assignment and say I'm going to work on it too, that changes your level of motivation quite a bit. You may say, 'What's the use.' Or, 'I'll try, but if I don't come up with it, I know he's going to

*Miles was using the critter, Speedy, as a mascot.

have the answer.' So you give it a shot and it doesn't work. That stunts the growth of the junior people."

What's more, Burrell found it very hard to get his work approved because of Burnett's creative review process. "I was a copywriter," Burrell explains, "and there was a copy supervisor, an associate creative director, the creative director, a group creative director, and, finally, the creative review board. Most of my work got past the account supervisor level, but very little got past the associate creative director." This lack of approval didn't change his views of advertising, though he did become a bit disillusioned.

"Even in those days, I looked at Burnett not as one agency, but as five agencies," he says. The creatives were assigned to groups depending on the kind of work they did. The group that handled the cigarette brands and beer ads was hot and dramatic. There was the group that created all the little critters like The Jolly Green Giant, and Charlie the Tuna. There was the hard-sell demonstration group; they had products like Secret, Lilt, and Ponds. And there was the cereal group, which largely used little people, but also functioned as the "warm fuzzy" soup group. Burrell was in the Pillsbury group. He felt he was in the wrong group.

After Burnett, Burrell left the country to travel. He wound up in Paris and stayed there for a while. "I was basically looking to fulfill an earlier dream of just hanging out in Europe," says Burrell. "I was getting older, and I figured I might as well do it."

As it turned out, he found himself hanging out with 18 year olds. "It was ridiculous," he says. "I was already too late." So he decided to find a copywriting job in Paris or in Belgium, but there was an obvious language and cultural problem, so nothing happened. In London, however, he wound up getting a couple of job offers.

He took one at Foote, Cone & Belding's London office to work on the British Overseas Airways Corporation (BOAC) account, now known as British Airways. This gave him quite an education. He learned how the industry differed between the United States and Europe. "An art director was paid paltry wages," Burrell says. "But they really loved words over there. And word play. They were selling the comfort of the seat and one line I wrote said, 'On BOAC, your seat will have an awful lot against you.' They loved that kind of stuff."

Burrell soon grew tired of the British wage scale and came back to Chicago in what was the middle of a recession. He was warned not to return. His friends said there were few jobs to be found. His response, "There may not be many jobs, but I only need one."

Within a week, Burrell was at Needham, Harper & Steers (NHS) working on Betty Crocker cake and frosting. "That was the best agency experience of my career," says Burrell. "I learned about marketing strategy and strategy-based advertising," he says, "and I learned the importance of basing your advertising concepts on a unique set of ideas."

Burrell found himself working for people who made sure the advertising was kept "on track." They wouldn't approve anything if it did not follow the direction they gave. (For more about tracking, see Chapter Thirteen.)

He was also forced to discover the unique characteristics that sold products. "I listened to cakes to see if they *sounded* moister," he says. "I was cutting them with spoons, with forks, with knives, with paper. I was looking for that extra 'little thing.' Is my frosting thicker? Sweeter? Richer?"

Burrell's intense relationship with Betty Crocker was mandated by his boss, who was not a creative genius. Instead, he was a marketing strategist. He expected Burrell to find that extra advantage.

For instance, on a special assignment for Schick shavers, Burrell remembers his boss looking for a way to demonstrate the product's superiority. "I stopped by his office and he was shaving a bar of soap, looking for slight variations between razors. He was shaving wood—and the furniture. I had visions of him at home after work, taking his shaver to all kinds of stuff to figure out how to demonstrate that it was better than any other razor. That was his way of thinking. He drove us nuts."

Eccentric or not, Burrell credits this person as being one of his mentors. "The interesting thing is that people in this business would sneer at him because he was so uncreative," says Burrell. "But he had the focus I needed."

This focus has helped Burrell run his own business. "I now have to evaluate other people's creative. And I have to do it on behalf of clients who have some very delicate, subtle messages that they want to get across. If I had not gotten any further than just creating, then I would not be able to evaluate the work as thoroughly as I do now."

In 1971, after four years at NHS, Burrell started his own agency, then known as Burrell-McBain, with an idea to specialize in reaching African-American consumers. A number of agencies targeting African-Americans had opened before Burrell's, but they did not consist entirely of people with extensive general market advertising expertise. "We were unique because we had the combination of the special insight that comes with being black," says Burrell, "and the kind of experience in general market advertising that brought a high level of sophistication and expertise."

Despite their level of experience, they did not have any prospects for business when they opened. Burrell's partner was committed to opening on a certain date even without a client. He felt if they waited until they got business, they could wait for a long time.

Nevertheless, it took them six months before they got their first piece of business—some public relations work for The Edison Theater Company on a freelance basis. They wanted to attract blacks to a nightclub for a Dixieland band. Says Burrell, "I can't tell you how far away Dixieland music is from black people and their interests. But we said we'd get them in."

They played it by ear, because they needed the $1000 a month they were to be paid. To fill the seats, they convinced their friends to come to the Happy Medium to hear the band. "It was incredible," says Burrell. "They fired us fairly quickly. They felt we didn't know what we were doing."

Eventually, their agency started attracting clients, including McDonald's in 1972.

Burrell bought out his partner in 1974 and rechristened his agency Burrell Advertising. He later opened public relations and promotions operations.

Today, Burrell says his agency is the way he had originally envisioned it. Now he rarely writes, although he does develop concepts. Despite that, and with all his successes and influence over the entire field of advertising (note his ideas on "positive realism" in the portfolio and advice sections of this chapter), Burrell is not sure his life is balanced. He's very mindful of his mental and physical health. To keep up his energy level, Burrell is a stickler for fitness.

But there's also another secret to his energy. "The more things you do that you enjoy, the more things you can do," says Burrell. "Because you just do them. If you had a job you didn't like and you kept looking at the clock, you'd find that five minutes seem like a half hour. But if you're doing what you like that's a whole different story. And I love what I'm doing."

A Very Logical Portfolio

McDLT

Burrell seldom found traditional brainstorming techniques helpful in developing concepts. "My way of coming up with ideas is through a process of deduction," he says. "I use logic."

To see how he works, let's look at the commercial. "The unique aspect about this product," says Burrell, "was that the cold lettuce and tomato were packaged on one side and the hot hamburger was packaged on the other. That was its advantage. It tasted good because you got all that hot, cold, crispy, and juicy all together. That's a very clear, unique selling proposition.

"To dramatize that, we came up with the concept of the package as a combination stove/refrigerator. We transformed this package—through the magic of television—into a little range on top with the meat and a little refrigerator on the bottom with the tomato and lettuce. And we asked, 'Wouldn't it be great if we could have a sandwich that's hot on the one side and cool on the other? Now you do.' We produced three commercials based on that concept. And they were very successful. Plus, all of them logically followed from the strategy."

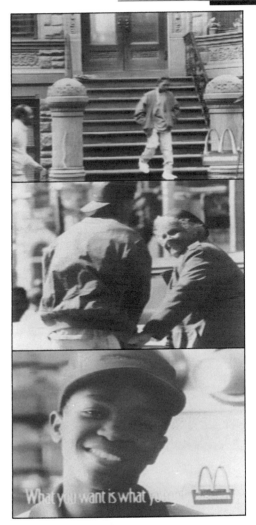

McDonald's Calvin Spots

*A hallmark of Burrell's advertising style is to convey a positive lifestyle. "We call it positive realism,"
says Burrell. "It's actually an exaggeration of realism. We look at ordinary, real life events and portray
them in a positive way. This is not true of everything we do, of course."*

*Burrell started this back in the early seventies. "Black people rarely saw themselves portrayed in a re-
alistic, positive way. We were accustomed to seeing ourselves in the mass media as either exaggerated,
acceptable exceptions to the rule, or as welfare recipients, criminals, and the downtrodden. The mass
media was missing the whole group of blacks who lived normal lives and had emotional, poignant kinds
of events happening to them. They have romances, they get married, they go away to the service, they
come back, they miss their families, they have grandmothers they love. We tried to present those images at
a time when people very rarely saw them. And it was relatively easy to do because you could take the
most commonplace occurrence in the black community, put it on film, and people would say, 'Wow,' because it hadn't been communicated before."*

Coca-Cola

Burrell's objective was to enhance the brand's image by showing it as hip and humorous. "It has nothing to do with talking about the brown stuff in the bottle," he says.

Burrell sees this spot as a lesson for beginning creatives. "The best work comes out of reality. Out of some truth. Some basic realities of life. Even if you exaggerate it or extend it.

"This is a Laurel and Hardy situation. Here, you have Charles Barkley, who's the bad, naughty guy of basketball. And you have Scottie Pippin, who's the good guy. It's an extension of that reality. You take it, lighten it up, and make it fun.

"One of the things that comes out of it is that you wind up liking both people more than you did before. It helps humanize them because they show they aren't just superstars. They're vulnerable. They're good sports. They're capable of laughing and having a good time with each other. Even though they compete with each other, they're friends.

"I would say that everything comes out of observing what's going on around you. Most good writers do that, whether they're writing advertising, comedy, or fiction."

Tide

For Burrell, good advertising is based on a sound marketing strategy. He doesn't believe that an ad can be effective just because it's creative. "Those are two separate things," he says. "It has to be effective and creative. It has to be focused on achieving a certain objective. And many times, you have to figure out what that objective is."

The process starts with a creative strategy, from which comes a creative concept. Out of that concept comes the execution. "I've certainly worked with people who don't subscribe to that," says Burrell. "They're successful ad people who believe that it's all execution. Do a great execution and, hey, people will pay attention.

"I want people to do more than pay attention. I want people to develop a specific attitude towards the product."

SOME POSITIVE ADVICE FROM TOM BURRELL

BURRELL THINKS ADVERTISING'S MAIN ROLE IS TO MAKE PEOPLE FEEL GOOD ABOUT A product. "The influence that advertising has doesn't always happen on a conscious level," he says.

But to create any type of good advertising (that will be seen beyond a job interview) a person must first break in. "It's harder today," says Burrell. "I think beginners have to realize that. One of the real sad facts about this business is that most of the training programs have gone to hell. My fear is that this business is going to be in deep trouble because we're not doing anything to develop new people. And today's advertising people aren't going to live forever."

To help develop your skills without a training program, Burrell has the following ideas and suggestions.

Determine what kind of good advertising you want to do

"It's very important to realize there are lots of good kinds of advertising," says Burrell. "I think people need to determine what kind they want to do. I don't put down the hard-sell advertising at all. I don't put down humor in advertising. All can be extremely effective. But, for instance, the group I was in at Burnett did not fit for me. You have to figure out what fits for you."

Target small agencies

"Small companies can't afford multiple teams working on an assignment. They need help, so you're more likely to get your ideas used," says Burrell. "If you start at a gargantuan agency, getting your ideas heard is more difficult."

Expand your advertising styles

"As your career progresses, very often you become a little bit more eclectic and have a broader perspective on the business. Certainly, we do at this agency. We've got all kinds of clients with different kinds of problems. Different corporate cultures. Different attitudes toward advertising. So we do image stuff. We do product-oriented advertising. We have to be flexible.

Make up products

"I remember one guy we hired—one of the best conceptual people I have ever worked with. He came up with products. He came up with football helmets for kids. He developed a unique selling proposition and a very fresh, new way to sell that," says Burrell. "He was hired on the basis of that speculative stuff. I never asked to see his produced work because I knew that was done for somebody else."

Show your conceptual abilities

"I'm looking for the ability to take a product and not only find that difference, but dramatize the advantages in a way that is innovative and fresh," says Burrell, "including the look, the sound, and the feel of the communication. That's the kind of thing I look for."

Be a Renaissance person

"You have to have a life outside advertising," says Burrell. "You have to know what's going on and be aware of what's happening. Because if you don't have a life outside, you don't have anything to bring to the job."

Know your audience in detail

"There used to be a magazine rack," says Burrell, "now there are magazine stores. There's a proliferation of different kinds of magazines for many different population subsegments. You even need a whole section just for women's magazines. You've got one for older women, for fashionable women, for young mothers, for women who run, for women into fitness, there's even one for women who run long distances. That's the way marketing is going. Since the world is getting so complex and competitive, you've got to figure out what piece of the pie you want. Which means when you're preparing to communicate something about your product or service, you'd better know who you're talking to in specific terms. Talking to women or talking to

men—or even to subsets of talking to black women or white men—is not enough."

Define your target audience

"When putting together a portfolio, write down a description of the subsegment you want to talk to," says Burrell. "You might even want to share it—what the product and the strategy are—with whoever is reviewing your portfolio."

Talk to more than one segment at a time

"If you're reaching a certain segment of the audience with an emotional message, invariably, it will have some meaning to some group outside of your primary target group," says Burrell. "So if you concentrate on communicating with the group you're targeting, the rest will take care of itself."

Expand your thinking

"The way the business is going, it is very important to stop thinking along the narrow lines of advertising creative," says Burrell. "Start substituting the term marketing communications instead. If you don't do that, you are not going to be ready for the new advertising. It's going to be more comprehensive. As a creative person, it is going to be very important to have as broad a knowledge base as possible."

Don't wait for inspiration

Burrell feels that creatives whose careers excel are self-starters and know how to generate ideas on demand. "There's too much dart shooting and sitting around waiting for an idea to come. That could take a day—or three weeks," says Burrell. "When it's time to do it, just get up and do it."

Create a feeling

"Advertising's role is to do more than just inform people," says Burrell. "Its role is to give people a feeling about a product. And the best way to do that is by striking emotional chords that build a bond between the audience and the product."

Determine the product's character

"Every product and service has a personality. For many of our clients, the product's character is based on a history of how people perceive it," says Burrell. "We have to understand the product's personality and the advertising should be within that context because the advertising is going to be questioned. When people drink a soft drink, they're not just drinking a sweet liquid. The product is an extension of them. I don't think you can build this personality. You have to find it."

Appeal to emotions

"Most products we use have some kind of emotional gestalt to them," says Burrell. "Although there are some products without an emotional appeal—like paper clips—in a competitive environment, you've got to establish an emotional connection. The product has to inspire fear, humor, love, romance, aspirations. Something."

Broadcast your plans

"If you have any pride at all, telling other people your plans will help you achieve them," says Burrell. "Once you commit to doing it, you follow through. I do that all the time. When I want to make sure that I'm going to get something done, I go out and tell other people that I'm going to do it. Then I'm expected to do it. Since I want to make sure I have a reputation for doing what I say I'm going to do, I do it."

Appreciate pressure

"Your future depends on your work being good because our growth as a company does. If you don't make it, then we're going to be in deep trouble. I know that's pressure. But people learn they are vital; they are necessary; they are critical. It forces them to use more of themselves," says Burrell. "Most of us use so little of ourselves. I try to push people to their potential."

Keep a lookout for creative talent

Creative talent is everywhere—but it's hard to find. If you move into a position where you are responsible for hiring creatives, you may discover talent in unconventional places. Burrell hired Anna Morris as a part-time bookkeeper in 1974. But her creative answers on her application hinted at a wealth of ability. Today, Anna Morris is Burrell's executive vice president/chief creative officer.

Postscript 1
THE DEATH OF MASS COMMUNICATION

THROUGHOUT THIS BOOK, YOU'RE HEARING HOW ADVERTISERS HAVE STOPPED TALKING TO the "general" mass market and have started targeting various market segments. Some have referred to this as the end of the mass market. For a deeper understanding, here's Burrell's explanation of how the three arms of his company operate, as well as issues to keep in mind when communicating with a segment of the marketplace.

"With Burrell Communications, advertising, public relations, and sales promotion are three separate companies. But at the same time, we work very hard toward cohesiveness. We make joint presentations. We look for opportunities for the other companies.

"How you handle integrated marketing communications is a big issue within the industry now. We think we have a jump on it because we've been dealing with this issue since our beginning. We're not into mass marketing. When you focus on segmented marketing, it is incumbent upon you to use all of the marketing communications tools you can in order to get maximum efficiency. And you have to make enough noise to be heard above all the noise that's being made by other communications.

"The people who are having a hard time are those who are into mass marketing. They've been taught that all you need to do is broadcast a commercial.

"Ideally, clients tell me their problem and their objectives. Then I come back with the solutions. Those solutions may involve advertising. They may involve advertising and public relations. They may involve public relations and promotion.

"Keeping a consistent image in marketing to different groups means looking for the common denominators. Sometimes they come in the form of a 'look.' Sometimes they come in the form of a central theme that works across the board. But if you're going to talk to various segments of the market, you can't be contradictory.

"However, because segmented marketing is becoming the norm, people are accepting advertising that is not aimed at them. The confusion factor is overrated.

"In my early days there was some concern about our selling a product to the black consumer market. Marketers were concerned about how general market audiences might react. Testing found that not only did whites like the advertising we did for the black consumer market, but that they recognized that the ads were for the black market.

"This was almost twenty years ago. Now you have advertising that is designed for seniors, youth, Hispanics, blacks, females—even working women and homemakers. People understand and accept that certain ads address particular segments.

"There's also an overestimation of how people think about advertising campaigns. The client is sitting here developing an overall strategy and campaign, looking for consistency. While the consumer is interested in what you're saying; nobody looks at television and says, 'Oh, wait a minute. That's not part of the campaign.' A campaign is not part of the lexicon of the consumer.

"You have to think about consistency in message. You don't want to say in one message that, hey, this thing is big and, in another message, that this thing is small. That's what creates confusion. So you have to strategically decide what's important about the product and build on that generality with more specifics that relate directly to the segment you're targeting."

. . . .

Postscript 2
DEFINITIONS TO HELP YOU FIND WHERE YOU FIT

WHERE DO YOU FIT IN THE FIELD OF COMMUNICATIONS? WHEN BURRELL JOINED BURNETT, he didn't know and ended up in the wrong group. To make your decision even more difficult there is the growing importance of graphic design, public relations, and promotions. To help you decide, here are some thoughts from Burrell.

"The first thing is to define advertising, public relations, and promotions. Advertising is publicity through paid media and is generally done for long-term returns.

"To complicate matters, I would rather classify retail and image advertising as intrinsic versus extrinsic advertising. Extrinsic advertising promotes an image of the product beyond its intrinsic properties. While intrinsic advertising focuses on product attributes.

"The next area, public relations, is generally—but not always—publicity through unpaid media. Promotion is the catch-all for various marketing tools not formally classified as advertising, publicity, or personal selling. They are short-term incentives to encourage the purchase of a product.

"Now, to help you decide where you fit, art directors are generally thinkers and conceptualizers who want to solve problems beyond simply the design aspect. A graphics person, on the other hand, may not care about the other aspects of marketing.

"On the writing side, a copywriter in advertising would be a problem solver. They need a certain level of creativity. With copywriting, what you write down in totally out of your head. If you are a public relations writer, you are basically a reporter. It's the difference between writing fiction and nonfiction. If you have a tendency to go toward the fictional, then you're more likely to be an advertising copywriter. If you want to report, then you're more likely to be in public relations.

"Promotions—if you're talking writing—is an extension of public relations. I know people who were advertising copywriters who went into promotions. They like the short-term aspect of promotions."

This Year, Packaged Goods Companies Will Produce More Of These Than The Department Of Defense.

Stan Richards

"I think people who go into advertising should do so because they absolutely love it," says Stan Richards, founder and leader of The Richards Group in Dallas, Texas. "These people watch television at night, paying little attention to the show, but perk up when a commercial comes on. They're so vitally interested in the way people communicate that they see it as a life's work."

Richards is truly someone who has made a life's work out of studying communications—from his days as a student in art school, to founding a leading Dallas design studio (some call him the father and ranking dean of Texas design), to turning his studio into a major player in national advertising.

His organization creates work that is consistently recognized as being among the best in the country—by *Adweek, The New York Times,* and New York Art Directors Club— working for such clients as Aetna Health Plans, Cellular One, G. Heileman Brewing, Memorex, Motel 6, Neiman Marcus, TGI Friday's, Wyndham Hotels, Zales Jewelers, and *USA Today.* His organization has also served a number of nonprofit organizations on a volunteer basis, including the March of Dimes and United Way.

Richards' early years were spent in Philadelphia and Atlantic City, settling in Dallas after graduating from Pratt in the mid 1950s. Today, he balances his business and personal responsibilities by setting aside evening hours for his family. He always leaves the office by 6:00 p.m., and if he has four hours of extra work he returns at 4 a.m. the next day. Richards has been married for 34 years and has two sons. One son heads a creative group at the agency and the other is finishing his Ph.D. in clinical psychology.

AN ENDEARING STORY

WHAT MAKES SOMEONE SUCCESSFUL IN ONE CREATIVE AREA AND NOT IN ANOTHER? IS IT nature or is it nurture? Whatever instills talent, Richards firmly believes that environment is what leads an individual to manifest one or another. "A designer is a designer in any medium," he says. "I'm convinced that if a great designer were taught the tools of musical composition instead, he or she could write a pretty nifty piece of music. The judgments are essentially the same. Designers just don't have the facility to use the particular tools that a composer uses. I believe the same talents apply to playwriting, sculpture, all the arts."

In this section, we're going to explore this concept—as well as see how this idea developed. Richards started his arts exploration very young. Even at 10 years old, he was one of those children who could draw better than anyone else in the class. (In fact, his mother was convinced that not only could he draw better than any kid in the class, he could draw better than every kid in America.) "That led me to believe that I was going to do something in art," says Richards.

Then, in high school, he learned from a teacher that he actually could make a living as a commercial artist. On a recommendation from this teacher, he went on to Pratt in New York. He chose that design school because it was the only one with a basketball team, an important consideration for him at the time.

The school consistently turned out students with great potential in advertising and design. Richards credits Herschel Levit, one of his teachers at Pratt, with greatly influencing him, as well as a group of two or three dozen other art students. Along with Richards, these people went on to have outstanding careers in advertising or design.

Levit helped Richards understand what graphic design was all about. "In the very first session," says Richards, "he marched us all down to the school auditorium, sat at the piano and explained, in great detail, Arnold Schoenberg's 12-tone row system for composition. He explained how Schoenberg built his compositions and the wonderful symmetry involved without explaining its relevance to the class. At the end of this class session, we were dismissed and it was never mentioned again."

This taught Richards his greatest lesson. Here was a group of people who planned to work their entire lives without having to ever write a piece of music. As he reflected on it over the course of his studies, he realized that Levit was saying that to be a great designer, *everything* you know is relevant.

"Every time I went to class, I never knew where the discussion was going to go. We could critique our work and then the conversation would move off into very interesting discussions of architecture or dance," recalls Richards. "All of us gained tremendously from those discussions."

Richards graduated from Pratt in 1953 and got some job offers in New York. But he noticed that some talented designers who worked in New York improved when they moved on to Los Angeles. "So I thought Los Angeles was the place for me," he says.

He headed out for Los Angeles, but took a detour to Dallas because he had seen terrific work being done by Neiman Marcus. The exclusive Dallas retailer's advertising design was ahead of the industry and very well regarded. "It was brilliant," he says. "It was always great fun and had a nice light touch." He decided to apply there, but although he received encouragement, he did not get a job.

This frustrated him. "I was this 20-year-old kid out of one of the best art schools in America," Richards says. "Maybe I wasn't the very best kid in my graduating class, but there were a few of us who dominated the class. I was coming to a city that was not much more than a frontier town. It had a very sedentary, quiet, unexciting advertising industry."

Richards' portfolio consisted of a dozen highly experimental pieces from school. "I sat down and talked with a creative director who headed the biggest agency in Dallas at the time. He looked at my work and got very excited. He offered what turned out to be extraordinary counsel."

He told Richards that nobody in Dallas would hire him because his work was too advanced. But Dallas was going to grow and flourish. "He said if I could stick it out through the lean years, I'd be in a position to dominate the market. Because I'd be responsible for all the good stuff."

The creative director's prediction made Richards's detour well worthwhile. He took this advice and started a freelance design and advertising practice. He won local advertising awards over the next couple of years. Then, in 1955, the head of the Bloom Agency, the second biggest agency in Dallas, called and asked if he'd be interested in working as a creative director there.

"I took the job there thinking I would enjoy heading up the creative efforts for a big agency," says Richards. "But I hated it. It was all the classic things you hear about advertising agencies. It was bureaucratic, hierarchical—a stultifying environment. It was one in which the account managers said, 'No, that's not what my client is looking for and so I won't show it.' Then we battled over it. I left almost a year to the day after starting and reestablished my freelance practice."

Richards had to struggle very hard to reestablish himself. He had virtually no income for several months, but soon his business began to flourish. Business from Dallas-area companies and agencies came first, then from around Texas, and soon from the rest of the country. Eventually he built up a 20-person staff.

His organization developed relationships with advertising agencies based on print work. Sometimes a television assignment would come up, and the studio would be asked to work on it. Richards would conceive it, write it, and storyboard it—and on some occasions produce it. "I always felt that it was the most natural thing in the world to do both advertising and design," he says. "I might sit down in the morning and work on a logo and in the afternoon, work on an advertising campaign." Over the next 20 years, his organization grew into an important creative resource for advertising agencies.

Then, in 1976, when his design firm was firmly established, the CEO of a major Dallas bank asked him if he'd be interested in handling their account as a full-service agency. "It was an interesting moment," recalls Richards, "because if we became an advertising agency, we'd say good-bye to all of our clients. So I thought long and hard about that one, and decided it was time to make the transition."

When The Richards Group became a full-service advertising agency, his design group was kept intact and moved a few blocks from the agency. Eventually, the business grew to also include groups that specialized in direct marketing, public relations, and sales promotion.

As an advertising agency, several factors set The Richards Group apart from other organizations. Richards doesn't run his business by patterning the organization after current trends or the traditional practices of other agencies.

"I destroyed all the departmental lines. An art director is just as likely to be sitting next to an account executive as he or she is to a researcher. That way, if an art director is working late and stands up to stretch, he or she will notice an account executive in the next cubicle working just as long and hard. There is infinitely more respect for each other. Each knows the other cares just as much about his or her side of the business. That's enormously helpful in avoiding confrontations," says Richards. He also prefers that his employees spend time with their families and avoid late hours. "It's a business that requires considerably more than nine hours a day on a fairly regular basis," he says. "So I learned early in my career to set aside my evening hours for my family. If I have extra work to do, I just come in early. Nobody at my house cared whether I was gone at 4:00 a.m., but they cared a lot if I wasn't home at 7:00 in the evening."

In addition, Richards expects all his creatives to present their own work. "We don't shield any of them from our clients," he says. However, this job requirement does not demand exceptional presentation skills. "Good work speaks for itself," he says. "You can be absolutely silent and put five ads on the table and a person sitting on the other side is going to find it pretty easy to pick the best one."

But, for creative people, the most shocking practice of Richards's organization is his dress code. No shorts or sandals there. "We dress in business attire—ties and, for the most part, suits," says Richards. "Nothing in the world is more important than doing a great ad. That's what drives this organization. But if I sit across the table from a client who sees me as a member of a different 'tribe,' then my counsel to him is less valuable and therefore less likely to be accepted. I don't tolerate barriers that make it difficult to do great advertising. I want to remove those barriers and have all the decisions based on the merits of the work."

But individual work styles are respected, too. Richards prefers to work alone, but recognizes that sometimes others need a partner to be productive. So some of his creative teams work in partnership, while others choose to work by themselves.

Looking back on his more than 40 years in communications, he says, "Advertising is an extraordinary business. Every morning I get up and I'm excited about coming to the office. There is no business that is as emotionally rewarding as the one I'm in—with the exception of being a performer. And the only reason is that with a performance, you get to hear the applause. We don't. We have to assume that there is applause."

In many ways those characteristics make one successful in any endeavor. "You legitimately want to please," explains Richards. "In dealing with clients, you want very much for them to sit across the table from you, listen to your presentation, and when you're finished say, 'That's wonderful.' That's the applause I'm talking about."

"I'd do this whether anybody paid me or not. I work with very, very bright people who care about their craft. We spend our days trying to figure out how to create something wonderful. What more could anyone ask for? And, I'm overpaid for doing it!"

A BEAUTIFULLY DESIGNED PORTFOLIO

Mercantile Bank

Mercantile Bank's business had stagnated for years while the other banks in Dallas grew dramatically. The bank brought in a new CEO, who decided they were not being served well by their current agency. He wanted to project a more aggressive image. He wanted to communicate a willingness to take prudent risks—not to be regarded as the bank that easily rejects new ideas.

The Richards Group won the account on their credentials without even presenting a campaign. The agency found the bank's stuffy, stodgy, old-fashioned image was hurting them. "Our first assignment was to develop a new graphic identity and apply it to all of the business papers, signs—everything," Richards says. When he finished presenting the mark, the CEO said he liked the work because "it captured a feeling of momentum." The CEO then asked if a campaign could be built using the word "momentum."

Richards went back to his office and wrote a couple of TV scripts and print ads. A week later, he presented the line, "Never underestimate the power of momentum."

Wanting to attract the business community—which, at the time, was almost 100% male in Dallas—the campaign presented analogies between business and sports. And the results were phenomenal. The bank grew from $900 million in assets to more than $23 billion in assets over the 12-year period this campaign was used.

Richards is also proud that the CEO offered the direction and the agency respected his idea. Says Richards, "Most agency people are so arrogant that if an idea comes from a client, it is automatically put aside as not having any merit."

Is It Live Or Is It Memorex?

Memorex Audio Tapes

The Richards Group has represented Memorex for two years. Most of Richards's Memorex work is print ads for audio tapes and headphones.

"We were a convenient hire for Memorex," says Richards. "They are headquartered in Fort Worth, but were dealing with Weiden & Kennedy, a fine agency in Oregon. They were experiencing the problems that often occur when an agency and client are a significant distance from each other.

When they won the account, The Richards Group inherited the tagline "Is it live or is it Memorex?", which was originally written by Leo Burnett. They recognized the line's value and great heritage. It was meaningful to people of all ages. So there was never a question of replacing it. But the new ads were visually very different from those done by Weiden & Kennedy, who had used rock stars. Richards chose not to do that, but has still created arresting and provocative work. This ad was art directed by Richards' son, Grant, who is one of the agency's creative group heads. "Once we decided on that photograph, there was only one way to lay out that ad," says Richards.

Motel 6

The most prominent campaign The Richards Group has created—and the most successful in the marketplace—is the one for Motel 6. In the early '80s, Motel 6 was only using outdoor advertising. They asked The Richards Group to help them expand into other media. "It was a big opportunity for us," he says. "We were asked to work for this terrific organization that was preparing to spend several million dollars in advertising. After looking at the research, however, the first advice we gave was not to advertise. The product needed to be fixed. At that time, there were no phones in the Motel 6 rooms. Guests were expected to go down the hall to make a telephone call. If guests wanted to watch television, they had to pay an extra dollar and a half. And there was no reservation system.

"Without telephones, televisions, and a reservation system, we felt their advertising dollars would be wasted," says Richards. "The advertising could entice consumers to try Motel 6, but the disappointed guests would never come back again."

Motel 6 management took Richards's advice and made an enormous financial commitment to upgrade their product. Just installing the telephones resulted in the biggest order AT&T had ever received at that time—40,000 telephones in all.

Then The Richards Group developed the concept for the advertising. "This came directly from what we learned from qualitative research," says Richards. "Focus groups consisting of 10 or 12 people who had stayed at Motel 6 were recruited. The participants thought they were only there to talk about lodging. The moderator began by talking about where they stayed when traveling. The participants said they normally stayed at Marriotts, Hiltons, Holiday Inns, and about 20 other hotel chains. Nobody was willing to admit they had stayed in a Motel 6. When the moderator pressed harder, one person admitted it. And, once one person in the room admitted it, others followed. They justified their stay by saying that it helped them save money to buy an extra tank of gas or eat steak instead of hamburger. Suddenly, people responded with enormous pride in being frugal and deciding to stay in a Motel 6."

Richards sat behind the glass and watched this great welling-up of pride. It became relatively easy for him to decide that the creative strategy should be to point out that Motel 6 was a smart choice for the economical traveler. With this strategy in place, the execution was simple.

Two years earlier, one of Richards' writers had come into his office saying he'd heard an interesting voice on National Public Radio. It was Tom Bodett. They agreed that Bodett's voice and personal style could be very interesting, and kept him in mind for a future opportunity. When Motel 6 came along, they remembered him and wrote the series of commercials for him.

:60 Radio—"Fiscal Responsibility"

Hi. Tom Bodett for Motel 6 with a few thoughts about fiscal responsibility. You know this bein' an election year and all, I got a suggestion. If you're runnin' for office and you're out there on the campaign trail, why not stay at Motel 6 and save a few bucks. What with money bein' too tight to mention and government tools costin' millions, it'll be refreshing to get a clean, comfortable room for the lowest prices of any national chain. And while stayin' at Motel 6 may not win you the election, it'll sure make you popular with us regular folks. And don't forget, with the free local phone calls you can rally support from some of those local constituents right from the comfort of your room. And with the free color TV, you can sit back, watch the headlines, and see how you're doin' in the polls. Well give it some thought. For the rest of you not runnin' for office, well, Motel 6 is still a heck of a deal, and who knows, you just might run into your next elected official. I'm Tom Bodett for Motel 6 with America's future on my mind.

Where to shop when you want to impress your fiancé's parents.

Apple Pie Baked Fresh Daily In Our Bakery. Reg. $8.95, **Now $4.95.**

Mousse Truffee. Reg. $11.95/lb., **Now $7.95/lb.**

Cornichons, Reg. $1.12/¼ lb., Now ¼ lb. Free with Each Pound of Mousse Truffee Purchased.

Simon David Fresh Beluga Caviar, 1 oz., Reg. $27.99, **Now $21.99.**

Moet & Chandon White Star Champagne, Reg. $22.99, **Now $14.99.**

Live Maine Lobster, Reg. $9.99/lb., **Now $7.99 Each,** 1¼ lb. Avg.

Simon David

Richards believes that "advertising should be endearing, rewarding and relevant. It should make the reader enjoy the experience of viewing the ad." This work for Simon David is a good example of those qualities. It is based on common experiences and attitudes. And communicates the message in an simple, personable manner.

"I want the viewers to go through an intellectual process," he says. "I want them to say to themselves, 'I like what you said. I like the way you said it. I therefore like you. And if I like you, I find it easy to do business with you.' It's not terribly different from the way you would sell something across the counter."

Where to shop once they become your in-laws.

Hamburger Buns Baked Fresh Daily In Our
Own Bakery, Package Of 6, Reg. 99¢, **Now 59¢.**

Farm Fresh Tomatoes, Reg. 99¢/lb., **Now 49¢/lb.**

Lipton Tea Bags, 24 ct.,
Reg. $2.33, **Now $1.29.**

Ground Beef, 73% Lean,
Reg. $1.28/lb., **Now 89¢/lb.**

Coke, Diet Coke, Caffeine Free Coke, Sprite,
12-pack 12 oz. Cans, Reg. $5.39, **Now $2.79.**

Bob's Texas-Style Chips, All Varieties,
7 oz., Reg. $1.39, **Now 79¢.**

When you combine a first-rate grocery store with a first-rate specialty store, you have a marriage made in heaven. And it's known as Simon David. Where you can find everything you need to make just the right impression. At special low prices sure to impress even the most budget-conscious mother-in-law. But you should come in this week. Because just like any honeymoon, these sale prices will soon be over.

Simon David
Your Speciality Food Store Since 1889

*Prices good Sunday, April 17 through Saturday, April 23, only at Simon David, 9722 Great Hills Trail at the Arboretum Market, Austin, Texas 78759. We reserve the right to limit quantities. **We also honor Tom Thumb advertised prices.** Open every day from 8 a.m. to 10 p.m. For home delivery, call (512) 338-4250.*

Because of this approach, Richards always looks for some endearing way to communicate the message—that's what distinguishes great work—in broadcast as well as in print. This endearing quality distinguishes Richards' work from some of the advertising in today's annuals, which he often describes as the "in-your-face" school of advertising. "In-your-face advertising is confrontational, highly provocative," Richards says, "and can gain an enormous amount of attention. But it's really pretty easy to do—and rarely endearing."

Butch Cassidy and the Sundance Kid

While still a design studio, The Richards Group was assigned the advertising campaign for a new movie. Richards received the script and thought it was brilliant. "I knew this movie was going to be a smash hit," he recalls. "So I did the ad campaign, sent it to California, and got a call from the director a couple of days later. He loved what we did in the ad campaign, and asked if we would be interested in designing the main title sequence. He said he was having trouble with that. I told him I'd be delighted. It was approved and became part of the movie Butch Cassidy and the Sundance Kid. *It's our only credential in the movie business, but it won an Oscar for best picture. So I have a great track record with the Academy Awards."*

How to Endear Yourself to a Potential Employer

Richards has an unusually honest approach in making his hiring decisions. "I hire people I like. That may sound stupid," says Richards, "but personality counts. Integrity counts. It's an intuitive process. I get a feeling for the beginner, not just for the work in the portfolio."

When he interviews, Richards wants to find out what the beginner is like. "I try to draw that person out—beginning with high school years," says Richards. "I want to find out if he or she played sports, was involved in politics, or what his or her folks do. I try to understand what kind of person he or she is. I want to be satisfied that, when I expose this person to my client, he or she will represent both himself or herself and our organization very well. And if I hire people I like, there's a pretty good chance they'll like each other, too."

In the portfolio, Richards looks for two or three pieces that are so brilliant he could expect to see them in the annuals. Says Richards, "If a beginner is capable of doing that, I'd hire him or her." Here is some advice that can help you get to that level.

Review the annuals

Richards believes this helps you develop your instincts and abilities to make sound judgments. "Spend time reviewing the CA annuals, One Show annuals, New York Art Director's Annual and Graphis," says Richards. "Those books help you to recognize what is possible in advertising. It's important they be current, but it's also useful to look at older editions to understand where advertising came from, why things are done the way they are done—and how we got here. "If you only read this week's *Time*, whose ads are 90% garbage, you won't ever develop a sense for really terrific work. Emulate the best work that's being done in the field."

Stir up your creative juices

To come up with ideas, Richards tells us that anything can trigger a stream of consciousness. "I can pick up a magazine, the annuals, or the Yellow Pages and make some sort of word association that starts a thought process. Something might trigger a whole string of thoughts and lead me to a place I wouldn't come to otherwise," he says. "Also, I'm a runner and when I'm running alone, I find that helps me to solve advertising problems."

Understand the customer's position

Advertising's primary mission is to sell a product or service. That's simple. But to do that means identifying the potential customer's point of view. Ideally, research will tell us that. "We need to understand what information will change a potential customer's point of view," says Richards, "and what information will motivate them to do business with the client."

Use familiar products for a spec book

Your portfolio should have ads for products anybody can understand. Says Richards, "If somebody comes in with an ad for some highly sophisticated software program, an ad that only he and an engineer understand, it's very difficult to evaluate the work. The simpler the product, the better it is. Also avoid fictional products. Presenting real products, with real marketing considerations, has more impact."

Include radio in a copy portfolio

Richards sees very little radio work in spec portfolios. However, he feels this is an important component of advertising. So he is always encouraged when a beginner presents some terrific radio. Richards recognizes that beginners should also include TV because some employers want to see it, but he believes TV is difficult to evaluate. "It's a collaborative medium. It involves many people. In a television spot, there can be 10 people who played a major part in the process," he says.

Match your style to that of the agency

Also, Richards recommends dressing like the person who is going to interview you. "If that person is wearing sandals and beads, and that's the place where you want to work, show up in sandals and beads," he says.

Skip the research

Richards believes that beginners shouldn't be concerned with finding research on which to hinge a strategy. "Research is difficult to find and they may not have the skills to make sense of it," he says. "That's another reason why the products in their portfolios should have very obvious marketing considerations. Suppose a beginner chooses WD-40. You don't have to be a genius to figure out that most households in America have a can of WD-40 sitting on a shelf. One can of WD-40 can last a lifetime. Therefore, the marketing strategy should be to motivate people to use it up. That's simple. And no one needs research to understand that."

Be prepared to talk about anything

As we mentioned earlier, Richards looks for people he will enjoy working with. He wants to work with people who will be able to work with his clients. "I ask applicants to talk about subjects they are unprepared to talk about," he says. "I prefer to hear about their parents, brothers and sisters, and what they like to do for fun, rather than the details of their last position."

Be a grown-up

Richards particularly wants to avoid hiring people who seem arrogant. "I don't believe in artistic temperaments. I think that's often an excuse for infantile behavior. In my own organization, I simply will not accept that. I won't accept arrogance, and I won't accept temper tantrums," he says. "We want to present the work. We want the client to respond. And we want to be able to respond to the client's comments and then make the changes that satisfy all of the concerns. That's hard to do with people who are arrogant or cocky."

Invite client participation

"We go into every client/agency relationship understanding that we'll never know our client's business as well as he knows it," says Richards. "But we'll know his customer better than he ever can. And we'll know advertising better than he ever can. But we will never know his business as well as he does because he has ways of casually picking up information that will never come to us. We want to take full advantage of that. So we want our client to be a participant in the process. Consequently, if he or she has reservations about an ad, we want to understand why. That insight will help us reach the best answer."

Put aside business-to-business (unless it's great)

Richards recognizes that it's difficult for people coming from business-to-business agencies to break into consumer advertising. Most often they have to replace their business-to-business portfolio with speculative consumer work. "Too often, I see somebody in a bad business-to-business

agency, doing bad work for bad clients, thinking their work will be enough to get them a job in a good consumer agency," he says. "It won't. Most often the problem lies in the fact that the work is typically expository. It has little imagination. But if someone presents terrific business-to-business advertising, I will instantly know their talent can translate into good consumer advertising."

Always question your work

When you finish an ad, Richards suggests asking yourself questions about its effectiveness. "Does the ad make a point? And does it make that point clearly? Does it make the point without the body copy? If it's an outdoor board, can it be read at 70 mph? All of those questions are important," says Richards.

Include only about a dozen pieces

"You can have a few more," says Richards. "But not many. Secondly, they ought to be the very best you've ever done."

Attend an art school

"I hire a lot of kids out of art schools," says Richards. "They do a marvelous job of preparing people to enter the business. They're, for the most part, highly competitive. Those who distinguish themselves in an exceedingly demanding environment are going to be successful in business. So it's about as predictable as anything can be."

Postscript 1
WHAT TO LOOK FOR IN A CLIENT

ONE OF THE GREATEST DETERMINING FACTORS IN PRODUCING GOOD WORK IS THE CLIENT. That's why Richards has a series of questions he asks when taking on new business. These questions are also valuable for beginners because they will set criteria that will help you produce your best work.

"The first question to ask is can we do great work?" says Richards. "Is the client open to great creative? Do they trust fresh ideas? And are they willing to provide enough input to get it?

"The next issue focuses on getting results. Can we measure how the advertising works or are we going to have to be satisfied that the client's spouse thinks it's nice. It's important to measure results. Being able to look at sales and determine whether the advertising did the job is important to effective campaigns in the future.

"Can we make a profit? The client understands we both assume the responsibility of helping each other to profit in the relationship.

"And, can we have fun? That's the human side. Do we like the people? Do they like us? When we show up for a meeting are we going to be treated with respect? Will we enjoy the experience?

"Also, avoid working for clients in multi-layered organizations where the work travels through an endless series of approvals. At each level of approval, reviews make the work weaker and weaker. That's frustrating for a creative person."

● ● ● ● ● ● ● ● ● ● ● ● ● ● ●

Postscript 2
FINDING YOUR PLACE IN ADVERTISING OR DESIGN

WHERE DO YOU BEST FIT: IN AN ADVERTISING AGENCY OR IN A DESIGN ORGANIZATION? While many art directors and even writers may be able to fit into both, the beginner who knows where his or her strengths are has an advantage. In the last chapter, we had Burrell explore this topic. Now let's have Richards shed some more light on it.

"The basic difference between the design organization and the advertising agency is that design work is done on a project basis," he says. "Even if the organization designed an annual report for a client for twenty consecutive years, it's still a project. We do his annual report and at the end of it, he gets a great annual report, we send a bill, and that's the end of it.

"With an advertising agency, it's a total relationship where concerns go beyond the advertising. The agency works to help improve the sales organization. Or understand the products and services enough to recommend enhancements. That way, creative people can have a profound influence on a client's business.

"Obviously designers in the design organization need superb design skills. In the case of writers, someone who can write an annual report, slide presentation, or a film may not necessarily have the skills to write an ad. It's a matter of style.

It's always been a lot easier for me to write ten pages than to entertain, excite, and explain in a seven word headline. Consequently, a writer in our design organization may be excellent in writing long assignments, but may never have written a headline in his or her life.

"This person who is likely to wind up writing annual reports is more interested in journalism or in writing the great American novel. He or she may love to read English prose or enjoy writing three page letters to erudite friends.

"Within the advertising agency, I look for great conceptual skills. A successful art director needs the right combination of verbal/visual skills. They have to be able to write headlines as well as conceive an ad or TV spot visually. The people I hire in my design organization will have superior design skills, but won't necessarily be able to sit down and write a headline. Several of our people are able to work in both areas comfortably.

When you come to Oslo, bring an open mind.

Amil Gargano

"There are a lot of people in this business with big reputations in big agencies who have done little to earn it," says Amil Gargano, founding partner of Amil Gargano and Partners. "These people pound their chests, talk about how great they are and exploit the work of people they supervise. While the work they create themselves is usually mediocre at best."

Gargano, on the other hand, has a big reputation for a good reason. He was the creator of numerous breakthrough campaigns for such clients as Volvo, Hertz, Pan Am, MCI and Calvin Klein. And he was the creative leader and co-founder of one of the hottest shops of the sixties and seventies, Carl Ally, Inc. (now known as Ally & Gargano). He has won hundreds of industry awards, holding the record for the most gold medals won in one year from The One Show awards, and he has been elected to the Art Director's Club Hall of Fame and to The One Club's Creative Hall of Fame.

In 1991, he founded his new agency with one client—Showtime. Today, his clients also include American Express and NYNEX.

In addition to agency responsibilities, Gargano serves on the boards of Helen Keller International and the Smithsonian Institution's Center for Advertising History, as well as on the creative advisory board for the Partnership for a Drug-Free America. Since 1973, he has also been a visiting professor at Syracuse University, where he teaches a post-graduate level communications course.

Residing in New York, he has been married to the same woman for the last 29 years and has one son.

A Very Relevant Story

WHAT ATTRACTS MANY TALENTED PEOPLE INTO ADVERTISING? GARGANO HAS A SIMPLE answer: nothing. Years ago, they would drift in from other careers. "A lot of people have wandered in with ambitions of becoming serious artists and writers," he says.

Gargano, in fact, was one of those people. As a child, he wanted to be a fine artist and, later, a commercial illustrator. He started working toward those goals in the fourth grade after a teacher identified his artistic abilities. She suggested that his parents send him to art classes after school. So every day, after his regular classes, he attended the William's School in downtown Detroit. And his father picked him up on his way home from work. "That's where I developed a real interest in art," says Gargano.

He then attended Cass Tech. in Detroit, a high school that emphasized art and music, and, later, he entered Wayne State University. But his education was interrupted by the Korean War. He wound up spending 21 months in the service, of which 15 months were spent on the front lines. "I was discharged early because I had combat experience," he says. "I started thinking about what I wanted to do and I found that I didn't have enough money to go away to school."

So, back home, he registered at Cranbrook Academy and financed his education with the help of the GI Bill and by working as a part-time salesman in a men's clothing store. "I was one of two veterans," Gargano says. "The school was in the suburbs of Detroit, an enclave of automobile executives. Everyone was affluent, and the surroundings were palatial."

Finding himself uncomfortable in these surroundings, Gargano stayed for only one year, and left to find a job. Friends suggested he apply at Chrysler. But his portfolio wasn't really cut out for a position in America's automobile capital. "I wasn't interested in drawing automobile parts," he says.

Nevertheless, he was offered a job designing the lettering for car interiors. "I didn't want to spend my life with a group of men in shirt sleeves trying to decide whether to use script, serif, or san serif type," he says, "so I rejected it. And the guy doing the hiring was outraged because the job paid $100 bucks a week—a lot of money at that time."

Then, he learned of a job at a place called Campbell-Ewald. "I thought advertising agency! What a terrible business," he recalls. "Advertising in the mid fifties was so bad, you couldn't even parody it because everyone would assume you were serious."

But since agencies commissioned artists for illustrations, he took the job, expecting it to bring him closer to achieving that goal. In his job, he cut mats, and completed mechanicals and patch work for the art directors. "I became their hands," he says. "And on weekends and evenings, I'd work to develop a portfolio that would land me a job in a Detroit art studio."

Then on Christmas, six months later, he tried to resign in order to look for a job as an illustrator. "I was so naive," he says. "My parents were direct, honest people who taught me to be up-front with everyone. I couldn't imagine looking for a new job on someone else's time. You didn't take advantage of anybody who had hired you. That would be immoral. Today, that seems ridiculous, doesn't it?"

But the aspiring illustrator's attempt to quit was met with protest. To his surprise, he was told by his boss, Al Scott, that he had been planning to promote him to assistant art director after the holidays. "He told me," says Gargano, "and this is what got me: 'In advertising you create the ideas and give them to an illustrator. As an illustrator, you wind up rendering art directors' thinking.' This intrigued me."

In January of 1956, Gargano took on his first assignment as assistant art director—doing industrial ads. "In those days," says Gargano, "a copywriter would give the art director a yellow piece of paper with a headline that had already been approved by the account executive. So I took the information, looked at it, and designed the hell out of it. The result didn't make much advertising sense, because the design had no relationship to a selling concept, but it looked interesting and different from the other ads being done. The agency loved it. I look back now and cringe."

After eight months, he was promoted to art director; then to group art director. At 27, he became vice president. "I was just beginning to understand what advertising was about," he says, "because I became immersed in it." He studied the New York Art Directors Annuals and began to notice the work of Doyle Dane Bernbach (DDB) and other up-and-coming agencies. He was impressed—more by the design elements than the concepts, but he began to understand how to really communicate with people—that what you say and how you say it is what gets people to read and believe your ad. "I began to examine why I stopped to read certain things," he says, "and what interested me. I knew other people would be attracted the same way."

He did not study television commercials because art directors had no part of the process. "Most of them were abominable, anyway," Gargano says. "They were predominately singing commercials. Not that things have changed much. They've just gotten a lot more slick."

He had always wanted to work in New York, and the work coming out of agencies like DDB was what motivated him further. He spoke to his group supervisor about wanting to move, saying he would prefer to stay with Campbell-Ewald and work in their small office there. "I told him if you ever need anyone in New York, you can count on me," says Gargano. "I'd volunteer."

And in less than a year, the opportunity arose. It happened because Carl Ally, then an assistant to the president of Campbell-Ewald, had his eye out for new opportunities and noticed how fast New York agencies were growing. He asked to be sent there to try to cultivate new business. With some reluctance, management agreed. In New York, Ally heard that the Swissair account was looking for an agency. He called them, made a pitch and won the business.

To service the account, Ally needed fresh talent. Says Gargano, "The New York office was a sleepy place where people were hiding comfortably." That was Gargano's cue. "Carl Ally was someone I had worked with sporadically back in Detroit," Gargano says, "and we hit it off extremely well." He moved to New York, along with Jim Durfee (also from Campbell-Ewald).

A few months later, the agency also got United Aircraft Corporation (United Technology). But the work they were doing wasn't what Campbell-Ewald management had in mind. Complying with clients was more important than vigorously defending ideas. Consequently, the trio left for other jobs agreeing that, should the opportunity arise, they'd start their own agency.

During his first few years in New York, Gargano spent much of his time becoming acquainted with the city. He became even more familiar with the work that DDB was doing and watched for it. "Most of the advertising at that time was not very compelling," says Gargano. "But DDB had tremendous appeal. They told things the way they were, did it in a way that was startingly original—in a language that everyone spoke."

Because DDB's work was so remarkably different from previous advertising, Gargano studied it to learn the elements that made it work. He'd walk to the subway station in New York and see the ads for Levy's Rye Bread. Or open *The New York Times* and see an ad for Orbach's. In the process, Gargano's attitude toward advertising changed from contempt to inspiration.

"There was a famous ad that Bob Gage of DDB did for El Al," says Gargano. "It simply said that El Al has shrunk the Atlantic by 20%. And they had this dramatic photograph of the Atlantic Ocean with the corner cut and rolled back 20%. At other agencies, this ad would have never been conceived or approved. Instead, they would feature a big, stupid airplane—like that was the thing people were buying. But people don't buy an airplane trip, they buy an experience. An airplane's just the vehicle to get you some place. Knowing that, DDB took advantage of a simple, powerful idea that people would find unusual and engaging."

In addition, he spent many hours talking with Ally and Durfee about advertising. "We were all from Detroit and trying hard to find our own advertising philosophy to help change the industry. We used to talk about why certain ads were effective. And what individuals were creating real innovation. We became students."

Much of what Gargano saw bothered him. Historically, the account person had absolute control. There was a definitive agency hierarchy. Copywriters were number two; followed by research and media. "The art director was last on the food chain—a renderer, a pair of hands," he says. "I was outraged by this caste system—mainly because there wasn't any overwhelming thinking taking place by any of these people to begin with." Bernbach, however, liberated art directors. He gave them equality to copywriters. That appealed to him.

In addition, the three of them had their own opinions. And their philosophy departed from DDB's humanistic, emotionally engaging approach. They took after a harsher, more combative style. They wanted to challenge the audience with reasons to buy one particular product over another, but in ways that hadn't been done before. They wanted to differentiate themselves—with a style that would be their own.

"We said to ourselves that information is the crucial element to creating persuasive advertising. It's a weapon. You can bludgeon your competition with the right information," says Gargano. "We believed in taking a consumer advocacy position. What's in it for them? We had a tremendous contempt for advertising of an insidious nature. It was often tasteless, patronizing, and mindless in its presentation to people."

In 1962, with those thoughts in mind, they pitched an unknown account, Volvo, and won the business. Carl Ally, Inc. was formed. "Because Carl was ten years older and had a strong personal sense of entitlement, he insisted that his name be on the door exclusively," says Gargano. "Our first advertising for Volvo pioneered comparative advertising. What we did for Volvo was define the character of the automobile to the public. Gave them a new set of criteria for buying a car: Durability, longevity, and safety. A strategy that endures 30 years later." The agency then went on to create some of the decade's most significant work.

By 1977, Gargano wanted recognition in the agency he had helped found. "Look, my contributions have equalled yours," he told Ally. "In fact, in some respects, I think they've exceeded yours, so I think my name should be on the door too." Ally agreed and the agency's name was changed to Ally & Gargano.

But then, in '78, the agency lost three major pieces of business and billings dropped from $54 million to $26 million in billings. Carl Ally had been chairman and CEO for 16 years and he suggested that Gargano take over the agency to revitalize it. Gargano agreed only if he was made the controlling shareholder, something Carl had insisted upon for himself in 1962. "We believed that we can function as equals within the agency, but someone has to ultimately make the hard decisions," says Gargano. "To his credit, I can't think of many people who could step aside the way he did. So I took over the company in April of 1978. And we got lucky and had five remarkable years of growth and recognition for our work."

By 1983, Ally & Gargano reached nearly $160 million in billings. "Then someone had the bright idea to take us public," says Gargano. "It sounded good at the time. But it was the biggest mistake of my business career. It was a disastrous period in my life. The whole company changed. We had always believed in a broad distribution of equity in the agency. We wanted people to feel it was their agency, too. The employees had a tremendous sense of loyalty to the agency. When we went public, that sense of camaraderie and family was lost."

Soon shareholders and analysts were coming at Gargano from every direction. His board of directors knew nothing about the advertising business. He was approached by a lot of agencies interested in acquiring them. By 1986, Gargano could see that the agency was vulnerable because of its size.

Marketing Corporation of America (MCA) provided a solution. They proposed an acquisition that would keep the integrity of the organization intact. After eight months of negotiations, MCA acquired Ally & Gargano. The two cultures were incredibly diverse, but MCA wanted an agency with a creative reputation and philosophy and was willing to defer. So, Ally & Gargano was to be dominant in the relationship. And MCA's name was to be dropped. "It's been fully integrated," Gargano says. "And the inevitable outcome was a completely different agency."

By 1991, Gargano wanted to run his own agency again, and so Amil Gargano and Partners was born. "I have strong feelings about entrepreneurship," he says. "What interests me is being in control of my own fate. If you don't own it, you don't control it. I just want to work guided by what's important to me—unencumbered by extraneous people. It sounds a bit selfish, but that's what makes me go. I need that. I'm pathologically incapable of working for someone else."

Forming a new agency also gave him an opportunity to get back to what he enjoys about advertising. "Years ago someone said that advertising is no business for a grown man. I'm bored out of my mind sitting in a meeting with 14 brand managers talking about inconsequentials for six hours. They start to dissect stuff that is absolutely absurd. I think, 'What am I doing here? Why am I sitting here wasting my time? My life is going by!' That's the part of the business I try to divorce myself from. And that's precisely why I'm getting back to what I enjoy. I came into the business doing art direction. That's what I want to go out doing."

COMPARE THIS PORTFOLIO

**You can hurt a Volvo,
but you can't hurt it much.**

This Volvo was bought new in Ann Arbor, Michigan, in 1956. Its owner paid $2,545 for it, complete. He has raced it, pulled a camping trailer halfway across the country with it, let kids climb all over it, and it's seldom under cover. It has 80,261 miles on it. The head has never been off, the brakes have never been relined, the original tires lasted 55,000 miles, the clutch hasn't been touched, the valves have never been adjusted (much less ground), and it will still top 95 mph. Total cost of repairs exclusive of normal maintenance: One hood latch, $4.50. One suspension rod, $30.00. Not all Volvos will do this. But Volvos have a pretty good average. One enthusiastic owner in Wyoming wrote us that he has driven his Volvo over 300,000 miles without major repair. We think he's exaggerating. It's probably closer to 200,000 miles.

Volvo

Volvo—when Ally, Gargano and Durfee pitched the account—was trying to enter the American market and did not have an identity. And they were up against Detroit, which was just beginning to downsize their products by coming out with compact cars like the Valiant, the Corvair, and the Falcon.

Their first commercial showed a Volvo, Valiant, Corvair and Falcon competing in a race and the Volvo was out in front. Way in the back were a Renault and a Volkswagen. The copy simply said, "Volvo will outperform Valiant, Falcon and Corvair and get almost the same gas mileage as the Renault and Volkswagen."

Later ads, like this one, talked about other ways this car was better than Detroit cars, taking Volvo out of the import arena. "Rather than compete with dozens of import cars that sell less than 50,000 units combined in the United States, we said, 'why not compete with cars that sell 2 million units in the United States. And we'd be the only ones competing with them.' That's the basis on which we tried to compete and redefine Volvo," says Gargano. "Instead of just concentrating on the craft of making ads, the real strength of Ally & Gargano was its ability to find new ways of thinking about a product or service."

Shearson Lehman Brothers

When Shearson awarded this account to Ally & Gargano, the investment community was under siege. It had lost credibility among investors. The problem then was, how do you restore confidence?

Gargano thought that by having Shearson profile the way investments can support companies who are working to improve things, investors would have a higher opinion of the company. "Our cities need rebuilding. Bridges are falling down, buildings are collapsing, and roads are horrible," says Gargano. "And Shearson has identified a company addressing this problem. So here's an opportunity for investors to make some money—because first of all, you have to appeal to their sense of greed—but they can also do something fundamentally worthwhile for society."

Ecology and health care are two other issues Gargano addressed for Shearson. "People usually make money at someone else's expense, but these ads give people a chance to make money while helping other people."

Gargano contrasts these ads to Shearson's major competitor. "Merrill Lynch says we're a 'tradition of trust' and they show bears getting transformed into bulls. And they spend millions of dollars to produce that transformation technique. Does that do anything other than engage in the technique of advertising?"

On the other hand, this campaign enabled Shearson to demonstrate *virtue and trust. "We were being responsive to a problem," he says, "not just making ads."*

Hertz

Avis, a DDB client, had been publicly ridiculing Hertz for four years, in one of the world's greatest ad campaigns ever. Even without using the name, everybody knew who Avis was talking about. And Hertz's market share was declining rapidly. Gargano believes the reason they got this business was because they were the only ones to tell Hertz management that it was time to tell Avis to shut up. "We were the ones who said you have to assault them because there's no virtue in being second."

In addition to attracting customers, the campaign provided impetus, philosophy, and stature for Hertz that management couldn't do with talks and rallies in their annual sales meeting. "We ran it for 90 days," says Gargano, "and it killed Avis's campaign. It was aggressive. Confrontational. No nonsense."

Gargano argues that this campaign was not risky (see advice section). "There's a lot of risk-taking going on now. The argument is it gets people's attention. I believe that work like Infiniti takes the wrong direction (see Chapter Four). I don't know how it was sold, but it took a big risk. I would never create or try to sell that to a client because I have no conviction about it," he says. "Instead, this hard-hitting response was a logical next step in light of Avis's actions. That is not risk taking. It's determining a strategy based on events and choosing the message that will provide the best results."

"To their credit," says Gargano, "Avis's campaign established a standard of how to conduct business in the rent-a-car industry. They promised a different, caring attitude by their people, clean ashtrays, windshield wipers that worked, a full tank of gas."

Pan Am

Gargano's goal for advertising is to make consumers say, "I never thought of that company that way."

Here's an example of how he did that for Pan Am. Since all of their destinations were offshore, and America is inhabited by immigrants, he created a campaign introducing the idea that foreign travel is an opportunity to discover one's heritage. It showed Japanese Americans visiting Japan. Western European Americans visiting Europe. And African Americans visiting Africa. "Air France was talking about serving French meals, TWA was offering three kinds of entrees and two different feature films, and Braniff was having their stewardesses wear different fashions," says Gargano. "But an airplane is supposed to take you someplace. Nobody gets on it for the ride."

For another example of finding substantive points of difference, Gargano looked at Pan Am's tag line. Since they pioneered commercial aviation—they were the first airline to develop international capabilities and they worked with Boeing to develop new airplanes—they had a line that said, "The world's most experienced airline." But when their account was with J. Walter Thompson, they dropped that in favor of, "Pan Am makes the going great." Says Gargano, "That's not an advantage. That's just a slogan. It's a line. Given the choice, what airline would you rather fly on? The world's most experienced airline or an airline—any airline—that makes the going great?"

MCI

According to Gargano, the first rule of comparative advertising is to have a superior product. "Otherwise, why make comparisons?" he asks. "You can only do that if you have a better product." MCI, for instance, offered people an alternative to AT&T at a 50 to 60 percent savings on their long distance phone bills. "That's a superior product benefit—a significant point of comparison," says Gargano. "It has enormous appeal. Most of the world is struggling to get by on their salaries. Telling them that they can save 50% on their long distance bills will get their attention."

ADVICE THAT WILL HELP YOU SEE ADVERTISING IN A NEW WAY

WHAT MAKES A GREAT ADVERTISING PROFESSIONAL? ACCORDING TO GARGANO, THE REAL issue is to use your creativity to find strategic, innovative ways to (re)position products. "Ad making is a craft," he says. "You can develop it over time by observing good work and developing your own writing and art direction skills."

To help advertising professionals and beginners alike focus on this issue, Gargano has been sharing his ideas with MFA students at Syracuse University since 1973 as well as spending many hours at schools lecturing, always emphasizing that strategic development is the foundation for all advertising.

"You have to build the strategic definition of the product or service within tangible parameters," he says. "It cannot be some big, innocuous strategy like 'quality and value.' You can go into any board room and hear the chairmen and the minions say the same, boring thing, 'We're quality and value.' Those are the watchwords of the '90s and they've been for the '80s—and the '60s and '70s. But that's not a strategy. That's an objective."

In his MFA seminars, his first assignment is to have his students pick a product they know and like, and then define an objective. "They have to decide what they want their ad to do," he says. "Who do you want to reach? What do you want for them to learn from the ad? Then, in just a couple of sentences, define a strategy of how they intend to accomplish their objective. Most of the time it's clearly articulated, but when someone shows the resulting ad, it bears no resemblance to what that person wanted to achieve."

Gargano believes this happens because advertising people have been trained in the business of just making ads. "They get caught up in puns, visual techniques; everything is tortured and manipulated beyond belief. It's frantic with the technique of advertising. That is not very different from what takes place in this industry day by day from New York to L.A."

To help you get beyond the technique of creating advertising, here is some of Gargano's advice:

Know your product

"Get immersed in your subject. Any good writer is going to do that," says Gargano, "and become extremely knowledgeable. Become so well armed with the facts, you can defend any position you take for a product. Simple, straight-line thinking. Simple, declarative language. That's the way it happens—not torturing a headline—or manipulating the graphics.

There is no substitute for knowing what you're talking about and being informed. And there are no short cuts. Get smart."

Analyze the features

"In forming a strategy, begin by analyzing the characteristics," suggests Gargano. "For example, if a boat or a lawn mower is manufactured in a special way, pay attention to the details. Take the collective pieces of information and try to find some overview. Then state in simple language—so you don't get derailed by your own cleverness—a summary of ideas that make the product important. Stick to simple language and, instead, put life into the concept. You can dress it up once you know where you're going. Then you can play with the language and the visuals, but not until you know you've got a vigorous idea."

Remember to make it compelling

"Nobody buys a magazine for the advertising. It's a chance encounter," Gargano reminds us. "You come across it purely by happenstance. If it's interesting, you read it. If not, you don't." Gargano makes his ads compelling by insisting that all his work provide some information. So consumers gain some value by reading the print ad or paying attention to the commercial on television. "If it has tremendous relevance and strikes some essential truth in people, an ad can produce astounding results," he says.

Pursue clients who want to shake things up

Gargano recommends working for upstart clients like MCI and Federal Express because they're innovators. They're companies whose leaders have the courage, brains, and conviction to want to change things. "We look for the kind of clients who want to change things, who want to do something, who want to be responsive, who do not want to settle for the status quo and business as usual."

Work without fanfare

"I admire guys like Bob Gage," says Gargano. "He said, 'I don't want to run anything. I simply want to do the work.' That has great appeal to me. The people who do the work and let it speak for itself are the ones I respect the most."

Get a good liberal arts education

"In college, I became as captivated by my liberal arts classes as by my art classes. I became as interested in English, history, and anthropology as in art," says Gargano. "A liberal arts education is an excellent foundation for any advertising person. Because in the course of an advertising career, you encounter diverse subjects which will serve you well in the future. You need a broad knowledge base from which to draw in order to respond effectively. And liberal arts tends to amplify and broaden your awareness."

Be as informed as possible

"I'm into information. I surely want to know what I'm doing. I want to be able to have a strong point of view and conviction about something, because that's what makes the difference," says Gargano. "I rely on market research during the learning period. What do people think? There are some people who tend to dismiss research or use it very sparingly. But I don't think you should resist information."

Use market research as a point of departure to something larger

"A lot of agencies and clients make the mistake of thinking that focus groups are going to provide new insights. At most, they're going to tell you what most everybody already knows," says Gargano. "If you ask somebody in a shopping mall for their opinion, they'll give you an answer; but it won't be *the* answer—it's only part of the answer. Research is a stepping stone to someplace else. There are certain things that people say that will strike familiar chords. But you'll never get a focus group that's so bursting with brilliant new ideas that you can say, 'That's it!' It doesn't work that way."

Tie the concept to the product

"Your product shouldn't be shoehorned into your commercial. It should not be something that, for example, makes people laugh and then says, 'Oh, here, by the way, is the advertiser's name.' That's film making. That's not advertising," says Gargano. "A good ad is something that brings out some fundamental piece of truth. When people look at it and unconsciously say, 'Yeah, that's true, that's worth considering,' that's the sign of a good ad."

Rework existing ads

In putting together a portfolio, Gargano suggests taking existing ads and improving them. "Many years ago a young journalist, who aspired to be in advertising, brought in his portfolio. He was a very quiet, introspective man, but I was absolutely dazzled by his ability to dig salient facts out of body copy and use them as the lead," Gargano recalls. "He took a series of ads and reworked them using what he found to be more pertinent information in the body copy. And he improved the ads. His art direction was terribly crude, but it didn't matter. He found new ways of positioning the products. It was the best beginner's portfolio I'd ever seen."

Avoid risks...

"When I'm on a panel at a seminar, what I hear repeatedly is 'We have to get clients to take risks.' But the worst thing you can do is tell a client to take a risk," says Gargano. "Clients don't want to hear about risks. They may be well established in their careers. They may have families, a mortgage, and car payments, the whole catastrophe. In comes a young art director and a copywriter who want them to take a risk. In effect, risking the client's job. That's not what they want to hear. Even some senior people with big reputations talk about taking risks. It's madness. Dumb. It's the wrong language to use with clients."

...Focus on the strategy instead

"Minimize the risks and go for a line of thinking that's progressive," says

Gargano. "So you can tell your client 'We've thought about your product very carefully and feel we have an opportunity to make tremendous inroads in our competition's market by taking this approach.' Get them to the point where they can comfortably say, 'Yeah, that's right. That will help my career. That will help pay for my kids' college years.' This doesn't mean your work can't be breakthrough. I've done a lot of breakthrough work, but never positioned it as risky."

Encourage accountability

"Accountability is essential," says Gargano. "We encourage it. Before a client spends $5 or $50 million on an ad campaign, find out what people think. Then afterward, find out how their perceptions have changed. Or put an 800-number on the commercial. The results will validate the strategy—and justify spending money on advertising. There is a definite correlation between running advertising in the marketplace and counting the results."

Find inspiration everywhere

"I'm stimulated by being alive and just observing life," says Gargano. "Last night I saw a 66-year-old tenor saxophonist who was filled with as much life and talent and zeal as any young jazz musician. He was funny. He was brilliantly talented. And I was inspired by the man. So where do you get the source for inspiration? All over the place."

"Comfort the afflicted and afflict the comfortable"—sign in Carl Ally's office

"Carl Ally liked the little guy," says Gargano. "That was one of the many things we had in common. We both grew up poor, not that we were wanting for clothing on our backs or food on the table. That may be a part of our iconoclastic, irreverant, but honest approach to the business. We didn't want to do traditional advertising—what was expected. We wanted to deal with the truth. The way things are. Warts and all."

Be the kind of person others want to be around

"I think that personality is as important as the work presented," says Gargano. "I've made the mistake of hiring some people who had great portfolios, but were arrogant people. Prima donnas without team spirit. Now I ask myself if I'd look forward to walking into their office and chatting with them for a few minutes. I want to be around people who enjoy producing everything from a commercial to a matchbook cover. These people love what they do. They're inspired. Alive. They have energy. And they make everything they touch important. So everything they do has a wonderful consistency."

Keep your values in check

"There aren't too many people I admire in this business," says Gargano. "But outside of this business, I have many. One of them is a successful ophthalmologist, who started an organization called Sight

Savers International. He's dedicated his life to curing blindness among impoverished people and regularly travels to Mexico and performs eye surgery. They come to him barefoot and wait for hours in a sweltering heat for their operations. A day or so later, these people, who've been blind for much of their lives, take off the bandages and can see. Talk about the heroes in this world—and nobody even knows who he is! And then you sit in meetings talking about shampoo and dandruff for hours."

Prepare yourself for instability

As a beginner, you may not earn much and some agencies may keep you around because you're relatively inexpensive. But as you move up, know that you have very little job security. "If you are lucky enough to earn six figures and have a good job, but haven't achieved superstar status, you're vulnerable," warns Gargano. When there are cutbacks, those people are often the targets. They're the ones cut out of the business and replaced by younger people who may not perform at as high a level, but will work for a third of the salary. "The pool of unemployed people who may never get re-employed in this business is big. It's a tragedy."

Explore different alternatives

"Advertising provides people with a background and the technical skills that can transfer to other related careers," says Gargano. "That makes it valuable as well as interesting." For instance, Gargano recently produced an award-winning documentary and even considered going into documentary filmmaking full-time. "As you progress in this business, you learn new skills and are provided with different job alternatives. So advertising has got to be one of the more compelling careers for young people. Unfortunately, the industry hasn't provided enough openings for beginners. We steal young people from other agencies and spend the other time firing the people who've been around for a long time."

• • • • • • • • • • • • • • •

Postscript 1
IN DEFENSE OF COMPARATIVE ADVERTISING

COMPARATIVE ADVERTISING HAS BEEN ATTACKED THROUGH THE YEARS BECAUSE, ACCORDING to some critics, it lowers the esteem of both products and, according to others, people don't remember which product was the better of the two being compared. But we have shown in this chapter that comparative advertising can be a very powerful technique. Here are some more of Gargano's comments on this topic.

"Comparative advertising usually gets a bad rap because, many times, the comparisons don't make any sense—like products with a huge pricing difference such as a Volkswagen and a Mercedes Benz; or it lacks strong distinctions in product comparison, so the consumer doesn't remember which product is really better.

"It's just like other forms of advertising that have been criticized because the people creating ads did not know what they were doing. Humor has been wrongly criticized because most of the ads aren't funny and don't try to sell anyone on the product. Everybody thinks they're a gag writer. And radio is the most abused medium of all. Because, many times, the junior people get the radio assignments and think it's their chance to become the next Mel Brooks. But research has shown that during the eighties humor was America's most popular form of advertising. When it's done right, it works. Look at Federal Express.

"And you can do a bad testimonial. You can do a bad demonstration. You can do a bad slice-of-life (which is usually redundant). And, you can do a bad comparative ad.

"Our criteria are simple. You have to compare reasonably like products. If you are in the market for a car at—let's say— between $12,000 to $15,000, what are your choices? What would you look for? Which cars are selling in that price category and are they of comparable performance characteristics? Of course, you must also have the superior product. Otherwise, why make the comparison?

"If the comparisons are weak or irrelevant, it only lowers the esteem of the products you're advertising. Look at Pepsi Cola, a BBDO client. Do you think that some of Pepsi's gain in market share was achieved only because they said they were the 'Pepsi generation?' That's part of it, but that message came in the context of aggressive taste comparisons. I bet you could see Coca-Cola's market share diminish as Pepsi's rose because people preferred Pepsi over Coca-Cola.

"The American Association of Advertising Agencies has published standards that explain the do's and don'ts of comparative advertising. There are some guidelines that make a lot of sense. You compare similar products of equal value. And you don't compare irrelevant features.

"I once gave a speech to the American Marketing Association and took the two advertising techniques that were most commonly denounced: comparative advertising and humor. I did a reel of comparative advertising and I showed the results. Then I did a reel of humorous advertising and showed those results. There was no point of contention. There are numerous case studies to prove that if comparative advertising is done correctly, it can be enormously effective."

. . . .

Postscript 2
THOUGHTS ON SOCIALLY RESPONSIBLE ADVERTISING

PROFESSIONALS IN EVERY INDUSTRY SOMETIMES FACE ETHICAL ISSUES. ADVERTISING PROFESSIONALS are no different. But advertising is seen by millions of people and decisions concerning ethical issues have immense impact. Although most of the people profiled in this book made a point of sharing their concern for sound ethics and social responsibility, Gargano spoke at great length on the direction advertising is taking and its impact on society. Here are some of his comments.

"I've often said that the kind of person you are is revealed in the most inconsequential acts you perform throughout the day. So people do reveal who they are through their work. And certainly when anyone creates advertising, they reveal a tremendous amount of information about their character. When I look at the work that is highly regarded by young people today, it tells me something about them. And, I find the bulk of today's work very disturbing.

"So much of it is created for shock value. All under the guise of being cool and hip and street-smart. I'm angered when an ad attacks my Italian heritage. Or, trivializes human suffering, minorities, the handicapped and even death.

"People think 'Hey, we're cool. Don't take it all that seriously.' But it's wrong. It's socially irresponsible because it trivializes. It's petty and degrading and encourages young people to embrace the same viewpoints.

"Death and violence have become something we casually accept because it's abundant on our television screens. A former president of Columbia Pictures noted that in a typical American film, 164 people get killed. And those deaths are never reconciled in the plot. No one ever thinks about the consequences of an individual's death—whether the individual was a villain, hero, pedestrian, bystander or whatever. Did he have a family? Did she have a husband? Were there children? What were the consequences of that death? It's never even brought up. The director simply cuts to the next scene.

"I can't believe those messages don't seep into our psyches. If children continue to get heavy doses of casual death on television, I gotta believe that over time it contributes to increasing crime and violence.

"Sometimes people lose sight of the power of mass media when they assume, 'You can do anything you want to. You can be outlandish and immoral if it's tongue-in-cheek.' I find that irresponsible and offensive. There has to be a sense of responsibility on the part of the people who create the ads and the clients who approve them."

CHAPTER TEN

Tomorrow morning when you get up, take a nice deep breath. It'll make you feel rotten.

It is said that taking a deep breath of fresh air is one of life's most satisfying experiences.

It can also be said that taking a deep breath of New York air is one of life's most revolting, if not absolutely sickening, experiences.

Because the air around New York is the foulest of any American city.

Even on a clear day, a condition which is fast becoming extinct in our "fair city," the air is still contaminated with poisons.

On an average day, you breathe in carbon monoxide, which as you know is quite lethal; sulfur dioxide which is capable of eroding stone; acrolein, a chemical that was used in tear gas in World War I; benzopyrene, which has produced cancer on the skin of mice; and outrageous quantities of just plain soot and dirt, which make your lungs black, instead of the healthy pink they're supposed to be.

At the very least, the unsavory elements in New York air can make you feel downright lousy. Polluted air makes your eyes smart, your chest hurt, your nose run, your head ache and your throat sore. It can make you wheeze, sneeze, cough and gasp. And because air pollution is responsible for many of those depressing "gray days," it may affect your mental well being. If you're a person who is easily depressed, prolonged exposure to polluted air certainly isn't doing you any good.

Of course, at its worst, air pollution can kill you. So far, the diseases believed to be caused, or worsened by polluted air are lung cancer, pulmonary emphysema, acute bronchitis, asthma and heart disease.

600 people are known to have died in New York during two intense periods of air pollution in 1953 and 1963. How many others have died as a result of air pollution over the years is anybody's guess.

Who is responsible for New York's air pollution problem? Practically everybody. Dirt, smoke and chemicals belche from apartment buildings, industrial plants, cars, busses, garbage dumps, anywhere things are burned.

But the purpose of this advertisement is not to put the finger on who's causing the problem. It's to get you outraged enough to help put a stop to it.

What can you, yourself, do about air pollution? Not much. But a million people up in arms can create quite a stink.

We want the names and addresses of a million New Yorkers who have had their fill of polluted air.

The names will be used as ammunition against those people who claim New Yorkers aren't concerned about air pollution.

If we can get a million names, no one can say New Yorkers won't pay the price for cleaner burning fuels, better enforcement of air pollution laws, and more efficient methods of waste disposal.

The cost of these things is low. A few dollars a year.

The cost of dirty air is higher. It can make you pay the ultimate price.

Box One Million
Citizens for Clean Air, Inc.
Grand Central Station, N.Y. 10017

Ed McCabe

"For a business that thrives on imagination, there's amazingly little of it in advertising," says Ed McCabe, writer, sportsman, adventurer, frustrated artist, and advertising legend.

Throughout this book, we've met creatives who've thrived because of their imaginations. In this chapter, we'll see how far you can go with just imagination—and some of the roadblocks that can come up along the way. McCabe has won almost every advertising award possible, winning more prizes in some years than entire creatively-based agencies, and was the youngest person ever inducted into the Copywriter's Hall of Fame.

McCabe's lack of formal training may have contributed to his success. "People tried to teach me the rules and I learned them all over a long and arduous period of time. And I learned all the writing styles, all the methods," says McCabe. "But I've never been a technique person. I try to identify the substance and put it in my work. I have an innate instinct for boiling things down to the most simple and naive way of presenting an idea."

When McCabe talks about the clients he's worked with, he talks in the first person. "We wanted *our* product to....They understood what *we* were doing....*Our* objective was to..." It shows his strong affinity for his clients' goals and may partly explain why longevity is a hallmark of his campaigns.

THE MAKING OF AN ADVERTISING LEGEND

LIVE BY YOUR INSTINCTS. MCCABE LEARNED TO FOLLOW THIS SIMPLE PHILOSOPHY EARLY IN life. At eight years old, after the death of his father, he got his first job. It was working in a Chicago newsstand. At 15, bored and with a history of juvenile delinquency, he dropped out of school. He was attending a tough public high school on Chicago's north side and felt he was only being taught how to survive. "And I already knew that," he says. These events forced him to rely on his instincts. "I had to make quick decisions. Friend or foe."

McCabe was first exposed to the profession shortly after leaving school. Needing a job, he went to an employment agency and the recruiter sent him on many interviews. But no one was interested. The recruiter tried everything. She even sent him to Spiegel Catalog to take an aptitude test for a copywriter position (the results said he'd make a better auto mechanic than copywriter, establishing McCabe's skepticism about testing right from the start). Finally, one day, the recruiter said, "I've got it. I'll send you to an ad agency. They'll hire anybody."

She advised McCabe to lie about having a high school diploma and sent him to interview at McCann-Erickson for a job in the mail room. McCabe got the job and earned a modest salary. But he kept his eyes and ears open. He took in everything and decided that the creative people have the most fun. He observed that the women were attractive, that the men were nice looking, and that they all drove nice cars and seemed to have a lot of money. McCabe was impressed.

After a few months, McCabe asked to transfer to the art department. There, he worked emptying water pots and cleaning brushes. The bull pen for the traffic department was nearby, which gave him an opportunity to get acquainted with the people in that area as well. He began to learn how the work flowed through the agency.

He also learned who worked on what account and how the work progressed. He noticed that one copywriter was perpetually behind in his assignments because he was having an affair with a woman in the art department. McCabe saw another opportunity. He went to the writer with a proposition, "I know you'd like to see your friend at lunch, but I also know you've got six ads overdue and a bunch of little trade ads to do. I'd like to try my hand, so why don't you let me help? What do you have to lose?"

The copywriter took advantage of this offer and gave him some assignments. His first ad was for International Harvester. A few months later the agency entered it in a competition and it won a merit award from the Advertising Club of Chicago.

McCabe continued to work on the copywriter's projects and, after about a year, he went to the copy chief with the portfolio he'd developed and asked to become a full-time writer. The copy chief refused to accept that anyone without a college degree—let alone without a high school diploma—could write ads. "I think it was an act of self-preservation," says McCabe. Since upper management had never sanctioned McCabe's writing activities and the copy chief had refused to grant him a promotion, he quit.

His next job was with Automatic Electric, a manufacturing subsidiary of General Telephone. The first ad he wrote there also won an award. Says McCabe, "I didn't know the rules, so I didn't get caught up in either playing by them or trying to break them." This gave him an edge in creating unusual—but appropriate—ads.

After two years at the telephone company, McCabe was attracted to the unique work being done at Doyle Dane Bernbach. He decided to pursue a career writing consumer ads. So he quit his job. "I always quit before getting another job," says McCabe. "I'm a dangerous kind of guy. I love to do things the hard way."

Once interested in advertising, McCabe read everything he could find on the field. He studied the people who were successful in the thirties and forties, people like James Webb Young, Raymond Rubicam, Claude Hopkins, and Albert Lasker. He observed that the greatest ads were simple, honest, and very obvious. He admired work like "A Hog Can Cross the Country Without Changing Trains—But YOU Can't!" for the Chesapeake & Ohio Railway Company.

McCabe also read Strunk and White's *Elements of Style* and the Harvard Classics. In addition, he had been writing Broadway-style shows, short stories, and poetry. In spite of his lack of formal education, he was clearly a writer.

But because there was a recession, he couldn't find a job. After more than seven months of unemployment, he decided to try his luck in New York. He went there with his then girlfriend. She was working as an assistant advertising manager of a bank in Chicago and wanted to learn copywriting. So McCabe helped her develop a portfolio. Says McCabe, "She comes to New York and gets a job as a copywriter at Macy's. The first day. Me, I can't get elected. I ended up as a cashier in Schrafft's."

For the most part, McCabe's portfolio consisted of trade and industrial advertising. Says McCabe, "There were not a lot of broad-minded people in advertising who could see how someone could make the transition to consumer." McCabe believes that this still is the case today because "people need to classify and categorize." Like Hayden (Chapter Six), his lack of consumer experience held him back.

McCabe finally took a job at an industrial agency, where he was asked to write 70-page technical brochures for such clients as General Electric. Topics included thermionic integrated micro modules. His goal was to convert what the engineers told him into English. Again, like Hayden, McCabe believes this experience helped him later in his career.

Still determined to do consumer advertising, McCabe continued applying to Doyle Dane Bernbach, as well as to other agencies. Around that time, Benton & Bowles introduced a campaign for Western Union that excited McCabe. It consisted of a picture of a telegram with the headline saying, "Ignore it." Then, on the telegram, it said, "Ignore a telegram? You can't." Says McCabe, "It was very powerful and epitomized everything I believed about good advertising."

So McCabe sent a telegram that said, "Ignore a telegram? You can't. That's why I'm sending this. I'm a copywriter and I need a job." Benton & Bowles called him for an interview. They kept him in a room for more than 45 minutes until he accepted a job. They kept bringing in new people to try to convince him to take the job. "They thought that DDB would hire me in a minute if they let me walk," says McCabe. "Little did they know."

What took so long for him to take the job? While waiting in the reception area, he began to have second thoughts about the agency because he saw some of their work that wasn't so terrific. Once on board, however, McCabe began working on television ads for Maxwell House Coffee and Gaines Dog Food. His first assignment was for Instant Maxwell House Coffee featuring an American theme using Norman Rockwell paintings. "It never ran," says McCabe. "But everybody loved it around the agency because it was unusual without trying to be unusual."

In another campaign, he had male celebrities like Edward G. Robinson and Vincent Price talking about cooking and coffee. "I was interested in cooking and thought that other men were interested in cooking, too," says McCabe. "And if I was going to use celebrities, I thought I should do something unusual and different."

At that time, Benton & Bowles was a hotbed of talent. McCabe worked with such creatives as Amil Gargano and Roy Grace. But aspects of Benton & Bowles, such as the politics and the feeling that he wasn't living up to his potential there, disturbed McCabe. His last straw, however, came during a client meeting. McCabe presented a print ad he'd written and tried to sell it to the client on the basis of its uniqueness. The client responded with a puzzled look and asked why uniqueness was so important. At that moment, after more than two years of employment there, McCabe decided there was absolutely no future for him at that agency. Says McCabe, "I couldn't work for any place that put up with a client that stupid."

McCabe still aspired to DDB, where he thought clients would be less conservative and stodgy, but they still wouldn't hire him. So he moved to yet another agency, and his career continued to grow. He won lots of awards for his work on such accounts as Elgin Watches and Chun King.

McCabe lasted at this agency for only six months. He quit because he disliked their management style. "I worked on projects and found out that three other guys were working on the same project," says McCabe. "I don't mind competition, but I don't like underhanded competition. Bosses would be selling their own stuff and using your work as a foil to feed their own egos. There's a lot of that in certain places in this business."

Again McCabe applied to DDB. And, again, no luck. So this time he took a job at Young & Rubicam, but he only lasted there for eight months. McCabe quit because he thought his Christmas bonus was too big. Says McCabe, "I tried to give it back because I thought if they gave that kind of money to someone who had only worked there for six months—and had done as little as I had—they probably gave other undeserving people all kinds of money. I inherently believed that you get rewarded for a job well done and not for simply occupying a seat. I told them so and they laughed at me. I decided to move on because, philosophically, I was a misfit."

Shortly before McCabe quit, a copywriter working under him said he was applying for a job at Carl Ally. This copywriter was only making $16,000 and the job paid $2,000 more. He applied, but wasn't hired. Since McCabe knew Amil Gargano from Benton & Bowles, he called him up and asked for the job. He had to cut his salary in half, but he took it.

While at Carl Ally, McCabe worked on consumer products (Salada Tea, Vespa Motor Scooters, Citizens for Clean Air) and won four major gold medals the first year and tripled his salary. "That's where I really made a big name for myself," says McCabe. Why was he able to make a bigger name for himself here than at his previous jobs? The management of the agency supported him, and he worked directly with the clients.

McCabe stayed at Ally for three years. "I created one of the greatest creative departments ever assembled. I had Marty Puris and Ralph Ammirati among others—it was all-star city."

But then McCabe received a long-awaited call from Bill Bernbach offering him a job. Finally. He met their key people, but when word got out that Bernbach was thinking of hiring him, middle management at DDB protested. Ten of them said that they were hoping to be considered for the position that Bernbach had offered McCabe. They weren't happy.

"I got wind of it and told Bernbach it would be very bad for his agency to hire me," says McCabe. "He agreed, and we were friends from then on."

But this offer gave McCabe the fire to seek more. Says McCabe, "It was my year. I felt I was very valuable to Carl Ally, Inc., and I wanted more stock than I had." He asked for a certain percentage, and they offered him half of what he wanted. Says McCabe, "I just couldn't see myself spending the rest of my life settling for half of what I wanted. I decided that the only way to get what I wanted was to work on my own."

Then Sam Scali called McCabe and asked him to recommend a copywriter because he and some others were thinking of starting an agency. "I called Scali back and said, 'Yeah, I have your man.' He said, 'Who?' I said, 'Me.'" So we negotiated for about five months. I told Carl I was leaving and announced that we were opening an agency.

Scali, McCabe, Sloves went into business in 1967—without clients or prospects. Their first client was Volvo, which happened to have been with Carl Ally. McCabe had done some work on Volvo, and they called asking if the new agency would be interested in pitching the account. McCabe said yes, they got the account and the agency was underway. Scali, McCabe, Sloves quickly became one of the top agencies in the world.

In 1978, the agency principals sold Scali, McCabe, Sloves to Ogilvy & Mather. Part of the agreement was that Ogilvy was barred from the premises. "We wanted to protect what we'd built," says McCabe. "They were good about it—as long as it worked. We ran it the same way we had always run it."

But eventually the focus shifted. As a division of a larger organization, pressure grew to maximize profits. McCabe felt that this was a mistake. He felt the goal should be to be the best agency. Then the profits would come. Suddenly, McCabe was taking the kind of clients he'd always wanted to escape—big companies who weren't interested in great advertising. Says McCabe, "As soon as you put profit ahead of principle, you're in trouble."

Consequently, in 1986, McCabe decided to take a few years off. He drove a car race in Africa, worked in a presidential election, wrote a book and went to art school. In 1990, he was drawn back to advertising and joined Beber Silverstein & Partners. Says McCabe, "I thought it would be nice to be in Miami half the year but after seven months I realized that was a mistake. I really need to run my own show."

In 1991, along with a group of investors, McCabe started McCabe & Company in New York. He quickly attracted a roster of clients that included Coleman Natural Beef, the School of Visual Arts, Maxell, Rally's hamburgers, and others.

McCabe says he doesn't know where he'd be if it weren't for advertising. He loves the field. Adds McCabe, "The most rewarding aspect of this business is the big successes; the most fun is the music sessions."

McCabe's Portfolio: Campaigns with Longevity

WHY DID THE CUSTOMER CROSS THE ROAD?

To buy my chicken.
Frank Perdue

I'm pleased to report that people are flocking to my chickens.

Good for me. But it may be bad for you.

Because if you aren't selling my tasty, tender, young Perdue chickens, many of your customers could be going over to the other side and buying from your competition.

This isn't just idle clucking either. I've got proof.

Between October 15th and November 15th alone, 10,000 New Yorkers called up requesting the names of the stores near them which sold Perdue chicken. Naturally, I told them.

A day doesn't go by when we're not swamped with similar requests by mail.

Recently, a New York chain tried a little experiment. They put my chickens on sale (?) at 39¢ a pound. Instead of their normal sale price of 29¢.

You know what happened? They sold just as many as ever.

All of which proves a couple of things.

People will go out of their way to buy a superior product.

And you can charge them a toll for the trip.

TASTY YOUNG CHICKEN
PERDUE
QUALITY GUARANTEED OR MONEY BACK

Call Tom Robinson, our Sales Manager, today and you can have your first shipment of Perdue chickens tomorrow. 212-245-8532.

Perdue

Perdue was the first branded chicken and Scali, McCabe, Sloves's assignment was to explain why it was better and worth more money than regular supermarket chicken. The solution was found in Perdue himself. "Frank Perdue was a fanatic about quality," says McCabe. "He was tough. He was insensitive and difficult, but it was all motivated by a dedication to quality."

McCabe didn't rely on research. He simply showed the man behind the product. "With chicken you buy in a butcher shop or grocery store, you don't know where it comes from," says McCabe. By using Perdue as a spokesman, McCabe humanized the product. To reinforce the image of quality, he included a money back guarantee.

Says McCabe about the campaign, "Six months after it was launched a copywriter asked me, 'Okay, you got Frank Perdue doing the advertising and winning awards. What are you going to do next?' I told him, 'That will still be running when you have blue hair.' More than twenty years later, it still is.

Coleman Natural Beef

McCabe got this account because the client had been at Perdue and knew that McCabe understood the product category. Also, it was in a category that McCabe believed in—natural, healthy foods. Says McCabe, "I was enthusiastic about it, which I think is critical."

McCabe had a great deal of information about consumers and their potential acceptance of the product. For instance, McCabe knew how much consumers would pay for it. However, he claims he couldn't have done it without further market research. He discovered some data that no one could have known, information that he built the entire campaign around.

One of the great revelations? While fat and cholesterol were issues, health-concerned consumers were really more concerned about food additives. They could control their fat and cholesterol intake through dieting, but they couldn't control their food additive intake if it were in everything they ate.

McCabe built the campaign in a week using the first research indications. Then he waited four more weeks for the full research to back up the direction he'd taken.

Says McCabe, "If someone would ask me how much time it takes to make an ad, I'd answer, 'five minutes.' But I may need six months to do the thinking that leads up to it. I mean, I could do a Marlboro poster in 30 seconds, but somebody spent two or three years beforehand thinking about developing the campaign. That's what's important."

One of the best
things about
new Goebel Beer
is that it doesn't taste
anything like
old Goebel Beer.

Goebel Beer

Early on, McCabe learned the importance of emotional appeal over intellectual argument. He was working on the Goebel Beer account. Says McCabe, "They had a horrible reputation in the Detroit market. Their beer had degenerated and become a joke."

To regain their foothold, the company launched a new beer. "It was fabulous," says McCabe. "It was the first draft beer in a bottle." McCabe created a campaign that made fun of the old product to convince everyone that this beer was better. Yet the sales didn't meet expectations.

One day, on the way to see the client, McCabe was talking to the cab driver and the subject of beer came up. "I asked him what kind of beer he drank," recalls McCabe. "He said, 'Bud.' I asked him if he ever tried Goebel. He said, 'Yeah, that's a great beer too.' And he played back factually and rationally every point presented in the campaign. Everything. You couldn't have asked for better research. So I asked, 'Then how come you drink Bud?' 'Cause I like Bud,' he answered. So intellectual doesn't do it. The job was to make him like the new beer more than he liked Bud. I don't know if that was possible."

FAT CARS DIE YOUNG!

Some cars destroy themselves in the mere act of carrying themselves around.

Burdened with tons of chrome and huge expanses of sheet metal, it doesn't take long for a car to collapse under the strain.

So in building a car that will live a long time, you must begin by acknowledging one basic fact. Fat on cars, as on people, can be fatal.

(1966—1970)

VOLVO. THE FAT-FREE CAR.

When we designed the Volvo, a lot of superfluous stuff was dropped.

A Volvo doesn't have five feet of trunk hanging out behind the rear wheels. Instead of a long, low trunk, it has a short deep one. It holds more than a Lincoln.

Do you think your car has to be that wide? No. It's only that wide because a designer wanted it to look low. We make a Volvo wide *inside*. By curving the sides of the body, including the windows.

A Volvo doesn't need a six-foot hood because it doesn't need a gigantic gas-guzzling engine to push all the fat around.

We use a smaller engine, chop off the hood and move the wheels out to the corners of the car for better handling. Like on a racing car.

That way we can also make the passenger compartment bigger. And end up with more front leg room than a Cadillac. More rear leg room than the biggest Buick made.

VOLVO LIVES!

Unfettered by fat, Volvos live to ripe old ages. We don't guarantee exactly how long that will be.

But we do know that 9 out of every 10 Volvos registered here in the last eleven years are still on the road.

If you don't believe us, look around. You can't miss an eleven year old Volvo. It looks a lot like a 1948 Ford.

Only not as fat.

Volvo

"Sometimes you have to develop the campaign based on where the market is going; not on where it is," says McCabe. When he first did the Volvo campaign, automobile advertising addressed styling and price. No one talked about safety and durability. "Research indicated that was the wrong way to go," says McCabe. The decision to position Volvo was based on instinct. "This is the artistry of advertising that most people still don't understand," says McCabe. "Advertising is about seeing into the future. If you can see into the future and put your product there, then you have a long-term success."

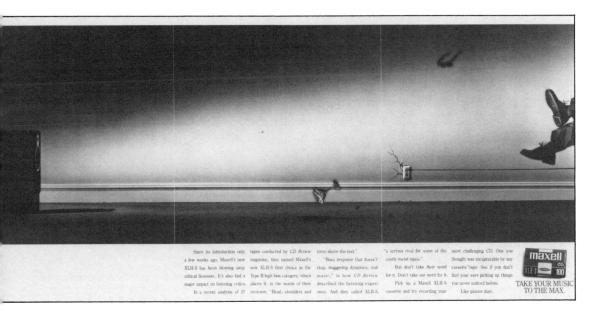

Maxell

Maxell is more a visually-oriented campaign. Says McCabe, "It's the one with the now-famous image of a guy being blown away in a chair." McCabe first handled this account while at Scali, McCabe, Sloves and, in 1991, his new agency took over the advertising. The trick of the campaign is to keep developing new ways of expressing the concept of being blown away by the sound quality. Says McCabe, "Any single image wears out, but the concept doesn't." The Maxell campaign has been running now for more than 15 years.

WORDS OF WISDOM FROM THE MOUTH OF MCCABE

HOW DOES MCCABE KNOW HE HAS A GREAT AD? THROUGH THE PRESSURE IN HIS STOMACH. Says McCabe, "If I don't get that, I won't even give it the intellectual time. I look for something uncategorizable. As soon as you categorize, you make it the same. It has to be something new, something that I've never seen before."

He hates advertising rules for the same reasons. Says McCabe, "As soon as you make rules, you've eliminated the whole concept of creativity. There are no 'no's' in advertising. There are understood tradeoffs."

"Of course, I read all the books," says McCabe. "Then I decided what I thought had merit and what didn't have merit. The problem is there are a lot of people who don't think. They just follow the stuff."

If you're ready to think, here are some ideas from McCabe to inspire you.

Know thyself

"Don't apply for a job in advertising until you know enough about yourself, what you believe and who you admire," says McCabe. "Then use some judgment in your approach. Do a little bit of homework." He says if you do a mass mailing of your resumes, there's almost a 100% chance he wouldn't hire you. Says McCabe, "It already shows a lack of judgment."

Know everything else

"You can't do anything until you know *everything*," says McCabe. "I execute under the gun, but I never conceptualize under the gun. It took five or six months to research Perdue and eight months to research Coleman. Sometimes it only takes three to five weeks. It depends on the complexity of the product." McCabe believes that's why speculative presentations are not a good and true test of an ad agency's skills. No one can possibly have enough information about the product or the market to effectively guide the creative. You need the research to direct you to a sound strategy.

Demonstrate how you think

"I want to see something indicative of the person," says McCabe, "his or her ability to be unexpected—yet sound. I'm not looking for off-the-wall ideas that make no sense. The answer should always grow out of the problem; and all problems are unique. I'm more impressed by someone who's done his or her homework than by someone with glib ads that aren't based on reality." McCabe realizes, however, that ads in a spec book may be a little off-base. Says McCabe, "No spec book is ever going to be as brilliant as work coming from people with the full facts in their hand."

Abandon the black book

Portfolios—and even how you approach an agency—should be unique the same way ad campaigns are unique. Says McCabe, "The answer should grow out of the problem." Unlike Ted Bell, he thinks the first step is getting rid of the black portfolio. "People are trying to convince me they are different, creative, and brilliant, but they've all got the same ads in the same black book," he says. He has been looking at books for 35 years and most don't hold his attention for more than the first 10 seconds. "The black portfolio inspires the first yawn. Then I open it and if I'm not absolutely blown away by the first ad, there's no reason in continuing because they've missed the whole point."

Build an image

"I'm not interested in day-after recall. I'm interested in a 10-year recall," says McCabe. He does that by maintaining a consistent image that builds brand recognition over time. "The ad is only one of the mediums you can use to build the image," he says. "When I get involved with a client, I try to get involved in all aspects of their image. We look at the uniforms employees wear, the design of the building, the graphics on the correspondence. Everything."

Make your own product assignments

"The selection process of picking assignments shows part of a beginner's creativity," says McCabe. "I think people should work on something they are knowledgeable about." When choosing products, stay away from the things everybody else selects—like insect repellants, No Doz, and Master Locks. "If I see another one of those, I'm going to jump out the window," says McCabe. "People tend to gravitate toward the easy products because there's an obvious story to tell."

Think simple

"I wasn't educated," says McCabe. "I was off the street, so I had an ability to talk straight to people without a lot of embroidery." That authenticity is what makes good advertising.

Aim to pass the "doorman test"

Not only does McCabe want his work to win awards, he wants it to create responses from real people. "It has to work on both levels," says McCabe. For instance, he knew that the Perdue campaign was a hit when the doorman of his building said, "I wish you hadn't done that campaign 'cause my wife keeps saying, 'Why can't you be more like him!'" The doorman's comments were a confirmation of the principles of the man in the campaign, which far transcends advertising. It has to do with making a national icon."

Be yourself

"I've hired more oddballs than anyone else in the business," says McCabe. He's hired a guy who drove a cab and whose pitch was he knew what makes people tick. He's hired a fallen priest. He feels anybody can learn to write copy. What he looks for is people who are able to cut through the boredom and humdrum of life and have a quirky way of looking at things. "You can teach a monkey to write the body copy for an ad," says McCabe. "But I can't teach anybody to think. Writing has to be in touch with humanity. There has to be a humanness to it, something that reaches people."

Speak honestly

Once, at Carl Ally, McCabe was interviewing a young art director and, as part of his questioning, asked which agency he thought was producing the best work. Instead of trying to be flattering and naming Carl Ally, the art director mentioned a different agency. This impressed and shocked McCabe so much that he hired the art director. Who was this art director? Mike Tesch, who went on to create some of the greatest campaigns at that agency.

Take on all types of projects

Some creatives have an attitude about the projects they're willing to work on. For instance, they think doing a matchbook cover is beneath them. "That never works for me," says McCabe. "Can you see Michaelangelo saying, 'I don't do ceilings.' I see that as juvenile idiocy." In fact, one of McCabe's favorite projects was writing copy for a matchbook. On the cover, the headline said, "Maybe you wouldn't smoke so much if you were happy with your job." Inside was information about a correspondence school.

Look for clients with potential

"I'm careful about choosing clients," says McCabe. "I look for products and companies that have the potential to explode in the future. At Scali, McCabe, Sloves, we took a lot of little clients and five years later everybody said, 'Where did you get all those big clients?' We made 'em big!"

Be wary of immediate acceptance

"If something is liked immediately, you should be very suspicious of it. As I said, advertising is about the future. Beethoven wrote a concerto and the violinist came in and said it couldn't be played. Beethoven answered, 'Oh yes, of course, it's meant for a later age.' That has a lot to do with advertising."

Work backwards

"There are many people in this world who look at something and see it for exactly what it is," says McCabe. "I don't know how to do that. I can only see it for what it could be. From there, I work backwards. Once you know where it could be, then you know where you're going." He adds that most people don't know where they're going. "That comes from taking the time to understand everything, from being able to form a credible and exciting picture of the potential. Once you know all that, it's easy."

• • • • • • • • • • • • • • •

Postscript
Advertising is Dead; Long Live Advertising

"You know why so much advertising is bad?," asks McCabe. "Because most agencies are corporations doing ads for corporations. But that's not what it's all about. We're in a business of communicating with people. Corporations can't do that.

"In the sixties work came out of Doyle Dane Bernbach as a breath of fresh air. People got excited."

McCabe thinks the advertising agency, as defined by most people, is a dead horse. "Ad agencies have no credibility outside of advertising."

As clients began recognizing the importance of such areas as direct marketing and sales promotion, advertising agencies were left behind. The big agencies, or "the mastodons" as he likes to call them, are too complex to accommodate rapid change. He says that only recently have agencies tried broadening their services. And they've only done it as a defensive measure. In order to catch up, they've tried buying existing companies.

"The communications thinking has to be across a wide variety of media, some of which might not be commissionable, but would add a great deal to the total message. I think that agencies should be paid a new way.

"I see this as a problem for agencies who have built their business, and their point-of-view on number crunching. They poured their money into broad-based media that returned easy money to them. But for agencies that realize there are different media vehicles to do the job, for creatives who are willing to take on all kinds of projects, the opportunity is an incredible one."

If this is your idea of a great catch,

this is your tackle box.

Contents™ Organizers have lots of cool ways to carry all your fancy lures.

C·O·N·T·E·N·T·S

Helps you carry it off.

Nancy Rice

"Make sure you merchandise yourself in your early years," says Nancy Rice, senior vice president, group creative director, DDB Needham/Chicago. "If you don't do this for yourself as well as you do it for your clients, then your career is not going to mean as much."

Rice is someone who knows how to merchandise creativity. She helped found two highly regarded creative agencies, Fallon McElligott Rice (FMR) and the former Rice & Rice Advertising, Inc., and has won numerous gold and silver medals in the Clios, The One Show, the Andy's, The New York Art Directors Club, The Athenas, Graphis, Print Case Books, and CA.

A 1970 graduate of the Minneapolis School of Art, Rice started with Knox Reeves Advertising (which merged with Bozell & Jacobs) as assistant art director and worked her way up to vice president, senior art director. She left the agency in 1981 to form FMR with four other partners and started Rice & Rice Advertising, Inc., in 1985 with Nick Rice. Rice joined DDB Needham/Chicago in 1992.

Rice lives in the Chicago suburbs. When she's not working, she enjoys using what she calls her "female skills"—cooking, remodeling, gardening, as well as raising her two teenage daughters. "I spend a lot of time with my kids outside of work. That can be, and still is, perceived as a negative in the industry—especially for females—but I don't care. My family is important."

A CAREER WITH ATTITUDE

WE'VE ALREADY LEARNED ABOUT PUTTING A PORTFOLIO TOGETHER AND CREATING GREAT ads—as well as other pieces of communication. Even what to expect in your first job. Now we need to explore ways to make your career blossom. We've already slightly touched on this subject when we looked at Susan Gillette's career (Chapter One). But in this chapter and the following two chapters, we'll focus more on ways to turn your talent into a successful lifelong career. Of course, we'll continue to look at great ads, as well as explore advice that will help you create them.

Nancy Rice didn't start out as someone determined to merchandise herself. In high school, she was the class artist, always drawing the posters to promote a function, and she simply figured there must be a way to make a living at it. To prepare herself, she enrolled in the Minneapolis School of Art. "It was not a terrific school for graphic design, much less advertising," says Rice. "But I met someone there who let me know about a job opening at a local art studio."

This studio did finished illustrations and provided keylining, comping, and rendering services for local ad agencies. After her second year of school, Rice landed a job cleaning their shelves and cutting mats. How did she get this job? "I could cut great mats," says Rice, "and I was willing to work for practically nothing."

But this gave Rice an opportunity to see how layout artists and illustrators worked and to get a feeling for what ads are like while they're being developed. "We'd get ads from local agencies to comp up so they could present their ideas to their clients," says Rice. "And I'd be mounting the comp ad and making it look all nice and I'd be saying, 'Can you believe this?' and 'What if they did this?' I rethought the projects the entire time I was there."

Nearing graduation, Rice planned to become a full-time employee at the studio. Instead, she was fired. Rice's supervisor—and one of the owners of the studio—said, "It's not that we can't use you. It's that we don't think this is what you should be doing. You really ought to be at an ad agency." To urge her in that direction, her boss offered her a list of people she could go see to get herself started.

Feeling hurt, she took his list and then went to the phone book to make a list of competing studios in Minneapolis. She planned to go work for one of them. "I'm going to show these guys," she thought to herself.

But with many recent graduates on the street looking for work at design studios, her competition was stiff. So her interviews included people from the list her ex-boss gave her. One of her last interviews was at an office building she had trouble finding. "The address just didn't make any sense to me," says Rice. "And I didn't have a car. I was on the bus and on foot."

She arrived an hour and a half late at the place—Knox Reeves Advertising—and met with Tom Donovan, who was the executive art director. "He seemed like a nice guy," says Rice, "and he asked me to wait so I could see the creative director."

When the creative director, Ron Anderson, came in and looked at her portfolio of student work, he hired her on the spot. But still determined to work at a graphic design studio, she figured she'd stay until she could find something better. Little did she know that she'd end up staying for eleven and a half years. "I started in May of 1970, a couple days out of art school, and stayed there until I left to form Fallon McElligott Rice," she says.

Rice says her book was not of the caliber that would get her a job in an agency today—or even back then. She believes she got the job because she could draw and their illustrator was quitting. "I think I was hired to fill the position of storyboard renderer," says Rice. "A lot of people can't draw coming out of art school in graphic design."

Rice also reports that she was aggressive about letting it be known that she needed a job, wanted the position, and wanted to start immediately. And she thinks the way she communicated during her interview helped. "It certainly was not my portfolio," says Rice. "I had some clunky package designs, some hand type renderings, and life drawings that were not particularly wonderful, and some keyline skills that were not marketable."

Most of what Rice did during her first year at Knox Reeves was assist other art directors by helping them comp their ideas and render storyboards. "A number of us there— about six or seven—were near the student level. We were not assigned to any particular piece of business. We were like buzzards looking for anything that would fall off the tables of more senior people," recalls Rice. "We took the projects they didn't want and tried to make something out of them."

Rice learned that the more she did, the more work her boss gave her. "It was like being thrown in a pond and getting a stone tossed to you. If you didn't sink, you'd get another one thrown to you," recalls Rice. "So the better you gave, the more you got."

Rice admits it wasn't a very nurturing environment. She didn't have someone to train her. "You had to go find it," said Rice. "Somebody else said this, but it describes my creative director's management style—'The Mushroom Theory'—which was keep 'em in the dark, feed 'em manure, and watch 'em grow." Her creative director did give feedback— if she sought it out. "The first time I asked for a raise," said Rice, "which was after about a year and a half, I was almost in tears. I asked, 'Am I doing OK or what?' 'Yeah, kid, you're doing great.' I had to ask for it."

In addition to her creative director (Ron Anderson, now chairman of Bozell), the executive art director also mentored Rice. "He was very patient, and he'd calm me down," Rice says. For instance, the first time she had an assignment to cover a photo shoot, she didn't know what to do. She wondered how to get from the layout to the final photo— and was afraid she'd get fired for not knowing. "I'd been working there a year and nobody told me what to do," says Rice.

She came in shaking. She wondered how to tell her boss that she didn't know what to do, and the executive art director took her through the process. "A lot of things in my early years were learned that way," says Rice. "And I'm still learning. I don't think you ever stop."

Since she didn't get much feedback from her bosses, she just did things that made sense to her and her writing partner. "We figured out what turned us on, what turned us off. We also talked about how we wanted to be spoken to as consumers," says Rice, "and we used those feelings as a guide."

For example, one of Rice's first campaigns was for West Publishing, one of the largest publishers of law books. West wanted to market their legal books to high school libraries. Since Rice and her writer teammate were closer in age to high school students than anybody else at the agency, they got the assignment. "We had to do ads that would pique the interest of high school library purchasing agents and key decision makers," says Rice. "We just did it from our point of view—why we'd be interested in reading an excerpt from a law book while in high school. They wanted to incorporate a direct response coupon. We didn't know anything about the science of coupons, so we didn't come in with any prejudices."

Their solution: a campaign explaining that students need—and want—to know their rights. In one ad, for instance, a row of people waited for a job interview with a Native American student in the foreground. The ad said that students should know their rights, and the laws against discrimination, when applying for a job. These and other issues affecting their lives are contained in these books. Another ad showed students protesting. A third one created controversy for the publisher; a visual of a pregnant teenager (in which Rice was the model). "We thought there was a growing need for kids to be aware of their rights," says Rice. "And it was very successful for them."

Like that campaign, most of the early campaigns Rice created were for clients of Knox Reeves' industrial division. "They didn't call it trade or 'business-to-business' advertising back then," recalled Rice. "And this division was in the basement—three floors down from the rest of the agency. The young teams were put on business that came out of that group. There were just a couple of people who worked down there. They were much older than the rest of the agency. And they were given all these down-and-dirty industrial accounts that noone wanted to work on except us. We saw these assignments as opportunities."

Rice and her peers were fascinated by the problem of trying to sell law books to libraries or refrigeration units to theaters. They'd ask themselves, how can we make this interesting? "I guess unattractive and dull products or products that were invisible to the consumer created a challenge we found exciting," says Rice. "It gave us the opportunity to do something wonderful and unexpected for the category and stand out in the publication. No one explained how a trade audience differed from a consumer audience, or what a sales force, a dealer, or a distributor was. They just sent us a job ticket, the size of the ad, and a stat of the logo. We had to figure it out for ourselves. Perhaps it was our naiveté that helped us do terrific stuff."

Rice realized that the people who bought business-to-business products were consumers, too. "Obviously if the product was good and performed a service, we would find its strength, where it could compete and win," said Rice, "and we did unusual, but relevant work."

The main thing Rice learned early in her career was that anything has the potential for being the subject of a powerful piece of communication, even with a small budget. "I've found that the bigger the budget, the glitzier the product or service, the more restrictions there are on the creativity," said Rice. "It's also harder to get through the layers of management on bigger pieces of business, both on the client and agency sides."

One of the first events that cemented Rice's attitude that an ad for anything can be great—and her first award-winner—was an ad she created for a little liquor store. Her first challenge was to create an ad that would be approved by the city liquor commissioner. The advantage was that this store had a huge selection with the lowest prices. However, state law prohibited them from directly stating that they were the cheapest. They had to figure out ways of communicating this message without actually saying it. Their solution: a visual of the price sticker on a wine bottle and the headline, "Of the 2,500 labels we sell, the most impressive is the one we stick on in the store."

The ad was also created on a very tight budget. Rice had to hand press the headline herself. She and a photographer went over to the liquor store, pinned up construction paper behind a bottle, and shot the photograph themselves. The newspaper created the half-tone. "The photo was done for a song," says Rice. "And it got all these awards." What's more, this ad won in a category the U.S. Army had entered—and Rice ended up with a higher award than they did.

"That was the first time it really, genuinely occurred to me that in this industry, it's the strongest idea that counts. It didn't matter that we produced our ad for about $100 and the Army had God knows how much," said Rice. "That told me I was on the right track. Don't be uptight if you don't have a flashy client or a big budget. What's important is the idea, how the idea is said, and that it's graphically refreshing."

During her eleven and a half years at Knox Reeves, Rice took on more and more responsibility. She worked with many different writers and became executive art director and one of the first female vice presidents within that organization. "That was where I met Tom McElligott," says Rice. "He was just another staff writer I worked with from time to time."

Her partnership with Tom McElligott led to the next stage of her career. Fallon McElligott Rice simply came about because three people got together and decided to start an agency. "Tom and Pat (Fallon) had worked together as freelancers," says Rice. "When I was approached, they had already decided to start an agency."

Rice took about a month to consider the move before she signed on. Once on board, however, they planned for a year before they resigned from their respective agencies and formed the business.

Within that year, they developed a business plan, and Rice and McElligott worked on some freelance projects, so they'd have accounts up and running as soon as the agency opened. Their goal was to have highly visible and award winning projects. They wanted to use these projects to set the tone for the agency. "A lot of agencies are built on a strong creative philosophy, but the philosophy isn't universally held by everyone in those organizations," said Rice. "We wanted to set up what we thought was the ideal situation—a situation where everyone involved in the agency truly believed that our only edge was creativity."

Rice says that having an entire agency built on that philosophy was something that all the principals hoped to achieve. "We wanted to be the best creative agency in the nation," said Rice. And they wanted to do it in Minneapolis. "All of us had families here," she adds, "and we didn't want to leave."

FMR was successful from the beginning. Some of their early ads won awards that brought them national headlines. They wanted the recognition for two reasons. First, they knew this would make potential clients notice the work they were doing. And they knew this would help them recruit top talent. "We merchandised ourselves through the national headlines we got by winning the awards," Rice says. "We liked that kind of visibility."

Rice's philosophy of advertising was manifested—as well as universally embraced—at FMR. "There wasn't an army of people who had different views of how an agency should work," she says. "Everyone was working together." Because of this, FMR was only small for a short time. "I guess the small and tight part was really only in the first year or two," says Rice. "Then we grew."

With FMR, Rice achieved everything she wanted—an agency totally committed to creative advertising. "It was a great experience," says Rice. "I loved the clients. I loved the staff. I started doing some of the best work of my career. We were able to attract a lot of national clients that we first thought would never come to the Midwest."

All of FMR's clients—from a little church and a company that made camping gear to *The Wall Street Journal* and *Rolling Stone* magazine—genuinely believed that smart, well-targeted, thoughtful advertising with a creative edge made a difference to their bottom line. "I found I did my best work for clients who truly believed that," says Rice.

Rice to this day refuses to go into detail about why she left FMR, saying only that it had nothing to do with the staff, the clients, the kind of work they were doing. She only states that there were growing ethical differences between her and her partners. So, after five years as a founding partner, Rice left to form yet another agency.

As a business, her new agency, Rice & Rice, Inc., made a conscious effort to support companies and seek out clients that had a commitment to social responsibility. "This was long before it was trendy," says Rice. "I've always felt strongly about environmental issues and parts of society that don't seem to get a fair shake." She and her husband, Nick, ran the award-winning agency for five years. I am champion of the citizens."

Today, Rice is with a much larger organization, DDB Needham, but her philosophy remains the same. "I'm still working with a group of people willing to do anything to do great work," she says. "I still believe, as someone said, that creativity is the last legal means of gaining an unfair edge over your competition."

Outside of work, Rice is family oriented. Most of her friends also work in the industry as art directors, writers, photographers, illustrators, and typesetters.

"It's really a fun industry," says Rice. She hopes that the bad times the industry is going through do not discourage beginners. "Budgets will get better," says Rice. "But it's not a good time to be a beginner right now. It's a good time to be a well-rounded profit center for the agency."

ADS CREATED WITH AN ATTITUDE FOR GREATNESS

Rolling Stone

The One Club called this one of the 10 best campaigns of the '80s, the only print campaign to make their list. It very simply repositioned the magazine in the minds of potential advertisers. This was one of the last campaigns Rice created at FMR.

Rice thinks that each piece of communication should have one idea and not try to say everything. "Have one strong message that can be communicated and acted upon or thought about," she advises.

Episcopal Ad Project

This campaign was started by McElligott and Rice a year before founding FMR, and was then claimed by them when they started. The client followed Rice when she went on to form Rice & Rice. The concept came about because a clergyman asked a simple question, "Why do I have to run classified ads that include lillies or manger scenes? Why can't I run bright, smart ads that tell people the way I think?"

Each ad explores a different position taken by the Episcopal church: that single people are part of the "family" and will find a home there; that it shouldn't just be parents who attend, they should also bring the children; that the church explores all aspects of life. "There were also some fairly strong ads against TV Christianity," says Rice. "That's the only form of worship we attacked and that was because of the clergyman who spearheaded the project."

Rice claims that this campaign is just another form of evangelism. "It's getting the word out in a way that's closer to selling a car, so people will be more interested in hearing what we have to say," says Rice. "All we're trying to communicate is that here is a community that feels a certain way, and if you feel this way too, come join us."

Without God, it's a vicious circle.

The Episcopal Church

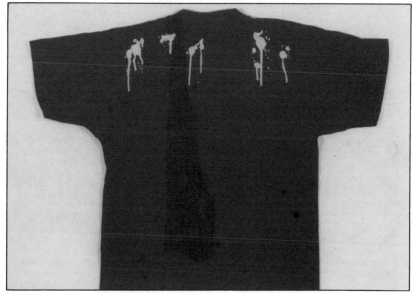

Chickens

"It's exciting to take a fresh viewpoint to solve a problem," says Rice. "Coming in without a lot of pre-conceived notions is an advantage." In this case, it's especially true.

Rice believes that ads should be treated like road maps to information. "The fewer detours and barriers you have, the better chance you have with consumers who have short attention spans and much better things to do than read ads," says Rice. "And you want to let them know you appreciate that they've taken the time to stop. You want to reward them by giving them something to take away that's going to be of value to them. That's the approach I take when creating ads."

Brainstorming roughs

This is how Rice comes up with ideas. She draws tiny boxes and sketches in the visual and headline. She and her writer partner go through the thumbnails and pick the best ones. They decide which will work best as magazine ads, as posters, as outdoor boards, or as another type of communications piece. "We ask ourselves which can use a photograph," says Rice, "and which can be done in all type."

Typically, this is as tight as Rice gets before deciding which ideas to present. Rice's next stage is to produce a bigger rendering by blowing up the thumbnails in the copier to keep the same balance.

Rice recognizes that everybody works differently, but thinks that generally this is as tight as you need to be in your portfolio. "Sometimes it's important to make them a little tighter," Rice adds. "It depends on what you're trying to show. Drawings are fine. There are no rules."

Agency announcement

Here's proof of Rice's attitude that any piece of communication—regardless of format, budget, dead-line, size—can be a gem. Many creatives look at little announcements as something to get out of the way quickly. Rice looks at them as chances to create an award winner. And this one has won many awards, including a One Show. "What's been most successful for me over the years is having the goal," says Rice, "to make something out of anything."

Farmers aren't about to let a lifetime of work slip through their fingers again.

The problems farmers face in the 1980s are different than the problems farmers faced in the 1930s. That's why the solutions have to be different.

Farmers aren't getting the answers they need from Washington. But they are getting answers from the farm. From a breed of farmer who's not afraid to take chances. Who is as likely to be raising mushrooms and alligators as corn and hogs.

At Successful Farming magazine, we think this farmer has something to say.

And we're going to help them say it. We're sponsoring ADAPT 100, a conference where farmers from across the country will get new ideas to help them adapt to a changing farm economy.

Thousands will attend. And hundreds of thousands more will read about it this February, in our special ADAPT 100 issue.

They'll be reading about the most exciting, innovative ideas to come out of agriculture in years. They'll be reading the ads, too. Which is why it's important for any company involved with farming to be involved in this special issue.

For more information, contact your nearest Successful Farming sales executive. Or call Gil Spears, collect, at 515-284-3118.

And call today. Before this opportunity slips through your fingers.

Successful Farming Magazine

"About 80% of my career has been selling business-to-business related products and services," says Rice, "and the other 20% has been selling to the general public." Rice says she likes selling to the public because of the high visibility of the communications. But she recognizes that business-to-business has its rewards, too. "You learn a lot," she says, which is one reason she has not yet considered going to the client side. "That seems so limiting, just doing one thing, working for one client."

Whatever the product, Rice always tries to look at it from a different point of view. She is not concerned when others in the industry think that it's a dull product (it's never dull to the people who need it). Finally, most advertising problems have similarities. "You apply many of the same principles no matter what the assignment is," she says.

Again, this was just a little trade ad, something most creatives would try to avoid or get out of the way. Rice, instead, created something that gained her and the magazine a lot of recognition.

SOME KERNELS OF TRUTH FROM NANCY RICE

YOU'VE ALREADY HEARD RICE'S MOST IMPORTANT ADVICE—THAT SINCE ANY COMMUNICA-
tions piece can be great, you should try to make the most out of every assignment you
get. "This attitude helped me when I started," says Rice. She thinks it's beneficial to create invitations for seminars, agency parties, little space ads, sales kits, materials for agency
pitches, mail aheads, leave-behinds, Christmas cards, and even birth announcements. "I'd
even give away my time to do it," says Rice. "It's amazing what you can make out of
them. And they start getting you some visibility."

Rice says she hears excuses like "I never get to meet the client," or "I never get to
sell the work." Her response: "Who cares!," she says. "If you decide that the account is a
dog or feel it's an insignificant piece, your attitude is never going to work for you." She
thinks that you have to sniff around and make it great. Once you have something, then
you have a right to complain. "The biggest barrier people face is a supervisor who doesn't
have the ability to recognize a good idea or carry it forward," she says.

But this attitude is not enough. There are other things you must consider. So to help
you along, here are some more ideas and suggestions from Nancy Rice.

Team up

Like Ted Bell (Chapter One), Rice thinks
that aspiring art directors and copywriters
should work together. "The majority of
good schools really push that team spirit
and let you know you are not all by yourself. It's your group that influences the
ideas that go into an ad," says Rice. "It's
smart to work with a teammate while
putting portfolios together. Sometimes
I've even said, 'Well, look up this person
we just interviewed the other day. Here's
her address. She has some good ideas,
you have some good ideas. Why don't
you get together and work on your
books?'"

Learn to be a quick study

In advertising, you have to be able to get
up to speed quickly. "The best way I ever
heard the demands put was by a copywriter who said, 'When changing agencies, I started one week finishing some
spots for Crispy Wheat and Raisins at one
agency and ended the week at a new job
writing trade ads for Honeywell Mach 4
torpedoes," says Rice. (Even within an
agency, you will have to change gears
quickly.)

Find good-quality products and services to work on

"It's hard for me to manufacture the 'up'
that I think is necessary to sell products
and services," says Rice. "If I think a

product is a dog or the people on the client side are dogs to work with, I have trouble providing a good service." Even early on, Rice turned down working on a product she didn't believe in. "If I thought it was genuinely bad," she says. "They'd find something else for me to work on."

Picture someone very specific

Rice believes you should be able to say, "Yes! This is the person I want to convince that this is a relevant piece of information about a service or product at this certain point," because this helps you focus your message. To do that, as well as to identify the strongest attribute and arena, Rice believes in research. For research ideas, see Chapter Five (Roy Grace). Rice's advice is similar. "In the beginning, it's not always possible to be very sophisticated about the research you do," says Rice. "You could pick a local dry cleaner, learn a little bit about them, go in and talk to the owner, and learn a little more."

Say only what matters

"I think it's important to find the strongest attribute of a product or service," says Rice, "to find an arena where you have a chance of winning." How? By knowing the product, the competition, and the people who will buy or use the product. "There may be 15 important things to say, but you must separate out those things and only communicate what will be perceived as a benefit."

Execute your ideas

"One thing that attracts me to a book is the ability to put ideas down; the fact that you don't need three assistants to render your ideas," says Rice. "I'm not talking about layout skills. I'm talking about how you create balance in a piece of communication. It's hard to teach that. It's less important to have things highly comped and rendered. It's more important to have a good idea in a rough form than a bad idea perfectly rendered, unless what you're going for is a rendering position, which is what I did."

Know where you're interviewing

Rice recognizes that not everybody wants to—or can—work in New York, Los Angeles, Chicago, or some other major advertising center. "It's more important to know about the agency and the creative director than the true market situation of the products or services in your portfolio," says Rice. "If you have a target city, get to know the agencies there and who's doing the good work. Get smart about your area."

Promote (merchandise) yourself

"I find that there's a lot of work out there that's very good, but the creative teams are fairly anonymous," says Rice. "Creative people should make sure they're visible with their work—whether it's through award shows or simply through joining advertising clubs and meeting people."

Get a job

"A lot of times, your first job won't be the best," says Rice. "But it gives you access to other talented people and some equipment. You can start building your book with your work. You might be in a group that's maybe not doing the best stuff, but you're getting a paycheck and experience. If you think, 'I can't believe what they're doing; it could be wonderful,' then do your own approach and put it in your book. If there's another person at the agency who has the same feelings—or even at an agency down the road—get together, talk about each other's accounts, and make it happen."

Make sure the team supports the idea

"Many times a team member will not have the same vision you have and will end up sabotaging the effort," warns Rice. "That's the most frustrating. When you sell an idea to a client, it's important that everybody supports it. Otherwise, it makes the client nervous."

Freelance

"There are a lot of decent little businesses that can't afford huge agencies. It's too bad a number of these places aren't a little smarter and advertise that they'd produce a good campaign if a young creative team wants to come in and do it," says Rice. "Find a client who won't burn you; make sure the client can at least pay the out-of-pocket expenses. Then use it as a way to get some work produced and to merchandise yourself."

Volunteer for pro bono work

"Good ideas are good ideas no matter who they're for," says Rice. "Actually, pro bono work is not that easy. You can run into a lot of committees who don't know much about advertising. But, on the other hand, it can be fantastic. It benefits a good cause and it gets you working with clients. Who cares whether you had to sit in a meeting and go through eight months of work to produce some advertising for someone. Is it good work? Did it do something for somebody?"

Enter awards shows

"There's been a lot of industry whining about whether creative people are doing real work for awards shows," says Rice. "They'll go and create some ads and give them to the local dry cleaner who runs them in the local newspaper. Then they enter them in shows and get a lot of publicity and awards. I think people who go around and create terrific things for little clients should be rewarded, not punished. You tend to find more of that being done in agencies where people aren't being given the opportunity to do good work; they'll go out and seek things like that." Since awards shows can get you publicity, you should consider entering them, too.

Treat vendors with respect

"Most people in this business have quite a few jobs along the way," says Rice. "The people who will stick with you and work with you wherever you go (as well as help you) are the suppliers—the printers, photographers, typesetters. So make sure they're treated as team members."

Rice warns that you should always remember you're building a career that will span many places and not one position at one agency. "I don't say that to be disruptive to team spirit," she says, "it's just that, although I've only had four advertising jobs, most people at my level have had six to twelve."

Be prepared for coincidences

"I've had my ideas show up in someone else's book. Once it was an ad that a client had rejected. There was no way the person could have seen it. So I hired him because I knew he was thinking along the same lines as me," says Rice. "But replicating an idea—either on purpose or by mistake—happens quite a bit. I've done it. I've produced an idea and then found it in a 20-year-old book. That happens. It's impossible to know everything that's ever been done."

Show you're hungry

Rice believes that your presentation is important. "If there were five people interviewing for a position and they all had great art direction and great ideas, the one that would get it is the one who showed the desire, drive. That person must really want the job," says Rice. "Show that you're willing to take any type of assignment and that you're aspiring to do great work. Most people come in wanting to work on the agency's prime accounts. The reality is, you're not going to get those."

Get a life

"It's important to have time away from your agency, time to travel, read, go to films, listen to music, play with the kids," says Rice. "If you want to think of it from a materialistic point of view, all those experiences will make you a better ad person. It gives you material to draw on. Dull people make dull ads."

Keep your eyes and ears open

"Ideas come from everywhere," says Rice. "Sometimes the best ideas happen on a boat or in a shower. It's your life outside the agency that gives you your ideas." Rice believes it's important to talk and listen to everyone. "Bounce ideas off other people," says Rice. "Not necessarily your creative teammate, but others in the agency—the receptionist or the accountant. Clients have wonderful ideas, your kids have ideas, even your next door neighbors have ideas."

Make unwanted advances known

"I was once removed from a piece of business because a client physically came on to me," says Rice. "I complained and ended up being taken off the account. That made me angry, but I was in no position to control my destiny at that point. That happens a lot in this business. It happens conversely, too. Clients go after young men. If it happens, go and complain to your supervisor and make it well known. Visibility is the best defense. If it's covered up at your agency—if that's their attitude toward young women or men—you should probably get the hell out."

Postscript
THOUGHTS FROM A CLASS

THROUGHOUT THIS CHAPTER, WE HEARD ABOUT THE ATTITUDE YOU MUST TAKE TO CREATE breakthrough work—no matter what kind of product or service you're selling. Since attitude plays such a big role in your early years, let's spend a little more time on this subject. Here are the thoughts that Rice presented to a graduate class she taught at Syracuse.

"Rice opened the three-day seminar with the following words: "The fact that you're paying money to be here at the high point of the tourist season tells me that you either really love the advertising business or you're having a very dull summer. Let's hope it's the first one.

"I understand that this group is composed of individuals who have probably spent a lot of time poring over years of advertising and design awards books like CA, Graphis, Print, One Show. And if you haven't, shame on you.

"On those pages, you'll find the best collection of what's hot and very little of what's not, and it may have already occurred to you that as you're paging through those books, you're seeing great work for clients like Levi's, Apple Computer, and Dove Bar, that it's going to be a long time before you'll ever get a chance to work on great products like those. They're probably spending about a zillion dollars on ads for television. How long will I have to wait before I can do great stuff like that? How long before I can get anyone to notice me? I want to work on a great account at my agency. I

want to work at a good agency. I want my first job. I want to change jobs. My creative director just doesn't get it. I've got great stuff in me now, I just don't know how to get it out. Because I have such small accounts. My accounts are dogs and I want to show what I can do.

"The problem is not your accounts. The problem is your attitude. Many of the people who you admire, who are doing those big accounts now, started just that way. And now we're going to do an assignment together. This is what we're going to do.

"I asked you to bring in the Yellow Pages from your hotel room. We're going to go through here, pick out a client and find out about that place. By tomorrow morning you are going to come back in and you're going to have picked the client, you're going to have called them up and we're going to fill in these positioning statements. We're going to decide who these clients are, who you're trying to reach, and what you want to tell them about your business. Whether it is true or not, it's going to be set in stone by the end of class tomorrow.

"And then we're going to talk about how to do some ads around it. And then we're going to come in with some sketches and that's as far as we're going to go.

Rice concluded the seminar with these comments: "This exercise was to just develop an attitude that no matter what it is, it can be exciting. We picked tiny little insignificant things. Some people picked brick manufacturers. A place that made American flags. A place that taught square dance. I did the assignment the night before I came and we picked a tattoo parlor (in portfolio section). The fact is, you can approach almost everything you do this way. No matter what it is, you can do something exciting.

"And that was the whole basis for the three days. That's what we talked about: The fact that you don't have to wait; that you can do terrific work on what you have right now; that you can start making yourself visible with what you have at your finger tips."

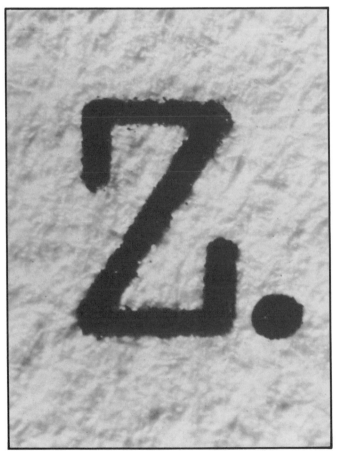

Lee Clow

"My portfolio is my credentials. It shows what I've been able to do in this business. So developing it is where I place my focus." That comes as an unexpected comment from a man who has worked at one agency for most of his adult life and is generally considered one of the most illustrious art directors practicing today.

Whether you plan to parlay your portfolio into a new position or stay in the same agency, Lee Clow, president/chief creative officer of Chiat/Day, emphasizes the importance of continually improving it. Throughout this chapter, you'll learn how focusing on your portfolio produces the best solutions for you—and your clients.

Throughout his career, Clow has demonstrated that his approach works. He has won numerous advertising awards, including a Cannes Film Festival Gold Lion. His work has helped launch the Macintosh for Apple, as well as produce outstanding results for Porshe, Nissan, Nike, Yamaha, Pioneer, and Pizza Hut. And under his creative leadership, Chiat/Day is considered to be one of the best agencies in the country.

A California native, Clow grew up on the beach with a surfboard, the sun, the surf, and a transistor radio playing Beach Boys tunes. That was Clow's youth, and it may have helped him learn to ride the waves of a volatile business. He feels lucky to be able to use his talents in such a rewarding and exciting way. And he feels lucky to have found a partner, whom he describes as his anchor. His wife of 24 years understands his intensity and passion for his work and encourages him to pursue it. He has two stepdaughters, who are now married, four grandchildren, and many dogs.

FROM SURFBOARDS TO ART BOARDS

ALTHOUGH MOST OF THE PEOPLE FEATURED IN THIS BOOK COMMUNICATED THEIR EARLY passion for creative work, that sense of drive isn't always a necessary ingredient for successfully beginning a career. Instead of the focused and uncompromising passion for communications that he'd later show, Lee Clow's early years were spent enjoying the sun and surf. His career goals were secondary. This doesn't mean he magically developed an interest in art later in life. In fact, this interest dates back to first grade.

Lee Clow was one of those kids who could paint a train and make the smoke rise in the right direction from the smoke stack. He was lucky enough to have a teacher who told his mother of his artistic talents—and a mother who encouraged him, rather than insisting he be a lawyer or a doctor.

By the seventh grade, he was sure that he wanted to be a commercial artist, but he wasn't sure what that meant. And by the time he went to Santa Monica Junior College, his interests broadened to include graphic design and advertising art direction. But he doesn't pretend to have been a dedicated art student. In fact, he was actually more dedicated to his surfing. "I thought someday I'd be a commercial artist, but not now," he says. "I was working in a bowling alley at night, so I could surf during the day. Those were my priorities."

He had learned about Art Center College of Design, but never had a burning desire to attend. Nor did his parents have the resources to support him as a full-time student in an expensive school. So, he worked to pay for art classes and enjoyed the beach.

Attending college in the sixties had benefits beyond an education. Full-time students were exempt from the military draft. So, like many people at that time, Clow enrolled in junior college as much to avoid fighting in Vietnam as to keep his artistic juices flowing. But because of his lack of academic enthusiasm, he let his credits drop below the "safety zone" and the draft board snatched him up.

Ironically, being drafted was good for his career. That's because the Army realized Clow's artistic talents and graced him with a peaceful position as draftsman/illustrator. "I thought it was kind of charming of the Army to offer me such a position before telling me to grab a rifle and fight," recalls Clow. He was assigned to White Sands Missile Range where he worked on a variety of design projects.

Without surfing to distract him, he actually became more committed to developing a career. He started investigating the options and discovered that Long Beach State College had a very good design curriculum and an excellent art department.

When he was discharged, he enrolled there. But Clow wasn't motivated enough to stick around for graduation—or for the portfolio development classes. "I still wasn't focused on what type of career to pursue," he says. "So I had a varied portfolio of everything from illustration to lettering to advertising design projects."

He considered becoming an illustrator, but after doing a few illustration assignments, he was frustrated. Says Clow, "I found it to be very one-dimensional and uninteresting to execute someone else's idea."

Finally, he found a job in a Santa Monica design studio doing mostly production. This gave him the opportunity to associate with trained graphic designers. One designer, who had graduated from Art Center College, talked to Clow about developing an advertising portfolio. He suggested Clow needed more focus. His work wasn't showing that he knew how to apply his talents. He also heard he should go to New York to break into advertising. But his affinity for the California sun and beaches would not allow him to sacrifice the West Coast environment for the concrete caverns of New York. He wanted to stay near the ocean while pursuing a career.

Working at the design studio gave him a chance to study *Communication Arts* magazine, as well as numerous awards annuals. He became absorbed in the difference between illustration, graphic design, and advertising. "I realized that graphic design and illustration were terribly one-dimensional career paths. What I really loved were the ideas," he says. Advertising art direction, both television and print, went beyond type, graphic design, and illustration to the development of a total message. In addition, advertising during the sixties was making many breakthroughs in communicating messages. That's what made it exciting to Clow, so he decided to funnel his enthusiasm into building an advertising portfolio.

Adding to his enthusiasm was another associate who had worked for Young & Rubicam and had become disenchanted with advertising. He shared experiences that gave Clow insight into how insane the business could be. One such story involved the McDonald's account. His friend, who had been working on the account, was in a meeting where the group was examining a dye transfer. All of a sudden he found himself in the middle of a heated argument. They were going crazy because McDonald's always put three pickles on a hamburger and the model only had two pickles. They would have to retouch the photograph for the print ad. The account people were tearing their hair out because the deadline would be missed and the account would be in jeopardy.

His friend, finding himself in this incredibly high-stress situation over a pickle, thought, "I can't deal with this. These people are about to have a heart attack over how many pickles should be on a hamburger. It's absurd. I gotta get out of this business." He moved to the design firm where his life was simpler and warned Clow about advertising's craziness. Clow felt a little intimidated, but the warning also challenged him.

This associate also offered advice on what to include in a portfolio—and what to exclude. Clow included some four-color jobs only because they demonstrated he'd actually had them produced. Yet, he admitted he wasn't too excited about the work. His friend explained that a portfolio should represent *the best* work, whether it's produced or not. He advised Clow to create his own assignments. "This is when I learned your portfolio is probably the most important piece of communication you'll work on throughout your entire career," he says. "It shows your level of quality, taste, judgment, and ability." That led him tobecome incredibly critical of the content.

To create a strong network, Clow then joined the junior advertising club in Los Angeles. Although most of the organization's members were account people, they took on pro bono projects, offering Clow the opportunity to produce creative work, as well as meet other people in the business. "When creatives work for free, clients can't be too critical of the quality of your thinking or execution," he says. "So it was a very good opportunity to learn what works."

Clow soon found a job at a small advertising agency, and quickly moved on to N. W. Ayer's office in Los Angeles. "At first, I felt intimidated," he says. "The large agency was filled with well-educated people wearing suits and ties." But Clow soon learned there are fewer talented people in the business than he expected. To him, it seemed their energies were motivated more by fear and defensiveness than smart thinking. "I found that lots of people were more worried about keeping their clients happy rather than finding the smartest answer to the communication problem. They were less the caliber of managers, executives, or administrators than I expected," he says. "So I wasn't as in over my head as I thought I might be."

Gradually, Clow gained confidence. He realized that many creatives just job-hopped, still doing the same caliber of work, and understood that that could stifle his career. Instead he polished his portfolio. His goal was to get into Chiat/Day. He wanted to work there more than anywhere else.

He called on Hy Yablonca, who was the creative director there, and customized his resume for the interview. The meeting was scheduled for noon, during his lunch break, but when he arrived, he was informed that Yablonca had just left for lunch. Clow decided to wait it out—for an hour and fifteen minutes. When Yablonca stepped off the elevator, Clow caught a flash of embarrassment on the creative director's face. Clow believes the embarrassment over missing their meeting may have been why Yablonca took an inordinate amount of time going through his portfolio. Even so, the interview concluded with, "I just hired a guy. I wish I had met you last week. Now, we don't have anything."

That was all Clow needed to hear. He was encouraged to continue sending samples to remind Yablonca that he was still available. Finally, Yablonca hired him as an art director, a move that he still wonders about. He's still not sure whether he was hired so he'd stop sending his monthly mailings or because they really wanted him.

"I often wonder if my life would have been different if Yablonca had remembered that first meeting and not felt a little guilty. He might have shuttled me in and out in 10 minutes in order to make his lunch date," he says. "To this day, Jay Chiat insists I only had one piece in my portfolio that he liked—and that was a menu design."

Clow swallowed a cut in pay to join the agency. But working there wasn't about money. It was about learning and opportunity. Chiat/Day was the "graduate school" of the advertising business—a great agency that cared about great advertising. It was an agency where everyone was expected to get up in the morning thinking up wonderful ads for their clients. With every assignment Clow thought, "I want this to be as good as anything that's ever been done in advertising." He worked as diligently as he could to create the work that matched the best in the business—which, at the time, came from New York.

But being a perfectionist is frustrating. "Nothing was good enough," recalls Clow. "I saw every wart and flaw." That insecurity, combined with an intense commitment to create the best work in the business, caused Clow's work to keep getting better and better. It wasn't long before Clow's recognition earned him the title of group art director/group creative director, and then creative director of the entire Los Angeles office.

"About halfway through my stay at Chiat/Day, I realized I am going to stay on this bus until it gets to the end of the line," says Clow. "So I was not going to try to parlay my portfolio into a new job or higher salary someplace else. But my portfolio is still important to me from an emotional standpoint. It always needs to be the focus."

Then came Apple. Steve Jobs, president of the computer manufacturer, was very intense and his standards were high. "Jobs was a cross between Leonardo DaVinci and John MacEnroe," Clow says. "He was truly a genius, one of the most brilliant people I've ever worked for, but he was incredibly demanding. And, at 25 years old, that was obnoxious. It was difficult to live up to his vision of what personal computers would mean. Jobs knew computers were going to change the world."

Jobs loved communication and realized the value of a consistent message. He put together one of the most complete internal design groups ever assembled. The Apple Design Group did everything—from trade shows and sales meetings and manuals to packaging. He insisted that Chiat/Day work with Apple's designers to evolve a consistent "look" and tone of voice. That brought the agency outside the realm of traditional advertising. And soon they were involved with all aspects of communicating Apple's message—from the manuals and brochures to dealer posters or a tee-shirt design. Everything had to be as great as the TV commercials.

"After meeting with Jobs, Steve Hayden and I felt like masochists," recalls Clow, "but we kept going back to try to satisfy his demands. We had a client who wanted great advertising. We'd be damned if we'd fail to deliver it for him. But the process of coming up with breakthrough ideas was grueling. We even had arguments about how much leading should be in the type."

Blending Jobs's genius with Chiat/Day's creative talents brought about a consistent style and tone and helped position Apple as an industry leader. It also helped Chiat/Day recognize how to best help their clients.

To win business, Chiat/Day tries to understand the client and pitch the business in an appropriate, smart, charming, and clever way. Clow recalls doing just that to get Nike's Los Angeles Olympics assignment. The agency had made their presentation. As a followup, the agency built a brick wall out of about thirty bricks and painted an athlete, Michael Cooper, bending over backwards across the wall. Then they sent a brick, individually wrapped and numbered, to each member of the Nike's marketing department. Each package had a note instructing the recipient to take the brick to the marketing director's office where they were to reassemble the wall.

Nike had said they'd let the agency know of their decision on the following Tuesday. But no one called. So on Wednesday Guy Day called Nike. He was told the marketing director was in a meeting and couldn't be interrupted, so Day left a message. But still no one called. By Thursday, the folks at the agency were starting to think the worst. Day left more messages that went unreturned. Finally, on Friday morning, the Olympic runner Mary Decker showed up in their lobby with a big bottle of Tequila. She said the marketing director suggested she come over and have a drink with the agency, because they would be working for Nike.

The marketing director decided the brick wall merited more than just a phone call as a response. He had to come up with something special. But Mary Decker was out of town, so he decided to stall everyone until she returned.

The pitch was characteristic of the agency's desire to involve their clients. The creative development process also requires client participation. It allows the agency to learn who the client is; to learn what their message is in order to come to an agreement about direction. But learning to incorporate the client company's personality into the advertising and create original new business pitches was just the beginning.

Clow also credits Chiat/Day with cultivating a management style that maximizes employee involvement. Although the Los Angeles office has 350 employees, they have open offices. Employees are grouped by account team rather than by function or department. And everybody's office space is the same as everybody else's—from Clow to Jay Chiat to the traffic manager—they're all there to make great ads.

They have also tried to avoid creating a hierarchy. "We didn't want people aspiring to corner offices and promotions 'upstairs.' Anyone can come to my office and find me," he says. As Chiat/Day grew, management put great effort into maintaining the horizontal structure—a structure that would generate uninhibited creativity.

Clow believes that most people succeed in what they really love to do—and can get incredibly passionate about. "Every day I consider myself incredibly lucky to have found a way to channel my love for art into something I can be so passionate and intense about. It's wonderful to be able to do something I find emotionally rewarding and make an incredibly good living at it."

THE EVER-EVOLVING PORTFOLIO

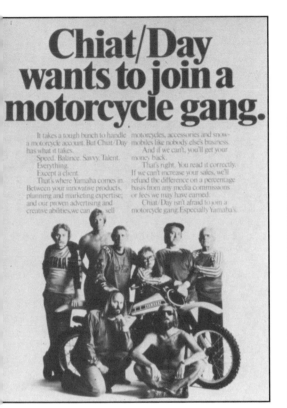

Yamaha

Like all companies, Yamaha needed advertising that was distinctive and relevant. They invited Chiat/Day to pitch the account. The agency enthusiastically plunged into developing the pitch and felt their presentation went well. But the client said, "Thank you very much," and hired the competition. Several months later, Yamaha asked for a capabilities plan to see how the agency would run their business. After the presentation, Yamaha gave the go-ahead to start producing the work they had seen the previous year.

This ad demonstrates how Chiat/Day brought distinctiveness and relevance to Yamaha advertising. Black leather, bandanas, and studded belts wouldn't work for Yamaha. Instead, with children, warm colors, and a light message, their ads would be distinctive in the world of cycling. For relevance, the message concentrated on engineering excellence and pointed out features and benefits.

On January 24th, we're going to let the cat out of the bag. And the mouse, too.

We're much better at building computers than keeping secrets.
Probably just about every magazine in your dentist's office has something to say about Macintosh,™ from Apple.™
So you probably already know that it's powerful, portable, flexible, versatile. And not very expensive.
And that it has a "mouse" – a clever hand-held device that eliminates typed-in computer commands.
Maybe even the fact that your authorized Apple dealer will unveil this phenomenal machine to the world on January 24th.
But did you know Macintosh has its own bag?
See, we *can* keep a secret.

Soon there'll be just two kinds of people.
Those who use computers and 🍎 those who use Apples.

Apple

Clow's task was to develop very simple, approachable advertising for Apple computers—advertising that would make people feel comfortable with the product. But Clow is often told, "You were introducing personal computers for the first time—who couldn't do that?"

Clow responds by saying, "It's never as easy as it looks on the surface. Creating great ads for Apple was hard work. It took great people working very hard to find a simple, obvious, great solution. It was one of the most incredible experiences of my career. And it was all worth it." Steve Hayden is still doing work for Apple that incorporates the personality developed in the beginning.

Nissan

The president of Nissan still talks about the work sessions that developed this campaign to advertise the Pathfinder, Nissan's four-wheel drive, all-terrain vehicle.

In the work sessions, it was suggested that Nissan have a man and woman start out in Chicago and drive the vehicle all the way through Central America into Brazil and on to Rio de Janeiro. Then each was to change into their tuxedo and gown and go dancing.

During the work sessions, the client and creatives talked through the logistics and decided on the number of spots. With a limited crew, the agency documented the couple's trip across the continents. The agency planned to air the spots on "Monday Night Football." Even though the budget wasn't very big, they ended up creating a big impression.

"If we had met with the president and announced we were going to have a couple drive from Chicago to Rio, and he had no part in the development, he might have rejected the idea. And the president's discomfort would be understandable. If anything went wrong, they'd waste a lot of money. But he was part of the decision—and he is still proud of that piece of advertising," says Clow. That's why he believes involving the client in developing the ideas is key.

Nike

Clow believes the job of the agency is to understand the personality of the company. "You become the spokesman for these companies and you have to accurately and faithfully translate their culture, spirit and point-of-view to the consumer," says Clow. "Nike is a great example. It's a company with soul and passion. And the spirit of their advertising is not born out of their agency—it's from them."

Although Nike works with Widen & Kennedy in Portland, they came to Chiat/Day for something special for the 1984 Olympics in Los Angeles. They disdained the commercialism of paying millions of dollars to be the "official shoe" of the Olympics and wanted to do something special to salute the Olympics, and athletes, in their own way.

To stay true to the brand and personality, Clow had to learn who Nike really was. "Portland is a very pure part of the world. They don't allow billboards there because they think they are visual pollution," he says. "But Nike was coming to celebrate the Olympics in the home of outdoor advertising—because in L.A., people live in their cars. Billboards line the freeways. It's the medium. If Nike was to be comfortable using billboards, the advertising had to be incredibly pure and simple."

Along with billboards, Chiat/Day found walls and murals to paint all over the city. The ads featured different athletes—a tribute to their dedication and focus. Post-production research showed people thought the ads communicated Nike's dedication and passion for quality athletic shoes without even using words. In the end, research also showed that 48% of the public thought Nike was the official shoe of the Olympics. Only 28% could name the actual Olympic shoe sponsor.

Energizer Bunny

When Clow was warned early in his career about the craziness of advertising, it wasn't an unfounded observation. Energizer is an example, but Clow's attitude is light-hearted. "It seems silly, but there is an incredible amount of pressure and energy spent to decide what the bunny should do next. A bunch of adults sitting around discussing what the bunny should or shouldn't do next—it's very entertaining," laughs Clow.

ADVICE FOR BUILDING YOUR PORTFOLIO

"IN ADVERTISING, YOU ALWAYS WORRY ABOUT THE QUALITY OF YOUR PORTFOLIO BECAUSE those who want to be great at this business never think that they are," says Clow. "That insecurity drives most good creative people. It's never good enough. It's never done. It could always be better."

To help you make it better, Clow believes you need to become a student of human emotions—and the communication of those emotions. To do this, he says television is a good resource. "It's is the most powerful medium on the planet," he says. "Sure, there's lots of garbage being broadcast, but if you look at all the books written in a year, how many of them are quality literary works? The percentages are probably the same. Be selective with television, in the same way you are with the printed word, and you open doors to new ideas.

"I was part of the first generation of television-watching kids. And I believe you can't help but have a much bigger and sometimes altered view of the world with that medium in your house every day. The time that most kids spend watching television gives them a broader view than kids growing up in previous generations without television—or the intellectual snobs who say, 'I won't own a television.'

"Television gave me an incredible understanding of communication. Whether it's Yogi Bear, PBS, or sports, it can help us understand how to communicate emotion. Just watching an important event or an exciting achievement in sports shows how much emotion you can pack into a few moments. When you see people feel intense emotions, whether it's patriotism inspired by the national anthem, or sympathy when hearing the plight of a family on "60 Minutes," you realize the power of television. It's that excitement that hooked me. It's more than being able to paint a train and make the smoke go in the right direction. It's having millions of people hear, feel, and react to something."

Once you've studied how to communicate emotions, advertising requires that you convey them in a very short time frame. Combine emotional power with simplicity and you get a whole different understanding of the business. "Then, you're not just a graphic designer, writer, or illustrator anymore," Clow says. To help you go beyond those job titles, here's some more of Clow's advice.

Show only the best

Your portfolio work is your credentials. Period. Nothing should be in there that you don't think is the best you can do.

Even once you're out of school and settled in your job, your portfolio should be the focus—and should be kept up-to-date. "It has to demonstrate what *you think* is good communication," he says. "It is the most important product of your career. It's the best of all your efforts."

Value all information

Clow believes you need to be attuned to the world. "To be a communicator—particularly in advertising where you talk to millions of people—means being aware of many things," he says. The "real world" experience you gain from living, interacting with the public, or in a liberal arts education, is critical input. Good creative people store information to draw on when creating advertising.

It's not the degree, it's the degree of quality work that counts

Education never held Clow back. And, he doesn't believe education is any substitute for a great portfolio. "Wherever—and however—you develop your talents is unimportant," says Clow. "Whether you have a degree from Art Center, Long Beach State, or Santa Monica City College is irrelevant. If your portfolio does not demonstrate an understanding of communication, you're not going to get a job. Even without a degree, if you have a portfolio that demonstrates talent, you'll find work."

Use spec or published—as long as it's the best

"If you put your work on a desk in front of somebody and ask him or her to judge it, then it should be the best work you've ever done—whether they're scribbles or tight comps, they should be your best solutions. If you aren't there to explain why you've included a sample, the interviewer will think that's what *you think* great design or writing is. Then, if the interviewer asks to see your work that has been produced—presenting it helps explain your experience level. Have published work with you as a tool."

Always focus on relevance and distinctiveness

"Good ads are made up of two things," says Clow, "a relevant message for the audience and the means to make the audience pay attention to it. You've got to figure out what the essence of the product is. Why should the consumer test drive the car or buy the six-pack? You have to find the reason why consumers should give your product their time. Then, because of the zillions of messages out there, you've got to find the freshest, most distinctive, most articulate way to communicate that message. A relevant benefit, stated in a mundane way, is invisible. It goes right past people. Conversely, you can produce the most outrageous commercial in history and if it doesn't say anything that people care about, it's a waste of money."

Find an agency where you can swim, not sink

Chiat/Day seldom hires people right out of school. "Beginners need a few years of real-world experience," warns Clow, "before we can throw them into the deep end of our swimming pool. If we threw someone in right out of college, I don't think they'd have the strokes down. They'd probably sink to the bottom. If they get a few years of experience at another agency, they can learn the ins and outs of the advertising business. They need to learn about account executives, clients, and budgets."

Regard your first job as an internship

"An education doesn't make you a doctor—or an art director. For a year or two, you need to learn what the advertising business is all about. The best way to do that is to be hired by an agency, so you can follow the 'doctors' around. When you get your first job in the business, don't be concerned with salary because you're really continuing your education. Look for an agency that has a real shingle on their door and makes real advertising for real clients, because you've only been in school making fake advertising for pretend clients," says Clow. "Then only change jobs when you think you've learned as much as you possibly can. Your focus should be to improve your talents as a communicator and to make your portfolio more complete and real."

Keep in mind, a bad agency can be a good experience

"You can learn a lot working at a bad agency—if you keep your focus." Clow's early jobs taught him what he didn't want to do. "I didn't want to work for an agency that was totally subservient to the client—an agency that didn't have enough integrity to believe their job was to sell great advertising. Sometimes that means taking a stand, rather than just giving them what they want." To make

matters worse, advocating the better concept is often perceived as being contradictory to the way agencies do business. "It was very frustrating to have a passion for great ideas and recognize the obstacle wasn't the client, but the agency who did not want to make the client uncomfortable!"

Diversify your talents

After getting a feel for the business, look for opportunities to diversify your talents. "Look for agencies where you can work on television if you need that experience," says Clow. "Or look for agencies that have different types of accounts. You want to round out your experience."

Look to the best

Steve Hayden regards Clow as one of his mentors. Clow feels Jay Chiat greatly influenced his career. "When I came to Chiat/Day, Jay Chiat opened doors for me and gave me opportunities," he says. "But I've always looked to the people who were doing the best work—in whatever category they worked at—as being the ultimate challenge. Whether it was George Louis, Bill Bernbach, Roy Grace, or Walt Disney, whoever was doing great things influenced me. Ultimately, Jay Chiat felt my work was up to the standards of the company he had formed. Doing ads that satisfied Jay Chiat made me what I am today."

Self-promotion should be arresting

Clow receives a myriad of self-promotion from aspiring creatives, but it's difficult to have any impact because there are so many. Understand the audience. Then, if you find exactly the right message to cut through the clutter, it works. The most exotic self-promotion stunt Clow recalls was designed by an Art Center graduate. "I had met her at a Christmas party where she gave me something to hold. As I left, some LAPD officers, who happened to be friends of the aspiring creative, said they'd heard I'd been trafficking in stolen items and mentioned the package. They really had me going for a minute, but when they said they'd take me in if I didn't look at her portfolio right then, I caught on." Clow looked at her portfolio.

Don't mistake a passion for profits as a passion for advertising

Clow reminds us that many people in the advertising business don't care about making advertising. They care about getting accounts, keeping clients happy, and making money. Great advertising is very low on their list of priorities. "I think I was lucky to have learned to recognize those qualities quickly. Chiat/Day was the only place that seemed moved by the excitement of advertising. They had passion," says Clow. "They didn't start an agency to get accounts and make money, but to do advertising."

Give 100% in everything because practice makes professional

Beginners seldom get the glamorous accounts. Clow sympathizes with that fact, but he urges them to "realize that every assignment gives you an opportunity to create the next great ad for your portfo-

lio. Don't think, 'This is only a trade ad, I want to do national television.' You're in training for a couple of years. Even with a dreary assignment, give it 100%. Your efforts will demonstrate intensity and passion, so ultimately you'll get bigger responsibilities." He also suggests getting your hands on briefs for projects that weren't assigned to you and then trying to solve the problem your own way.

Draw the personality from the company, not yourself or your agency

Distinctiveness should come from the personality of the product or company, not the personality of the creative person or the agency. Nike, Apple, and Nissan are all examples of how the personality of the company comes into play in creating a great ad. The advertising must be true to their personality, their tone of voice and who they are, warns Clow.

When in Rome...dress appropriately

Chiat/Day is well known for its "California style." Says Clow, "I grew up in California. I love the warm climate and the casual dress that goes with it. One of my heroes is a guy who started a surfboard shop, invented the Hobie Cat, and wore shorts to his board of directors meetings. We have comfortable and unusual facilities here in Venice, so I don't feel awkward wearing my shorts into the office, even if a client happens to drop in for an unscheduled meeting. But, when I go to Nissan or American Express, I don't wear shorts. I put on my coat and tie. My goal is not to be in people's faces."

Don't sell out

"Some people say creatives burn out after a point. Their work is no longer fresh. I think it's because they sell out," says Clow. "They lose touch with their craft and try to become 'good business people.' They rationalize that they're contributing to the agency's best interest by keeping clients happy, but the only reason you're in an agency is to make great ads."

Go beyond traditional advertising— to all forms of communications

"I've always wished that we could lose the word 'advertising.' It seems incredibly limited," says Clow. "I love all facets of communication that contribute to a company's position and value in the mar-

ketplace. Sometimes public relations is the tool; sometimes it's direct mail. Sometimes traditional television and magazine advertising works best. We do our best when we think of ourselves as communicators for our clients."

Look for new communication avenues

A communicator's job is to figure out the fresh, new ways to get the message across," says Clow. "Apple introduced the Macintosh with a 60-second Super Bowl commercial. That had never been done before, but it's not a breakthrough approach anymore. As a matter of fact, I'm not sure the Super Bowl is even the medium it used to be because now it's so cluttered."

· · · · · · · · · · · · · · ·

Postscript
GETTING CLIENTS TO BUY INTO CREATIVE WORK

CHIAT/DAY IS KNOWN FOR PRODUCING RISKY, BREAKTHROUGH ADVERTISING. ACCORDING to Clow, that reputation is the result of their ability to strike a balance between *creative* advertising and *effective* advertising. "In the early days, we were a bit arrogant. Too often we thought, 'We do creative work. If you don't like it, tough.' That's a very immature, creative-boutique mentality," says Clow. "We realized that you have to strike an honest balance between wanting to do great advertising and thinking that you're an artist working for clients.

"Chiat/Day went through a maturing process. We learned a long time ago that you can stay small and petulant and tell clients to go away if they don't like the work, or you can do special advertising that clients are as proud of as you are. But if an idea doesn't intimidate or scare a client a little bit, then probably it isn't good—it isn't breakthrough."

Here's how Chiat/Day gets clients to buy into those great ideas.

"The early stages of the process are when we learn our clients' opinions and gauge their comfort level. We call them strategic and creative work sessions," says Clow. "We ask our clients to spend a lot of time in the development phase of advertising. In the strategic sessions, we often come up with insights that may be different from the way they see things. We talk about it.

"After we begin to share an understanding of the approach, we start developing the advertising. In creative work sessions, we brainstorm and show a number of ideas in very rough form. We're looking for something special.

"There may be really bold ideas that are a little intimidating, but the client is assured they can really be great. They respond with reservations like, 'I'm really not comfortable with the spot,' and 'It's focusing on the negative side of the problem rather than the solution,' or 'I'm worried we're not showing enough of the product.'

"At other agencies, if a creative does something daring and the client gets nervous, the defense mechanisms kick in. The creative department is pressured to come up with ads that will please the client. The creative is told, 'you've had your shot at the solution. Now figure out what the client wants and give it to him.' The result is that the client gets advertising that's very safe and comfortable. Because when the client is happy, the account is safe. But the creative people are frustrated.

"Here, if a client doesn't like an ad, instead of putting pressure on the creative department, we try to figure out *why* the client didn't like it. Then we figure out what solution is still distinctive, unique and special. We have to find out what the client *wants*, then figure out what the client *needs*. Then try to make the client want what is needed. In stages, they come to accept what advertising will work best for them.

"It's like being an architect. If the architect does only what the client wants, the client can end up with fairly mundane architecture. On the other hand, other people passively put their faith in the architect's talents or the architect takes total control of the project. In those cases, the architect is the only one comfortable in the house.

"In these cases, if an architect goes away for three months, comes back with a solution and asks the clients to sign off on it, the clients may look at each other and say, 'We hate Spanish. We don't want to live in a Spanish house.' A successful client/agency relationship strikes a balance by understanding the people who are going to 'live in the house' and then 'building them a house that they'll enjoy living in," says Clow.

It's building and developing the advertising together that allows clients to embrace fresh, daring ideas. "They've made some contribution to the development of it," says Clow. "They are a part of it."

CHAPTER THIRTEEN

The one on the left will finish high school before the one on the right.

Adolescent pregnancy isn't just a problem in America, it's a crisis. To learn more about a social issue that concerns all of us, write: *Children's Defense Fund, 122 C Street, N.W., Washington, D.C. 20001.*

The Children's Defense Fund.

Tom McElligott

"I hate advertising," says Tom McElligott, cofounder of Fallon McElligott and its former creative director (see Chapter Eleven). "I hate watching bad commercials. I despise most of them. I really do. Ninety-five percent of the advertising out there is either just wallpaper or is aggressively bad. But then there is about 5% that is mildly pleasing—or sometimes is absolutely wonderful. At that point, it's art. Yes, it's selling, but it's selling artfully."

When it's great, he loves it. And he loves creating it. McElligott injects humanity and originality into his writing. He wants his work to touch people. And it certainly has touched the advertising community. Clios, One Show pencils, and New York Art Directors awards are just a few of the prizes that his creative genius has brought him throughout his career—more than enough to earn him a place in the One Club's Advertising Hall of Fame in 1991.

McElligott's high standards, idealism, and integrity also led the American Association of Advertising Agencies to choose him to develop an ad campaign aimed at improving the industry's image.

But despite his enthusiasm for the craft of advertising, he keeps a realistic outlook. "Frankly," he says, "I'm not prepared to die for this business. I love it—and I love to work hard—but some sanity has to enter the picture." For sanity's sake, he enjoys reading, camping, canoeing, and sailing. He now resides in Hawaii.

DRIVEN BY THE NEED TO SUCCEED

LOW SCHOLASTIC PERFORMANCE? AN UNSUPPORTIVE, DYSFUNCTIONAL FAMILY? No connections in the business? Those are typical reasons people use to explain a lack of success. But they shouldn't really hold anyone back. Just look at McElligott's career. He experienced all of those conditions, and instead of looking at them as a reason for failure, he used them for motivation.

As a high school student, McElligott was a classic underachiever. He graduated at the bottom of his class—a very large class at Fargo Central High School in North Dakota. "I surely didn't study," he says, guessing that his lack of academic achievement was a result of his home life. "I came out of an incredibly screwy family; I think quite a few creative people do," he says. "That led to low self-esteem and a lack of confidence."

But his high school years were not totally unproductive. In fact, when he was 14, he restored an old car. "This was a very creative project," he says, "because I made something happen. I would call up companies in Detroit and ask for car parts. I've thought about it in recent years and realized that that project was a lot like working in an ad agency."

After high school, McElligott spent three years in the Marines where he turned his low self-esteem into confidence. He left with a determination to put his intelligence to use. "I learned that I didn't want to carry a rifle the rest of my life," he says. He entered the University of Minnesota and, to his surprise, enjoyed a successful academic career as an English major. He discovered 18th century literature and made plans to go to graduate school so that he could teach it. But those plans were expensive because the GI bill, which had financed his pursuit of an undergraduate education, would not apply to his graduate degree.

McElligott had other financial pressures. It was the late 1960s, and he and his wife were expecting their first child. The role of husband and father weighed on him and he felt a rising need to make money, but had little idea of how to apply his education.

Meanwhile, he worked evenings at a local brewery as a tour guide. It was at one of the brewery's parties that he discovered a classified ad for copywriters in a copy of *Advertising Age*. The job paid $12,000 a year—which was double the salary he expected to earn as a teacher. Consequently, he decided to take a detour from graduate school until his wife could resume her career as a nurse. He planned to write ads while working out a financial plan that would enable him to return to graduate school.

"I had never studied advertising. I thought copywriting was something you'd do in a law firm," he recalls. "That's how little I knew about the business."

Later, McElligott looked in the classifieds of the local newspaper and found an ad for a position at Dayton Hudson's, a department store in Minneapolis. The position had been open for a long time because the copy chief, a perfectionist, had sent each candidate home with several ads and asked that they be rewritten. If the copywriter improved the ads to the copy chief's satisfaction, he would be hired. Apparently the copy chief wasn't impressed by anyone he'd seen. McElligott took him up on the challenge.

"That evening I sat at the dining room table rewriting the ads and discovered what I had been missing in the first 25 years of my life. I absolutely loved it. I had a wonderful time writing them." McElligott returned with his ads and got the job.

In retrospect, McElligott feels his ads weren't really very good. "I'm sure I'd look at that work today and wonder how I ever got hired," he says. "But they were probably a little better because I was so passionate about writing them. So they showed enough promise to get me hired."

McElligott loved writing for Dayton Hudson's, even though he wasn't very clear on how to do it. He was a good writer, and he had good ideas, but most of his ads were derivative. "What I managed to get on paper was taken from this room in my head that was full of slogans, headlines, and graphics that I had accumulated over the course of my 25 years," he says. "They weren't fresh and they weren't like the work I'd later do. But they were good enough. And I was one driven, passionate young guy who desperately wanted to do great work."

At Dayton Hudson's, he was asked to produce everything from two-page newspaper ads to small quarter-page ads. He found this to be great experience. "The wonderful thing about starting in retail is that you're forced to write quickly and produce a lot," says McElligott. "Many copywriters don't know what it's like to have a tremendous work load. In an agency, an ad or a campaign can consume weeks of their time. There's nothing like coming into your office on Monday morning and knowing you're responsible for producing 18 different pieces of work by Friday."

Within two months, he was promoted, and he began supervising people with much more seniority. Eventually, he also wound up writing all the broadcast for the store. And he loved it.

The next stage of his career happened by accident. At a local garage sale, he met a copywriter who suggested that he consider working in an agency; the copywriter said that retail was no place to spend an entire career.

But McElligott was still very naive. And he was happy writing and too busy working to investigate alternatives. Yet he realized that the retail industry was small. If he wanted to work for a quality organization, his choices were limited. In addition to his employer, there was only Neiman Marcus, Bloomingdale's, and a few others.

Consequently, he took the copywriter's advice and researched and found several ad agencies in the Minneapolis/St. Paul area that interested him. He applied to Campbell-Mithun and Knox Reeves, plus Leo Burnett and Needham Harper & Steers in Chicago. "I sent copies of my ads, which were not good at all, but they were good enough to get responses."

At Campbell-Mithun, he was offered a job with a very good salary. And, later the same day, he was offered a position at Knox Reeves for $1,000 a year less. "I took the job at Knox Reeves because it looked like it offered more opportunity," he says.

"It was a more creatively driven agency in those years, but it was not great. Ron Anderson, who became my friend, was creative director, and he clearly had a passion for creating advertising," says McElligott about his long-time friend. "When you find someone to share that with, that's something."

Ron Anderson inspired McElligott as a mentor and provided him with insight, stability, and editing over the next eight years. More important, he helped McElligott develop the ability to critique advertising, to distinguish his better efforts.

"Some work tickled me more than other work, but I couldn't tell which ads were good or just dumb. Ron could." One night McElligott left Anderson about 50 rough ads for the Minneapolis Police Department. "When Ron returned from a meeting, he was so excited. He called me and said, 'There are a couple of ideas here.' And I responded by saying, 'Oh really? Which ones?' I really didn't know," he says. "I'd had a pretty good afternoon at work and was generally pleased, but Ron knew which ads were stronger."

Over the years, McElligott has cultivated a greater sense of competency in judging his work. But even today, he has others look at his work. "You never stop needing an editor," he says. "I firmly believe, even if you're pretty sure, you owe it to yourself and your client to let other people look at it and to listen what they have to say about it."

Around this time, the creative director of BBDO noticed McElligott's work, called him up, and invited him to talk. "He complimented my work, but said that it looked like Minneapolis work. He then said that as long I compared my work with the best work being done in Minneapolis, I'd never be better than Minneapolis. That was key. It was like an epiphany. He suggested that I buy all the awards annuals I could find, and study them."

The eager young writer followed this advice and spent evenings poring over the outstanding work of the time. "I was absolutely knocked out by the work of Ed McCabe, Neil Drossman, David Altschiller, and Martin Puris—all the wonderful New York writers. And Bill Bernbach—the greatest ad man of our time," says McElligott. It was a different league of work. He found it to be powerful and honest and wanted to emulate it.

Meanwhile, his career kept progressing. With help from Anderson, he was made copy chief at Knox Reeves in 1974. This forced him to manage projects that he felt were over his head, but he was ambitious. And he accepted the position after Anderson agreed to be his partner. After years of working together, McElligott continued to find Anderson's presence reassuring.

"Being promoted at Dayton Hudson's and Knox Reeves was very helpful in both cases. It pushed me," he says. "And it did some good for my self-esteem."

McElligott's talent was honed enough to earn him a creative director position after Knox Reeves merged with Bozell and Jacobs. The agency had offices in Chicago, Dallas, Los Angeles, and Montreal and McElligott's role was to act as a troubleshooter, which required him to travel with Anderson to those offices either to save accounts or acquire new ones whenever necessary.

"I was living quietly in Minneapolis with my family. Everything Midwestern and intact. Yet every other week I was getting on airplanes to work on major national accounts—British Airways, Max Factor—which is no easy trick in this market," he says. "It was an opportunity to be exposed to account responsibilities I would have had to go to New York to find."

As a result, McElligott was learning that creating a good campaign wasn't enough, that he'd have to embrace the side of the business he most wanted to avoid—the marketing side. He had to become more sophisticated about marketing strategies in order to defend his work. That realization came after presenting campaigns he felt were terrific, original, and powerful, but were rejected.

"Ron (Anderson) and I would fly off to Dallas with a satchel of wonderful work, present the work to the client and have it dismissed. I didn't like that. I had worked hard. I wanted to see the fruits of my labor mean something. That's when I began a real transition. I began to really think about the client's product in the competitive environment and approach selling powerful, original work in a completely different way. It quickly became obvious to me that good writing was good salesmanship. I would track its success. I'd provide the client all the comfort I could. So they could understand that I was a disciplined, responsible steward of their dollar."

By 1979, McElligott began asking his staff to present their work in the context of the marketing strategy. "I'd have my staff bring me the strategy, put it on the wall and put their work next to it, and I had them tell me how their work tracked from the strategy. And then whether they had created something original," says McElligott.

With this change in his outlook, McElligott was ready to move on. He considered moving to New York or Los Angeles. But, instead, he chose to put the needs of his family first and stay in Minneapolis. He had established solid working relationships with Nancy Rice and Pat Fallon—freelancing with them in the evenings—so the three of them decided to start their own agency.

"I had grown out of room," he says. "I wanted a real agency with real accounts. I also wanted to create an environment where things *could* happen and direct a creative staff that would *make* things happen."

The goal of Fallon McElligott was simply to create fresh, original, powerful advertising—that was strategically sound. "My contract with people coming into the agency went like this: 'I want you to do the very best work of your life—or don't come. If you put in the time and are committed, I guarantee I will sell your work, maybe not all the time, but most of the time. If we have an account that consistently will not buy great work, I'll not let you suffer. I will not have you go off and turn out wonderful work that I've asked you to do and then have it shot down again and again. We'll resign the business.' Virtually every creative person I hired heard me say that," says McElligott. "I did not want good people continually bummed out after turning out brilliant, disciplined work."

That was a major commitment, but Fallon McElligott lived up to it. "We resigned a fair amount of business," he says. "So I got people to produce wonderful work."

McElligott operated very simply. When something didn't meet his standards, he had the creatives go back and do it again. If they still defended their work, he would take a group of six to eight people, go into the agency's conference room, and have them select the best three or four pieces. He then usually selected the final ad from that group.

"I'd discuss my picks with the team and if they disagreed with me, I'd change," he says. "I make mistakes. And I didn't want to stand in the way of good work or stop interesting things from happening. Quite the contrary."

Partly because of this process and a shared feeling of fairness, there was little turnover at the agency. "We believed that if an ad was terrific, it should get produced. In fact, if it was terrific and it didn't get done, everybody in the agency knew about it and was sympathetic. No one went off to his or her office alone feeling terrible."

Eventually, Fallon McElligott's innovative, effective, and creative work helped them grow to 140 employees—and put Minneapolis on the advertising map. Their success also attracted many companies interested in acquiring them, and the partners finally sold to Scali, McCabe, Sloves (SMS) in 1985.

Within a year, McElligott could see the agency changing. It was still a good agency with good people doing good work, but it wasn't the same to him. SMS had paid a substantial amount of money for the agency, forcing them to shift their focus from developing the best creative to improving the bottom line.

"We weren't in a position to resign Federal Express when they became the world's most obnoxious client. I saw reams of work go off to their office in Memphis. I promised the staff that wonderful work would be sold, but our sell rate plummeted from 80% down to 20%. For some agencies that isn't bad, but we weren't used to working that way."

This upset McElligott. Unlike Lee Clow, who is not opposed to presenting more work until the client is satisfied (Chapter Twelve), he believes that if a great ad is created—one that is strategically sound—then it should sell, unless, of course, the client has a good reason for not buying it. "I may redo an ad a few times because this is a service business," says McElligott, "but I despise it."

Unhappy with the direction the agency was taking, McElligott broke his contract in 1988, which forced him to take a year away from the industry.

McElligott returned to the industry in 1989, joining Chiat/Day, where he spent nine months. He had arranged to spend a week in Minneapolis, then a week in New York, London, Toronto, or Los Angeles. But within a few days, he could see that he'd be perpetually on the road. "Chiat/Day is a very interesting agency," he says. "And I continue to admire their work, but it is basically 'loony time' there."

So after being away from his son for more than five months and earning 163,000 miles on Northwest Airlines in nine months, he knew he couldn't continue with

Chiat/Day. "I decided I had better return to Minneapolis," he says. "In fairness to Chiat/Day, they bought me a wonderful place in Greenwich Village. But my wife and I made a commitment to put our kids through school in Minneapolis. My family has remained intact throughout the ups and downs of my career. It's a huge part of my life.

So, in 1989, McElligott found himself again starting an agency with several other partners: McElligott Wright Morrison White (MWMW) in Minneapolis. But he wanted to create a difference between his new agency and Fallon McElligott. "At Fallon McElligott, especially in our early years, we were happy just to create a good ad," he says. "The difference at MWMW was that we were looking to make those ads fit within a brand personality, which sometimes meant giving up brilliant moments. It also meant forgoing the pleasure of knocking off one wonderful 30-second spot that didn't fit the brand personality or tone of voice."

For an example of an agency producing work with long-term brand personalities, McElligott looked to Leo Burnett. "What they've done is commit to not only a strategy, but a brand personality that is pretty consistent—and recognizable by the consumer—over many years," says McElligott. "Given the great amount of advertising that consumers see, the only way to build equity with them is to have a reasonably consistent brand image."

But those mutual goals at MWMW eventually faded, and within a few years after the group had opened its doors, McElligott's agency partners instigated a "palace coup" while he was away judging the 1992 Cannes Film Festival in France. They tried to remove him from his creative director position and fire his copywriter. Their actions led to the quick demise of the agency. And the last we heard, McElligott was writing a book under a tall Hawaiian palm.

A PORTFOLIO WITH POLISH AND PASSION

In Minnesota
we have graffiti, too
It just happens
to be 800 years old

Everywhere you go in Minnesota art surrounds you.

You find it among the half-hidden caves and waterways where Sioux and other tribes left it hundreds of years ago.

You find it in stunning sunsets filtered through pine trees towering high into the sky.

You find it in a deer that darts through the bush, a fish that leaps splashing from the water, a loon that breaks the misty morning silence with it's eerie call.

You find it in the lush parks, tree-shaded boulevards, and exquisite malls of Minnesota cities.

You find it in the wide variety of professional and amateur theater, music, and dance throughout

Minnesota.

And, of course, you find it in the museums which Minnesotans have filled with art objects from Minnesota and around the world.

Art. It's all there waiting for you in Minnesota. Enough to fill a lifetime of vacations.

Indoors, or outdoors.

Minnesota
Lakes. And a whole lot more.

State of Minnesota, Tourism Division, 1978

Early in his career, McElligott learned that great ads need to have a dominant element that communicates very quickly. "Whether it's a headline, a startling photo, or something else, it has to be sufficiently original and arresting to stop you and get your attention," he says. "Then it has to be honest enough and intriguing enough to keep your attention while moving the ball forward in the selling process."

He believes that good creative people have an understanding of how the page works. They understand that adding elements to a page reduces the importance of every other element, while removing an element raises the importance of the remaining elements. "It's a simple rule," he says.

McElligott learned this from Tom Donovan, the executive art director he worked with at Knox Reeves. "He was a great teacher," says McElligott. "If you pushed him, he would say things like, 'I don't want to use that visual because it will rob the headline of its importance' and 'If you make the headline bigger, you're going to ruin the photo.' So he knew what had to happen."

This ad, created in 1978, is a result of that schooling. There are many elements to this ad, but each is proportioned in a way to easily guide the reader through it. "If nothing in the ad is very important," says McElligott, "then it's not a very important ad."

The Wall Street Journal

"There's nothing like watching television and having an absolutely terrific commercial come on," says McElligott. "It's a wonderful thing and it's well worth pursuing." And he has pursued it himself. Like this commercial for The Wall Street Journal. Notice the fair amount of humanity in his writing. "A good ad or commercial restates a problem that dozens of other people have tackled, but finds a different way of saying what others have said," says McElligott. "It's far easier said than done."

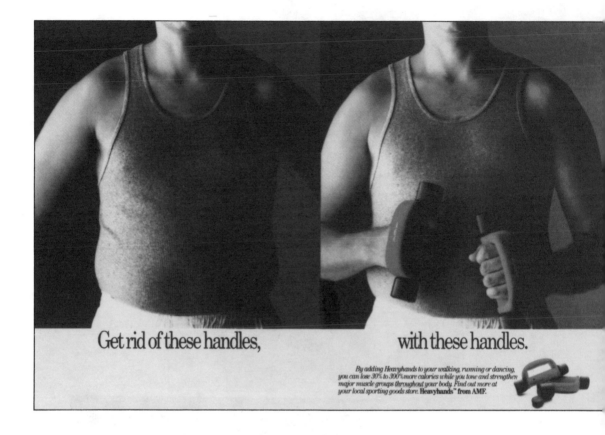

AMF, 1984

When creating an ad, McElligott likes to limit the amount of information that he includes in it. "For many years—and to some degree today—clients had a tendency to want to cram more into an ad. They're paying for it. So they want to give every possible piece of information that can help them make a sale," he says. "But if you pile on six different type faces, four different visuals, a logo, three pieces of copy, and God knows what else, the ad won't have any real power." For example, notice how sparse yet powerful this ad is. Now imagine what it would have been like if the client wanted to add little boxes of information about weight loss, as well as information about the company.

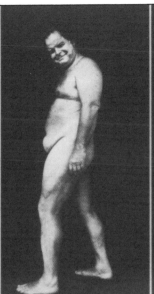

HOW MUCH WEIGHT DO YOU HAVE TO LOSE BEFORE YOUR INSURANCE COMPANY NOTICES IT?

Anyone who's ever tried knows that losing weight can be a real struggle. You go to bed hungry. You wake up hungry. You learn to despise lettuce. You exercise until you ache.

The good news is that according to recent studies, people who stay trim and exercise regularly live longer and are better life insurance risks. So now, ITT Life has come up with a Good Health Bonus* for non-smokers and people who are trim and fit. Which means that if you don't smoke, you could earn a 65% insurance bonus. With no increase in your insurance premiums.

If you stay trim and don't smoke, you could get a 100% life insurance bonus. And over half of the non-smokers who apply meet the special underwriting criteria for the Good Health Bonus.

Look. You work very hard to keep your body trim. Isn't it about time you got the trimmer life insurance premiums you deserve?

For more details call free: **1-800-328-2193** and ask for operator 901. In Minnesota call us at 612-545-2100. Or mail the coupon to us today.

ITT Life Insurance Corporation
Post Office Box 130, Minneapolis, Minnesota 55440   901
___ Please give me a free estimate of the low premiums I would pay for $_____ of life insurance with the ITT Life Good Health Bonus. My age is ___
I now pay $_____ in premiums per year.
I smoke cigarettes. Yes ☐ No ☐
I exercise at least 3 times weekly. Yes ☐ No ☐
Mr. Mrs. Ms. _____
Address _____ Apt. ____
City _____ State ____ Zip ____
Phone (include area code) _____

ITT Life Insurance Corporation ITT

ITT Life, 1983

Here was a product innovation that needed announcing to potential customers—reduced insurance premiums to nonsmokers who were fit and trim. In typical style, McElligott wrote hundreds of headlines before choosing which ones he'd use in the campaign. In addition, like most of the ads he writes, this one shows his tendency to use dry wit and irony when communicating. By the way, the photographs for this ad—all of the same man—originally appeared 10 years earlier in a magazine article that McElligott and Nancy Rice had remembered seeing. They tracked down the photographer and bought the rights.*

*Print Cases Book 6: The Best in Advertising, Bethesda, MD: RC Publications, 1984, pages 44–47. Tom Goss.

It beats analysis.

Some people believe you must confront the pressures of a mature, professional lifestyle head-on.

We, on the other hand, believe in outrunning them. Which is why we created the Porsche 944 Turbo.

With a 0 to 60 time of 5.7 seconds and a top speed of 162 mph, in the time it would take to describe an ink blot, you can leave your troubles far behind.

Stop in for a test-drive. You'll find it definitely beats analysis. And you may well find the 944 Turbo less expensive.

PORSCHE

Porsche

According to McElligott, advertising is pleasing when makes its point in an original way. "Originality is wonderful," he says. "When I see originality in a book, movie, architecture, or painting, I'm delighted. There's too little of it in this world."

Advertising isn't much different. "It has to sell, but if it sells with wit and originality, it's delightful," he says. "In the mundane daily life we all live, when you're in your car and look over at the side of a bus and see a truly wonderful piece of advertising, it's a moment of pleasure. You don't have to know anything about advertising to be delighted by it. And the pleasure of that moment reflects on the product. That's the greatest thing that can happen to the product because it gets the credit for delighting people."

In addition to showing how originality can sell, this newspaper ad is an example of communications developed within a long-term brand personality. All of the Porsche ads created at Fallon McElligott communicated with this attitude.

ADVICE FOR CREATING A SUCCESSFUL CAREER

WHAT MAKES A GREAT ADVERTISING PERSON? MCELLIGOTT SPECULATES THAT IT'S PASSION, intensity and a strong drive to succeed, more than education or even talent. "There are a lot of talented people around," he says. "But without the fire in their guts, a good talent can go to waste."

So when hiring, McElligott looks for an aura of intensity. "I am not talking about good salesmanship," he says "Quite the contrary. I'm talking about somebody who is so intense I'm not sure I want to be in the same room with him or her. I was a driven, intense guy with an enormous, dysfunctional need to succeed. It's not unlike the great American entrepreneurs outside of advertising. Success is a way of overcoming other things in their lives."

When he sees people with intensity, combined with drive, a sense of originality, and an ability to see things differently than other people, he feels that everything else can be taught—the strategizing, and the ability to write good sentences and paragraphs. "Over three or four years of copy chiefing, you can make a kid literate," he says.

But does this mean that he is endorsing an advertising education for these intense individuals? No. In fact, he remains unimpressed with most advertising schools.

"Maybe I'm not being fair, but I've concluded that the old adage—'Those that can, do; those that can't, teach'—is especially true of advertising. That's because advertising is not a profession. It's a craft. So the people doing it should be the ones teaching it. And generally, they are too busy making money and are under too much stress to teach."

So if you're extremely driven—and want to be guided by one of advertising's greatest practitioners—here are some ideas and suggestions that may help you along.

Don't be afraid to take an unconventional path

"People who create effective advertising have the ability to come at problems from a fresh perspective," says McElligott. "They have a slightly askew point of view. And often travel unconventional paths, which force them to stand at the sidelines and see something from a slightly different perspective. I can't make this a blanket rule, but it's a pretty good one."

Take a course in art direction

"Art direction is more methodical than copywriting," says McElligott. "It's a little closer to a profession. It's still a craft, but art directors have to have the basic mechanical tools. They have to know typography, composition, and all kinds of things that begin to resemble a body of professional knowledge."

Know the rules—and break them

McElligott believes that good advertising is about breaking rules. If you create within the rules, you can't be fresh. And freshness is what disarms consumers. That means, according to McElligott, "Great advertising should make your client's palms sweat a little." But when you break the rules, McElligott warns, "know the consequences. Certain things simply have to happen in a print ad or commercial," he says, "So breaking rules is great, but first understand the trade-offs."

Study the annuals—again

Like so many of the other creative geniuses found in the pages of this book, McElligott believes the best way to start a spec book is to get the One Shows, New York Art Director Annuals and Communication Arts Advertising Annuals—and study them. "Start to understand why some of these ads are really special," he says. "If you bring the annuals into your life, in effect you're bringing in the graduate school of advertising. You're getting a glimpse into the minds of some very good creative advertising people. You have to start somewhere. Even Picasso was influenced by other painters. His early work was derivative."

Identify products you want to advertise

"Get into the Zen of thinking about concepts," McElligott suggests. "Pick five or ten products you might like to advertise—pens, cars, batteries—anything. Start a file for each one. Put all your roughs in there. Start thinking about each product. Relax. Page through the annuals and consider whether an interest-ing approach to one problem would make sense for your product. For example, would an approach for BMW make sense for Shaeffer pens?"

Collaborate

"A beginning art director should enlist the help of a beginning copywriter, so the copy will be as crisp and effective as possible. Beginning copywriters need the help of a beginning art director who, in turn, will help the visual be as powerful as possible," says McElligott. "Even when putting a beginning book together, it's important for the art director and copywriter to share a firm grasp of the concept and how it applies to the goal of the campaign."

Be resourceful

"There's a lot to be said for using scrap art. Use existing photos. Get stats made and type set," says McElligott. "You can put together a pretty convincing ad with very little money and it'll look close to a real one. We do that for presentations. I know that we have more resources, of course, but good spec ads don't have to be expensive."

Polish your portfolio

"Beginners should strive to create ads that are as original and polished as the ads I see in The One Show or the D&AD. That's the fastest way to get a job. If you show a book that has six or eight ads close to that caliber, you'll almost certainly get a job. In a way, creating a good portfolio is a huge accomplishment, but it's not that complicated,"

McElligott says. He also thinks polishing the ads is important for another reason. "I like to think I can see an idea. But, sometimes, I'm amazed at how terrific some ads become when they're executed," he says. "And I suspect I'm not the only creative director who sometimes does not fully appreciate where an idea can go when it's in its roughest form."

Share with your partner in a way that works for both of you

"I've never been the sort of writer who wants to sit in a room staring at an art director for five days. When working with Nancy Rice, for example, she'd go away. I'd go away. Then we'd meet, share ideas and tweak the ads until they did what we wanted them to do," he says. "It was a strong collaboration. It often works that way for creative teams."

Go for volume first

When McElligott writes, he churns out a huge pile of ads, sometimes 30 different variations on the same concept. This helps him move past the easy solutions and loosen up. "You have to get past the stuff everybody else does," he says, "and that requires a lot of hard work." Sometimes he creates five or six hundred roughs before he finds four or five ads he loves. "I'll look the next day," he says, "and usually one of them is far, far better."

Talk to the consumer one-on-one

Advertising is most effective when it speaks to one consumer rather than to an enormous audience. "The problem with so much advertising," he says, "is that it speaks from a podium. I think—with rare exceptions—advertising copywriters tend not to understand that it's an extremely personal thing to sell something to somebody. Of course, the best writers find that out fairly quickly. But if you look at the whole body of American advertising, you will find very little that actually touches people."

Use simple and casual language

McElligott believes writing should reflect the kind of dialogue you hear between individuals. When it does, it has a truthful, special quality that lends the advertising credibility. "It quickly became obvious to me that good writing was good salesmanship," he says, "so the less formal the language is, the better it is. And if you're writing in the vernacular, sentence fragments are appropriate."

Fulfill the strategy

"I don't know that young people have to be fully familiar with the entire process of strategizing, but I think they at least need to have respect for it. They must have a general awareness that they are responsible for fulfilling a strategy. So the work should never be so obviously wacko that it would never stand a chance of being produced," says McElligott. "Then, once in an agency, it must track. It's a very, very shallow victory for some kid to go off to an awards show and pick up a gold medal for something that didn't work. That can't last a lifetime. And that's not good for a career."

Make your work defendable

McElligott believes in pre- and post-testing. "So I'm at the point now where I will absolutely not take a piece of work to a client when I can't strategically track it. I want to be able to take clients through the strategic process. Ultimately, something has to happen in the marketplace. Because what we're doing is selling. And if we're not selling, then we're doing something wrong and we can't be proud of it."

Seek advice

"At some point, you'll have so many roughs that you'll need to have some objective input to help evaluate which ideas have the most potential," says McElligott. "Without feedback from others it will be difficult to create a spec book. So this is where you need to be pretty resourceful because editing or mentorship is not easy to come by, especially from really good people." McElligott says he has helped several beginners through this process, reviewing their work and helping them decide on which rough concepts to pursue, as well as which changes to make.

Persevere

"Getting into the advertising business requires resilience and tenacity," says McElligott. "You can't be crushed when people don't return your phone calls or letters," says McElligott. "Simply hang in there. And then do some brilliant ads for your spec portfolio. And you'll surely get a job."

Keep up

The speed at which the advertising industry changes hinders effective advertising education and also complicates the advertising professionals' need to keep up. "When I returned to advertising after a year away," says McElligott, "I was astonished at how fast things had changed. It took me six months just to catch up."

Trust your instincts when hiring

Many good creative directors can sense the kind of intensity and originality that fuels a beginner's career. McElligott has relied on his ability to sense these qualities in people he has hired. And his instincts have paid off. Many of the writers he has hired who exhibited drive have become extremely successful. While they had varied levels of education, they all shared an intense need to succeed.

• • • • • • • • • • • • • • •

Postscript
COMMENTS TO PREPARE YOU FOR THE STRUGGLE

THROUGHOUT THIS BOOK, WE'VE HEARD THAT ADVERTISING IS A SHRINKING FIELD, THAT many experienced people are looking for work, and that it's getting harder to break into the field. Let's hear about that from someone who has experienced those ups and downs.

"A lot of people are drawn to advertising today. There are hundreds of wonderful applicants coming and going who I can't hire and I feel very badly for them. There is virtually no place for them because the business has become considerably smaller in the past twenty years. Far smaller. When I started out, it seemed tough. But it wasn't as tough as it is now. Whatever I did in 1970 was good enough to get me into the city's premier department store. But not today. Not with what I had to show them.

"In fact, with what's happened in this business, I doubt I would get in. I had a lot more enthusiasm than I had ability. Today, I see young people with fairly polished starting books who are relentless in their pursuit of success. It's that combination—really—that does it.

"The most important thing about the whole ad game is to be damn sure you're really passionate about it. It's no place for people who aren't sure they want to be there. There are a lot of mid-career advertising people on the streets of New York, Chicago and Minneapolis who are having a very tough time—and it's especially bad to have a tough time when you're in your late thirties or in your forties.

"In the last five years, the advertising industry has taken a hell of a beating. Yet, it still attracts people for all the right reasons. I was attracted to it because it can be great fun. It's creative, it's challenging, and it changes every day.

"So I don't want to discourage anybody, but people have to be prepared for real ups and downs. To get into the business without that knowledge would be a big mistake. It's pretty commonplace for people to lose their jobs a few times during their advertising careers. And, unless you understand that—really understand it—advertising can be brutal."

Afterword

BILL BERNBACH IS DEAD
by Tom Monahan

The VW Bug is a relic.

The Beatles broke up more than 20 years ago.

Hip huggers are unhip.

The entire cast of Star Trek is old.

Johnny Carson is retired.

John-John Kennedy is a lawyer.

Mick Jagger is a grandparent.

It's hard to find vinyl records.

Dionne Warwick does infomercials.

Opie is bald.

Twiggy isn't.

Sean Connery is being cast as an old man.

Little Stevie Wonder is 42.

Angie Dickinson has wrinkles.

The Beach Boys aren't.

Univac is a museum.

Tie-dyed is out. Again.

"Laugh In" isn't funny.

Merlin Olsen does flower commercials.

Vincent Price is a sweet old man.

Rod McKuen is starting to make sense.

Crosby, Stills & Nash aren't young.

Jerry Garcia is fat and gray.

M*A*S*H reruns are in rerun.

Christie Brinkley has posed in her last bikini.

Space age is old age.

Edsels are desirable.

Gordie Howe is Gordie who?

Ol' Blue Eyes really is.

Joannie no longer loves Chachie.

Pittsburgh has clean air.

Mr. Potato Head is Mr. Plastic Head.

The Cold War has thawed out.

Basically, it's not 1965 anymore.

I have to start by saying that I have more respect and admiration for Bill Bernbach than for anyone else in the business world.

He made the advertising industry respectable. He gave creative people status.

Tens of millions of Americans, and billions of people around the world, most of whom never heard of this ad industry Goliath, are indebted to Bill Bernbach for showing respect for them as readers and viewers and for cleaning up the media.

Bill Bernbach is Babe Ruth, Elvis, and Albert Einstein. He is Henry Ford, Picasso, and Neil Armstrong. No one has ever done, nor will likely ever do as much for this industry I've chosen as my profession. Thank you, Mr. Bernbach. And rest in peace.

Bill Bernbach is dead.

He died many years ago. But there are too many people in our industry who, in the name of respect, won't let him pass.

I read, with great dismay, a piece in *Adweek* recently that had many of our industry's leaders ragging on the "80s excess" and preaching a return to "traditional values" à la Bernbach. (It's kind of funny how a rebel of 30 years ago represents tradition today.)

Creative bashing has become quite fashionable. A popular way for veterans of our industry to endear themselves to the sentiments of risk-averse client types is to disassociate themselves from the "creative excess" of today's "boutique" creatives, and look to the tradition of the '60s as a time "when advertising tried harder," to quote the title of a book that romanticized that great era of 30 years ago.

Yes, the '60s can teach us a lot about advertising. But, it's not 1965 anymore. It's a different world we live in. And if we try to hold onto the past too tightly, we're going to miss the present.

"Think small" was a great, great ad. It, more than any other ad, is why I'm in this crazy business.

But, "Think small" might not work today. We'll never know. Just like we'll never know whether my boyhood idol Bob Cousy could play in the NBA of the '90s.

I returned to the home I grew up in recently. The hill in the back yard used to appear so high and so steep. We used to slide down that hill in the winter like it was Mt. Everest. Today that exact same topographic formation is barely a bump on the back lawn. But it used to be so huge. What's changed?

In *Communication Arts* Steve Henry recently wrote that having the same old players judge award shows could be causing us to perpetuate the same old standards. I couldn't agree more.

In another recent issue of *Communication Arts* (August 1992) Marty Cook asked us to open our eyes and minds to the new, young talent who seem to be making a stir, and try not to judge them with our established rules. I will add my voice to this plea.

Nineteen ninety two is a different time than 1965. And we can't change that. Technology has made us different. Environmental consciousness has made us different. MTV has made us different. ("You don't look at rock 'n roll, you listen to rock 'n roll," says a voice in the back of my head. "Sorry," a more honest, aware voice says, "today, you look at rock 'n roll, too."

One of the great ironies of this whole "new wave creative" bashing is that a lot of the people who are criticizing the experimenters of today, and who "don't get" what these new, weird kids are trying to do, kind of forget that 30 years ago they were the experimenters whom their establishment "didn't get."

"There's a return to traditional values," the demographers have been telling us the past few years. Fine, but that doesn't mean we can turn back the clock.

Ed Sullivan just won't play today. "And now for your entertainment pleasure... Topo Gigio..." Yeah, right.

I love what the '60s did for advertising. I love what the '60s did for the world. But the times they have a changed. And those who try to preach a return to '60s Bernbachian values are just showing their age.

As for those who preach the Ogilvy values, well,...sorry, but the man in the eye patch just doesn't cut it anymore. Not even close. When I hear the ranting and raving of that old man who lives in the castle in the vineyard in France...come on, who's out of touch, here?

The leaders of yesteryear were great for their time. Jerry Della Femina told us to ride the subway to get in touch. Today, one might say to watch MTV or FOX to feel the heartbeat of our culture.

Now, I'm not ready to flush everything the '60s stood for down the toilet. Some of the basic truisms still relate, but only in a '90s context.

Just like Jesse Owens' training methods might be as appropriate today as in 1936 when he was "the world's fastest human." Yet, sadly, even though his methods might still work, the great Mr. Owens couldn't place in most college track meets today. He might not even place in some high school meets.

It's a different world.

Jesse Owens is dead. Bill Bernbach is dead. And it's very dangerous to pretend otherwise.

This viewpoint, might be just a tad controversial for some people. I'll add gasoline to the fire by saying, if you bristle at some of these thoughts, it only serves to prove how attached you might be to these 30-year-old ideals, and how out of touch you might be with where the world is at today. And more importantly for our business, where the consumer's head is at.

I heard someone say recently that every generation thinks the music of its time was the best. My folks think swing was the best. I, of course, know that '60s rock is the best. My nephew, poor kid, thinks metal is tops.

(I wouldn't be showing my age, would I?)

When we ignore the values of youth, we start missing where our planet is heading.

The surest way for advertising to miss the future is to hold on to the present, or worse yet, the past.

Maybe the reason so many people in the business are looking back to the golden age of advertising is because there isn't a lot of true innovation today, creatively.

I might suggest that maybe there isn't much innovation, because too many of us are looking back.

To all the people in their 40s, 50s, and 60s in the ad business—remember how unhip your father was when you were growing up? Well, today, you're older than your father was back then.

Don't hold on to the past so desperately. Embrace the present. Be open to the future.

Sorry, but that's really all we have.

I love almost everything Bill Bernbach stood for. I also love bell bottoms, VW mini vans, and souped-up Pontiac GTOs. As long as they're kept in their proper perspective.

One important thing Bill Bernbach's professional life stood for was letting go of old concepts and reinventing. In a letter to the owners of Grey Advertising where he worked just before he started Doyle Dane Bernbach, Bernbach wrote that he was "...worried... we're going to follow history instead of making it...." And, "We must develop our own philosophy and not have the advertising philosophy of others imposed upon us."

In another context he wrote, "for creative people, rules can be prison."

I suggest that the best way to truly keep Bill Bernbach's ideals alive is to let him rest in peace.

Amen.

Contributor's note: This piece originally appeared in a regular column I write for *Communication Arts*, and is reprinted here with permission. In the context of this very valuable book, this chapter serves as a punctuation.

Within these pages you get a glimpse into many great ad giants' minds. They represent many diverse styles, philosophies, opinions, ideals, convictions,... (...only kidding). In their own way, these leaders of our industry are their own Bernbachs. What they share with Bernbach and with each other is an unwavering respect for the power of creativity in advertising, or in life, for that matter.

They are followers of Bernbach. From the Belles and Graces who were so directly influenced by the great one, to the Clows and McElligotts who got the religion more indirectly.

And they are Bernbachian heretics, as well, all of them. Because you simply can't achieve any kind of greatness in the ad business unless you change the business, or add something to the business, or redirect the business, or reinvent the business, or simply break the rules of the business. Because that's what creativity is.

So, to the young people in the ad business, those whom this book is primarily designed to serve, know that Bill Bernbach is dead, know that the first violinist's chair is always open to a new tenant and that there have been so, so many individuals who have sat in that chair at one time or another since Bernbach. Because that's the way creativity is. And that's the way the ad business is. Always looking for new ways to think and do. Always looking for new thinkers and doers.

TOM MONAHAN
Formerly of Leonard Monahan Lubards & Kelly

How This Book Came to Be

Writing this book was an act of selfishness. As two young copywriters, struggling to develop our own portfolios, we wanted advice. We felt that by learning about the formative years of the top people in the field, we'd gain some career strategies and inspiration. We also wondered if what it takes to succeed was the same as what it takes to break into a consumer agency.

Both of us have made every possible mistake. We have created reams of meaningless pun ads and shown tons of published business-to-business work. That's because neither of us started our careers with strong mentors in the creative field.

As part of this struggle, Larry Minsky had a chance to meet Joel Hochberg, then president of DDB Needham/Chicago. The highlight of the interview was not the critique of his very rough beginning portfolio—Hochberg graciously avoided that. Instead, Hochberg talked about his early days writing catalog copy for Spiegel and how hard it was for him to throw everything away to create a spec portfolio that would get him a job in an agency.

Since Larry's portfolio was filled mostly with materials targeted to the education market—valid, but inappropriate—he was inspired by Hochberg's story.

That experience led to the concept for this book—advertising greats talking about the lessons they learned during their formative years, how they overcame struggles, and what they look for in advertising. With this book, we could ask questions that *beginners* and people early in their careers need to know.

With a burning desire to produce this book, Larry again postponed creating his spec portfolio and took a job at a small outpost of a large trade show promoter. Admittedly, it wasn't what he wanted to do, but at least this gave him the opportunity to string words together. Sometimes the punctuation even fell in the right places.

Meanwhile, Emily was on the fence about which direction her career should go. She didn't realize how important it was to express herself creatively until, after more than a year in a design firm as account executive and marketing director, she began to have opportunities to develop communications materials. It was wonderful. She decided that she, too, could develop her creative talents. She felt that advertising was one of the few ways to express herself creatively—and still make a living. She was also fascinated by people who managed to reach prominence in their careers through creative excellence.

Together, Minsky and Calvo kicked around these issues, put together a proposal for this book and won a contract. With his portfolio long on hold, Larry hooked up with Phil Gaytor, a creative director at Leo Burnett, and finally had an opportunity to gather some guidance and feedback on his work. More important, Gaytor gave him the assurance that perhaps he did indeed have something to offer the advertising industry.

Early in the research stage of the book, Minsky and Calvo met with Susan Gillette. Her descriptions of bad in-house environments she had encountered encouraged Larry to leave his job at the trade show promoter and eventually find a job at a consumer-oriented agency. That was just the beginning of many pieces of advice that helped both authors get closer to their goals.

Over the years it took to finish this book, they've had many more experiences under their belts. Here are some additional thoughts that may help you down the road to success in creative advertising.

Use the Standard Directory of Advertising Agencies

This book references agencies' addresses, phone numbers, billings, accounts, and principals, alphabetically and by geography. You can find the book in the library and use it to target organizations for which you want to work. Make sure the directory is current. Agencies change their names, are sold, merge, and go out of business faster than restaurants in a trendy neighborhood. In addition, some agencies inflate reported billings and staff size to look better to potential clients. Copy as many as you can. Circle the ones that appeal to you. Keep the other names, you'll probably need them, too.

Keep your portfolio fresh

When Larry met with Gaytor he was told to keep adding to his book with fresh spec work. This was especially important when returning to an agency for a second or third interview. Even if a spec ad is new and truly great, because it has been seen before, it won't seem fresh the second time around.

Understand the difference between working at a small firm and a large one

Small firms are more hungry to use their resources. Most of the time, you can gain added responsibility, though not necessarily a bigger paycheck. That offers you the opportunity to learn how the organization functions—wins new business, develops proposals, and creates the communications materials from concept through execution. You learn how to manage multiple projects. Sometimes you even learn how to hire and fire. You also learn office management, billing, media, and public relations. On the negative side, however, you may not be as well paid as you would be by a larger organization. Raises come sporadically and benefits are erratic. But what the heck, you need the experience. And the work can be just as great.

Make sure your talent is part of the product in an in-house agency

If you are considering the client side, try to work for a company that regards your function as fundamental to the bottom line. The more distantly your skills are seen to relate to profitability, the less pay, respect, and opportunities for advancement you'll find. However, in some ways, a job on the client side may offer you more creative freedom than an agency job. On the client side, you can present ideas that agency account executives may be too afraid to show. The corporation has made an investment in you. They're paying for your benefits. They've trained you in their markets and product lines. If you present a wild idea, you may get thrown out of the VP's office and told to go back to the drawing board, but they won't lose your account.

Keep working

It is important to remember that you're never done. There's no perfect job, client, boss, or product. So you must keep working on your portfolio even after you have a position. You never know when you'll need to show it again.

Pay attention to your gut feelings

Ted Bell says he interprets anything but a black portfolio as kind of "show-offy." Ed McCabe, however, says if you come in with a black portfolio, you're missing the point. After reading this book, you might be feeling confused at the conflicting advice the creatives offer. Good. You're right where you need to be to plot your next move: Take direction from your gut feelings. The purpose of this book is to get you to decide for yourself the best way to get a job and become successful. The contradictory suggestions in this book helped us develop a fuller view of the industry. We hope it did the same for you.

The Advertising Classics

Doyle Dane Bernbach Agency

Doyle Dane Bernbach Agency

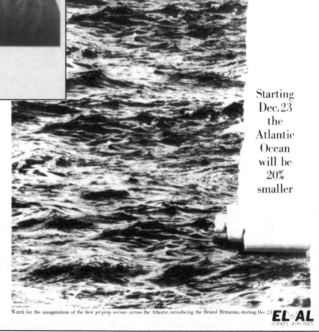

Doyle Dane Bernbach Agency

What Should I Read to Find Out More About Advertising?

EVERYTHING. YOU SHOULD IMMERSE YOURSELF IN POPULAR CULTURE. READ ALL KINDS OF magazines and books. Likewise, you should also see as many movies and plays as possible. Listen to all kinds of music. As Lee Clow pointed out, anytime you gain a deeper understanding of any form of communications, you become a better, more versatile advertising creative.

Pay attention to all kinds of publications about advertising. You may later decide to ignore then, but it always helps to know what is being said, who is saying it, and what is being produced. To get started, you may wish to review the following publications:

PUBLICATIONS OF THE AMERICAN ASSOCIATION OF ADVERTISING AGENCIES

The 4As—the national trade association of the advertising business—has several very basic publications on the industry that can help you get started. They include *Go For It! A Guide to Careers in Advertising* and *Advertising Agencies: What They Are, What They Do and How They Do It.* Some 4As publications are free and others have a small cost. You should contact them in New York for details.

MAGAZINES

Advertising Age
Crain Communications
740 Rush Street
Chicago, IL 60611

Adweek
BPI Communications
1515 Broadway Avenue
New York, NY 10036

Archive
American Showcase
915 Broadway Avenue
New York, NY 10010

Art Direction Magazine
Advertising Trade Publications, Inc.
10 E. 39th Street
New York, NY 10016

Communication Arts (CA)
Coyne & Blanchard, Inc.
410 Sherman Avenue
Palo Alto, CA 94306

ADVERTISING ANNUALS

There are many awards shows and awards annuals in advertising. Read as many of them as possible. At least the latest ones. The three annuals probably most often mentioned by the people featured in this book—and probably the three easiest to find—are:

Communication Arts Advertising Annual (December issue of *Communication Arts Magazine*). See publishing and address information above. The annual comes out each December. *Communication Arts* also publishes helpful annuals in design, photography, and illustration.

New York Art Directors Annual and International Exhibition. Switzerland: RotoVision S.A.

The One Show. Switzerland: RotoVision S.A.

BOOKS

Advertising's Ten Best of the Decade 1980–1990, New York: The One Club for Art and Copy, 1990.

Bendinger, Bruce, *The Copy Workshop Workbook*, Chicago: The Copy Workshop, 1993.

Bolles, Richard Nelson, *What Color is Your Parachute?*, Berkeley, CA: Ten Speed Press, published annually.

Burton, Philip Ward and Scott C. Purvis, *Which Ad Pulled Best?*, Lincolnwood, IL: NTC Business Books, 1993. (Be sure to purchase the *Answer Key* along with the book.)

Ganim, Barbara, *How to Approach an Advertising Agency and Walk Away with the Job You Want*, Lincolnwood, IL: NTC Business Books, 1993.

Higgins, Denis, *The Art of Writing Advertising*, Lincolnwood, IL: NTC Business Books, 1985.

Hoff, Ron, *I Can See You Naked*, Kansas City, MO: Andrews and McMeel, 1988.

Ind, Nicholas, *Great Advertising Campaigns*, Lincolnwood, IL: NTC Business Books, 1993.

Kessler, Stephan, *Chiat/Day: The First Twenty Years*, New York: Rizzoli, 1990.

Levinson, Bob, *Bill Bernbach's Book*, New York: Villard Books, 1987.

Marwah, Raj, *Buy this Book!*, Chicago: American Marketing Association, 1991.

Mayer, Martin, *Madison Avenue U.S.A.*, Lincolnwood, IL: NTC Business Books, republished 1992.

———, *Whatever Happened to Madison Avenue?* Boston: Little, Brown and Company, 1991.

Ogilvy, David, *Confessions of an Advertising Man*, New York: Atheneum, 1985.

———, *Ogilvy on Advertising*, New York: Vintage Books, 1985.

———, *The Unpublished David Ogilvy*, edited by Joel Raphaelson, New York: Crown Publishers, Inc., 1986.

Reeves, Rosser. *Reality in Advertising*, New York: Alfred A. Knopf, 1961.

Schultz, Don E., Stanley I. Tannenbaum, and Robert F. Lauterborn, *Integrated Marketing Communications*, Lincolnwood, IL: NTC Business Books, 1993.

Seiden, Hank, *Advertising Pure & Simple: The New Edition*, New York: Amacom, 1990.

Sharp, Bill, *How to be Black and Get a Job in the Advertising Agency Business Anyway*, Atlanta: Sharp Advertising, 1969.

Souter, Nick and Stuart Newman, *Creative Director's Sourcebook*, Cincinnati: North Light Books, 1988.

Strunk, William, Jr & E. B. White, *The Elements of Style*, New York: Macmillan, 1959.

Wasserman, Dick, *That's Our New Ad Campaign...?* Lexington, MA: Lexington Books, 1988.

Wells, William D, *Planning for ROI: Effective Advertising Strategy*, Englewood Cliffs, NJ: Prentice Hall, 1989.

Young, James Webb, *A Technique for Producing Ideas*, Lincolnwood, IL: NTC Business Books, 1975.

CREDITS

Chapter 1
Boxed Ties, Chivas Regal: Ted Bell, Copywriter; Charles Picirillo, Art Director; Bill Bernbach, Creative Director; Doyle Dane Bernbach Agency.

BankAmericard: Ted Bell, Copywriter/Art Director.

Yukon Jack: Ted Bell, Creative Director; Tinker, Dodge & Delano, Agency.

Volkswagen (Thing): Ted Bell, Copywriter; Reinhold Swenk, Art Director; Bob Levenson, Creative Director; Doyle Dane Bernbach, Agency.

Volkswagen (Rabbit): Ted Bell, Copywriter; Reinhold Swenk, Art Director; John Eding, Creative Director: Doyle Dane Bernbach, Agency

Memorex ``Is It Love'': Ted Bell, Copywriter; Reinhold Swenk, Art Director; Leo Burnett, Agency.

McDonald's Sounds of Summer: Ted Bell, Copywriter; Bob Taylor, Art Director; Norm Muse, Creative Director; Leo Burnett, Agency.

Chapter 2
American Cancer Society, Fry Now Pay Later: Susan Gillette, Copywriter/Creative Director; Needham Harper Steers/DDB Needham.

Polaroid: Susan Gillette, Copywriter/Creative Director; Needham Harper Steers/DDB Needham.

McDonald's First Kiss: Susan Gillette, Copywriter/Creative Director; Needham Harper Steers/DDBNeedham.

AIDS Prevention: Susan Gillette, Copywriter/Creative Director; Needham Harper Steers/DDB Needham.

Michelob: Susan Gillette, Copywriter/Creative Director; Needham Harper Steers/DDB Needham.

"Feminine Protection" and "Fight Cancer" are from Susan Gillette's early portfolio.

Chapter 3
501 Print: MIke Koelker, Copywriter/Creative Director; Chris Blum, Art Director; Foote, Cone & Belding, Agency.

501 TV: Mike Koelker, Copywriter/Creative Director; Leslie Caldwell, Art Director; Foote, Cone & Belding, Agency.

Women's 501s: Mike Koelker, Copywriter/Creative Director; Mike Salisbury, Art Director; Foote, Cone & Belding, Agency.

Levi's Dockers: Mike Koelker, Copywriter/Creative Director; Leslie Caldwell, Art Director; Foote, Cone & Belding, Agency.

Chapter 4
John Hancock Financial Services: Bill Heater, Copywriter; Don Easdon, Art Director; Hill Holiday Connors Cosmopulos, Agency.

Wang: Bill Heater, Copywriter; Don Easdon, Art Director; Hill Holiday Connors Cosmopulos, Agency.

Infiniti: Bill Heater, Copywriter, Don Easdon, Art Director; Hill Holiday Connors Cosmopulos, Agency.

Budweiser: Bill Heater, Copywriter; Don Easdon, Art Director; Hill Holiday Connors Cosmopulos, Agency.

Chapter 5
Paint the Paint, Volkswagon: Charles Ewell, Copywriter; Roy Grace, Art Director; Doyle Dane Bernbach, Agency.

Trouble, Volkswagen: Charles Ewell, Copywriter; Roy Grace, Art Director; Doyle Dane Bernbach, Agency.

Mobil One: John Noble, Copywriter; Roy Grace, Art Director; Doyle Dane Bernbach Agency.

Alka-Seltzer Spicy Meatball: Charles Ewell, Copywriter; Roy Grace, Art Director; Doyle Dane Bernbach, Agency.

Can You Spot the Copycat? IBM: Roy Grace, Art Director; Doyle Dane Bernbach, Agency.

Fabulous Jack, American Tourister: Marcia Bell Grace, Copywriter; Roy Grace, Art Director; Doyle Dane Bernbach, Agency.

Ranger Rover: Diane Rothschild, Copywriter; Roy Grace, Art Director; Grace & Rothschild, Agency.

J & B On the Rocks: Diane Rothschild, Copywriter, Roy Grace, Art Director; Grace & Rothschild, Agency.

Chapter 6
We're Losing Our Minds: Steve Hayden, Copywriter/Creative Director; Mike Moss, Art Director; Steve Hayden, Creative Director; Chiat/Day, Agancy.

Bendix: Steve Hayden, Copywriter; George Scott, Creative Director.

KFAC: Steve Hayden & Brian O'Neill, Copywriters; Tom Tawa & Doug Smith, Art Directors; Steve Hayden, Creative Director; Boylhart, Lovett & Dean Agency.

Baked Apple: Steve Hayden, Copywriter; Rob Janoff, Art Director; Hy Yablanca, Creative Director; Chiat/Day, Agency.

Apple Insert: Steve Hayden, Copywriter; Brent Thomas, Art Director; Steve Davis, Creative Director; Chiat/Day, Agency.

1984 Apple: Steve Hayden, Copywriter; Brent Thomas, Art Director; Lee Clow, Creative Director; Chiat/Day, Agency.

Lemmings: Steve Hayden, Copywriter/Creative Director; Chiat/Day, Agency.

Apple Welcomes IBM: Steve Hayden, Copywriter/Creative Director; Chiat/Day, Agency.

Chapter 7

Mc Donald's: Tom Burrell/Art Director; Burrell Communication, Agency.

Coca-Cola, TV and print: Tom Burrell/Art director; Burrell Communication, Agency.

Tide: Tom Burrell/Art Director; Burrell Communication, Agency.

Chapter 8

Mercantile Bank: Bob Dennard, Art Director; Stan Richards, Creative Director; The Richards Group, Agency.

Butch Cassidy & the Sundance Kid: Jim Jacobs, Art Director; Stan Richards, Creative Director; The Richards Group, Agency.

Simon David: Doug Rucker, Copywriter; Gary Gibson, Art Director; Stan Richards, Creative Director; The Richards Group, Agency.

Motel 6: Thomas Hripko, Copywriter; Stan Richards, Creative Director; The Richards Group, Agency.

Memorex Audio Tapes: Grant Richards, Copywriter; Todd Tilford, Art Director; Stan Richards, Creative Director; The Richards Group, Agency.

Chapter 9

Volvo: Amil Gargano, Chairman/Creative Director/Art Director; Carl Ally Inc/Ally & Gargano, Agency.

Shearson Lehman Brothers: Amil Gargano, Chairman/Creative Director/Art Director; Carl Ally Inc/Ally & Gargano, Agency.

Pan Am: Amil Gargano, Chairman/Creative Director/Art Director; Carl Ally Inc/Ally & Gargano, Agency.

MCI: Amil Gargano, Chairman/Creative Director/Art Director; Carl Ally Inc/Ally & Gargano, Agency.

Hertz: Amil Gargano, Chairman/Creative Director/Art Director; Carl Ally Inc/Ally & Gargano, Agency; ©Hertz System, Inc., 1966.

Chapter 10

Citizens for Clean Air: Ed McCabe, Copywriter/Creative Director; Ron Barrett, Art Director; Carl Ally, Inc., Agency.

Perdue: Ed McCabe, Copywriter/Creative Director; Sam Scali, Art Director; Scali, McCabe, Sloves, Inc., Agency.

Coleman Natural Beef: Ed McCabe, Copywriter/Creative Director; S. Bowden, Art Director; McCabe & Company, Agency.

Maxell: Ed McCabe, Copywriter; Lars Anderson, Art Director; Scali, McCabe, Sloves, Inc. Agency.

Goebel Beer: Ed McCabe, Copywriter; Gargano, Art Director, Carl Ally, Inc., Agency.

Volvo: Ed McCabe, Copywriter.

Chapter 11

Rubberrmaid: Nancy Rice, Creative Director; DDB Needham Worldwide, Agency.

Episcopal Church Project: Tom McElligott, Copywriter; Nancy Rice, Art Director; Fallon McElligott Rice, Agency.

Rolling Stone: Bill Miller, Copywriter; Nancy Rice, Art Director; Fallon McElligott Rice, Agency.

Gold 'n Plump: Tom McElligott, Copywriter; Nancy Rice, Art Director; Fallon McElligott Rice, Agency.

Tatoo Parlor Roughs: Dick Thomas, Copywriter; Nancy Rice, Art Director.

Rice & Rice Announcement: Nancy Rice, Copywriter, Nancy & Nick Rice, Art Directors; Rice & Rice, Agency.

Successful Farming: Jim Newcombe, Copywriter; Nancy Rice & Nick Rice, Art Director; Rice & Rice Advertising, Inc., Agency.

Chapter 12

Yamaha: Brian Butler, Copywriter; Lee Clow, Art Director; Jay Chiat, Creative Director; Chiat/Day, Agency.

Energizer Bunny: Lee Clow, Creative Director; Chiat/Day, Agency.

Nike: Gary Johns, Copywriter; Jeff Gorman, Art Director; Lee Clow, Creative Director; Chiat/Day, Agency.

Road to Rio, Nissan: Dick Sittig, Copywriter; Lee Clow, Creative Director; Chiat/Day, Agency.

Z intro, Nissan: Brain Belevant & Steve Bassett, Copywriters; Pat Cunningham & Mike Mazza, Art Directors; Lee Clow, Creative Director; Chiat/Day, Agency.

Chapter 13

State of Minnesota, Tourism Division: Tom McElligott, Copywriter/Creative Director; Nancy Rice, Art Director; Bozell, Agency.

ITT Life: Tom McElligott, Copywriter/Creative Director; Nancy Rice, Art Director; Fallon McElligott Rice, Agency.

Porsche: Tom McElligott, Copywriter/Creative Director; Mark Johnson, Art Director; Fallon McElligott Rice, Agency.

AMF: Tom McElligott, Copywriter/Creative Director; Dean Hanson, Art Director; Fallon McElligott Rice, Agency.

The Wall Street Journal: Tom McElligott, Copywriter/Creative Director; Nancy Rice, Art Director; Fallon McElligott Rice, Agency.

Note: Every effort has been made to trace and acknowledge all relevant parties. We wish to apologize for any omissions.

TITLES OF INTEREST IN
ADVERTISING, SALES PROMOTION, AND PUBLIC RELATIONS

For further information or a current catalog, write:
NTC Business Books
a division of *NTC Publishing Group*
4255 West Touhy Avenue
Lincolnwood, Illinois 60646-1975 U.S.A.